AF655993

From the book:

"O India, how I love you! What mysterious force in you calls forth my love? You are not always clean outwardly, your climate is not the best, your heat is unbearable, your rains are miserably uncomfortable, your creature comforts are nil as compared with the West; but you have a towering spiritual strength, and there is the tenderness of the Mother in you as you welcome all visitors to your shores." - ***Sri Daya Mata***

"Of all the things that happened to me in India – and there were many wonderful things – the most lasting and most important was the softening of the heart, that opening of the heart. There is a place for individuality, but that exaggerated sense of self-importance begins to dissolve in India, and for that I am eternally grateful." - ***Swami Atmarupananda***

"India is, and always will be, a land of living saints. The rich spiritual tradition, and the esoteric knowledge of yoga and meditation that is inherent in the culture, allows evolved souls the capacity for continued spiritual growth and attainment."
- ***Swami Mangalananda***

"To receive Her greatest blessings you must go to India with a spirit of humility and reverence. Then everything becomes magical. In the Bhagavad Gita, Lord Krishna says to Arjuna, "You cannot see Me with your present eyes. Therefore I give you Divine sight by which you can behold my mystic opulence." If, through God's grace, you are able to get even a tiny glimpse of that Divine sight, a whole new India is open to you." - ***Kaisori Devi Dasi***

"Welcome to India"

Where Souls Dream GOD

Westerner's Perceptions of Spiritual India

Sundaram La Pierre

Originals

Delhi

First Published 2009 by:
Himalayan Heritage, California, USA
Reprinted With Permission 2018

Copyright © Sundaram La Pierre
Cover Design by Colin Kenney

ISBN 10: 81-8454-207-0
ISBN 13: 978-81-8454-207-3

Published By

Originals

A-6, Second Floor, Nimri Commercial Centre,
Ashok Vihar Phase-4, Delhi - 110 052 (India)
Tel.: +91 11 2730 2453 Fax: 011 4706 1936
Website: www.Lppindia.com, e-mail: info@Lppindia.com

This Edition is for Sale in India Only

All Rights reserved under International Copyright Conventions. No part of this book may be copied or translated or transmitted in any form or any manner or by any means including uploading in any database or otherwise without the written permission of the Author.

Printed At

D K Fine Art Press P Ltd.
Delhi-110052

PRINTED IN INDIA

**Hail, mother of religions, lotus, scenic
Beauty and sages!
Thy wide doors are open,
Welcoming God's true sons
Through all ages.**

**Where Ganges, woods, Himalayan caves
And men dream God –
I am hallowed; my body touched that sod.**

From **"My India,"** by Paramahansa Yogananda

Himalayan Heritage

PO Box 235713
Encinitas, CA 92023

Contents

Bharat Mataji
Mother India

Dedication

This book is lovingly dedicated to the life of my life, my divine Gurudeva, Sri Sri Paramahansa Yogananda; and to our lineage of God-realized masters who have shown the way to the kingdom of God within.

To Self-Realization Fellowship, whose principal aim is to preserve the true teachings of our Guru for all who are drawn to follow this path.

To my beloved wife, Hilary, who has so gracefully joined me in our India adventures. When I was younger I prayed for Divine Mother to come to me as a soul companion that I may love Her in human form. She did.

To my soul-friend – my *bhaiyya* – Gangadas (Craig Bell). It was through his kindness and generosity that I made my first acquaintance with the holy land of saints and sages. We began in SRF at about the same time, and have been chanting and meditating together ever since.

To Drs. Thomas and Victoria Parker, founders of Polestar Tours, who, over a period of more than 25 years, introduced hundreds of SRF devotees and friends to the wonder and glory of our Guru's native land.

To the avatars, sages, saints and bhaktas of India and the world – each and every one.

OM SHANTI OM

Foreword

By Swami Mangalananda

India is a land of Saints. It always has been, and by God's grace, will always be. One great Master told me, "Every generation will have its Saints. God will never leave Himself without a witness in India!" Yet these great Beings generally live away from the disturbing sight of the world and pursue their God-intoxicated lives in the solitude of caves, jungles or hidden retreats. Though American by birth, I have lived in India for many years. I have sought out the Saints, Yogis, and Masters in my travels, spanning the height and breadth of this divine subcontinent. I've encountered Saints in their caves high in the Himalayan peaks, and in secluded ashrams in the dense jungles of the Plains. I have received their blessings and listened to their esoteric teachings while huddling around a small *dhuni* fire or sweating in the tropical heat of the jungles. And by the great and undeserved grace of the Mother, I have had the blessing of knowing, traveling with and receiving Initiation from the divine Sri Anandamayi Ma, one of the greatest spiritual luminaries of India. Hence when my dear friend, Sundaram, asked me to write a short introduction to his wonderful book, I readily agreed.

I first met Sundaram and his wife, Hilary, when they visited our Mata Anandamayi Ashram in Omkareshwar, Madhya Pradesh, in Central India, several years ago. We at once felt a deep affinity between the three of us. Since then we have kept in contact with mutual visits between California and India, and through correspondence. The selfless work they do in promoting the true ideals of *Sanatana Dharma* in the West through their *Himalayan Heritage Magazine*, and their work with devotional music and *kirtan*, is of great importance in today's western society. It has been my privilege to contribute several articles to their magazine, and to sing *kirtan* in their temple, the Jyoti Mandir, during my visits to Encinitas.

One can pursue the spiritual life in any environment. Indeed, we must begin walking from where we are right now. It is not necessary to put on a loincloth and endure the hardships of living in India. Yet for those who practice Yoga and study Eastern thought and philosophy, a visit to India is to find the authentic source and spring of those ancient teaching that have become diluted or "over-adopted" for presentation in the West. A few westerners with strong Indian *samkaras* (deep impressions from previous births) have benefited from residence in India for the purpose of pursuing an intense and one-pointed spiritual endeavor.

On a superficial level, India is currently in a state of unbalance and unrest. With the intrusion of much western influence and the rapid blossoming of technology, there is a much-needed growth in material prosperity and an updated 'practical side' of life. Yet India's deep, ancient and eternal culture is rising up to counterbalance this current trend. It will certainly predominate. If a visitor can penetrate the quiet heart of India – in the ashrams and temples, the small villages and towns, they will find ancient India intact and thriving.

Once while visiting a very old temple in Jagannath Puri, I was sitting under a tree enjoying the intense spiritual atmosphere of the place. I had the experience that the 'Real India' is not a place at all but a spiritual state. It is a vibration of intense holiness and eternal stillness. On this inner blueprint, as it were, the external culture, religion and the nation are built. That changeless, inner India is always accessible to those who will endure the sometimes intense elements, and the apparent confusion and chaos that a visit to India often may bring!

Someone once noted that the whole world is the Lord's Temple, but that India is the holy inner shrine where the Deity resides, the 'inner sanctum,' as it were. Religion in India and her culture are inseparably intertwined. It can be said that *Sanatana Dharma* (Hinduism, in its highest expression) is not so much a religion but a way of life. The devotion, divine love and sacrifice of the people of India does not come into play only during a few hours of the day, or on a certain day of the week. It interpenetrates every moment of their lives. It is this element that has fostered the devotion, the renunciation, the surrender and the love that has created the Saints of each and every generation. The holy shrines of pilgrimage that dot the map of India shed light and power throughout this land; the ones that have dedicated their lives to the continuity and preservation of this spiritual current send their blessings to the entire world.

I believe that this present book of Sundaram's will be an inspiration to many, and an encouragement for all of us to live our lives in that same divine spirit wherever our destiny has placed us. *Where Souls Dream God* – let the journey begin!

Bharat Mataji ki Jai!

Swami Mangalananda
Mata Anandamayi Ashram
Omkareshwar MP, India

Introduction

This essence of Truth – the Sanatana Dharma, or eternal principals of righteousness that uphold man and the universe – was given to the world thousands of years before the Christian era, and preserved in India with a spiritual vitality that has made the quest for God the be-all and end-all of life and not an armchair discussion.

– Paramahansa Yogananda, *The Second Coming of Christ*

It has been said that all truly great spiritual masters of the world are universalists. They have risen above religious and cultural limitations to embrace all of humanity. They belong to everyone. They bear the message of universal brotherhood and sisterhood, asking us to break down all man-made boundaries between children of the one God.

In his quintessential poem, *My India,* Paramahansa Yogananda writes: *I love Thee, O my India! And thy love I shall give to every brother nation that lives. God made the earth; Man made confining countries and their fancy-frozen boundaries. But with newfound boundless love I behold the borderland of my India expanding into the world...*

The title of this book is in direct reference to Paramahansaji's poem; in fact, to the final words that the great master spoke in this life. He had often told his disciple that he wanted to die, "...with my boots on, speaking of God and India." And so it was that on March 7th, 1952, at a banquet in honor of the visiting ambassador from India at the Biltmore Hotel in Los Angeles, the great master, who would become known to his disciples as a *Premavatar* (Incarnation of

Divine Love), spoke these words from his thrilling poem ***My India***: "Where Ganges, woods, Himalayan caves, and men dream God – I am hallowed; my body touched that sod." Lifting his eyes, his body slumped to the floor in *mahasamadhi*.

These are the words of the Master. It is true that a few people have objected to the use of the pronoun "men," in this and other writings, and I honor their point of view. Yet no one could honor women more than the great masters of the world who are merged in the One Mother-Father God. It is valuable to observe that Paramahansaji left his organization in the capable hands of his advanced women disciples, especially Sri Daya Mata, who has guided Self-Realization Fellowship / Yogoda Satsanga Society of India for more than fifty years.

Sri Ramakrishna Paramahamsa's work was continued by his wife and consort, the Holy Mother Sri Sarada Devi. Sri Aurobindo Ghosh was succeeded by Mother Meera; Swami Muktananda Paramahansa by Gurumayi Chidvilasananda; and Dhyanyogi Madhusudandas by Shri Anandi Ma. Some have said that this is the age of the Mother. In recent years there has come a wave of divine souls from India led by the "Divine Mothers": Amritanandamayi Devi (Ammachi), Vijayeswari Devi (Karunamayi Ma), and Sri Maa of Kamakhaya. It is the motherly qualities of compassion, forgiveness, acceptance and love that are so desperately needed in our world today.

Potentially, all women are manifestations of the Divine Mother, and saints, especially, honor them as such. In Paramahansa Yogananda's time, for better or for worse, the word "men" was used as a synonym for "all humankind." Let us understand it in its all-inclusive sense as referring to every incarnated soul equally, as the Master undoubtedly intended.

Two Indias

In writing this book, we are fully aware that there are actually two Indias. There is political India: modern India jumping about on the international scene struggling to keep pace with the western world. There is an India of corruption and immorality. There is an India of poverty and despair. Let us call these aspects the India of mundane affairs. We will leave them to other authors. The India you will read about in these pages is the India Paramahansaji is referring to in his poem when he says:

Though mortal fires raze all her homes and golden paddy fields, yet to sleep on her ashes and dream immortality, O India, I will be there!

This is Spiritual India. Just as the holy *Ganga,* while appearing to be contaminated with refuse and debris, ever retains Her pristine purity, so Spiritual India, impinged as it is over the grossness of mundane 'reality,' remains eternally pure and present, welcoming "God's true sons through all ages."

India, we shall find, is more than the sum total of the holy vibrations left there by Her countless saints. From the beginning of time great souls have graced Her spacious boundaries. They come for Her. India does indeed give *darshan* of Herself!

My India

By Paramahansa Yogananda

Not where the musk of happiness blows,
Nor where darkness and fears never tread;
Not in the homes of perpetual smiles,
Nor in the heaven of a land of prosperity
Would I be born,
If I must put on mortal garb once more.

Dread famine may prowl and tear my flesh,
Yet would I love to be again
In my Hindustan.
A million thieves of disease
May try to steal the body's fleeting health;
And clouds of fate
May shower scalding drops of searing sorrow –
Yet would I there, in India,
Love to reappear!

Is this love of mine blind sentiment
That sees not the pathways of reason?
Ah, no! I love India,
For there I learned first to love God
and all things beautiful.

Some teach to seize the fickle dewdrop, life,
Sliding down the lotus leaf of time;
Stubborn hopes are built
Around the gilded, brittle body-bubble.
But India taught me to love
The soul of deathless beauty in the dewdrop
and the bubble –
Not their fragile frames.
Her sages taught me to find my Self,
Buried beneath the ash heaps
Of incarnations of ignorance.
Through many a land of power, plenty and science
My soul, garbed sometimes as an Oriental,
Sometimes as an Occidental,
Traveled far and wide,
Seeking Itself;
At last, in India, to find Itself.

Though mortal fires raze all her homes
and golden paddy fields,
Yet to sleep on her ashes and dream immortality,
O India, I will be there!
The guns of science and matter
Have boomed on her shores,
Yet she is unconquered.
Her soul is free evermore!
Her soldier saints are away,
To rout with realization's ray
The bandits of hate, prejudice, and

patriotic selfishness;
And to burn the walls of separation dark
Between children of the One, One Father.
The Western brothers by matter's might
have conquered my land;
Blow, blow aloud, her conch shells all!
India now invades with love,
To conquer their souls.

Better than Heaven or Arcadia
I love Thee, O my India!
And thy love I shall give
To every brother nation that lives.
God made the earth;
Man made confining countries
And their fancy-frozen boundaries.
But with newfound boundless love
I behold the borderland of my India
Expanding into the world.
Hail, mother of religions, lotus, scenic beauty,
And sages!
Thy wide doors are open,
Welcoming God's true sons through all ages.
Where Ganges, woods, Himalayan caves, and
men dream God –
I am hallowed; my body touched that sod.

©Self-Realization Fellowship
Used by permission

Song of India

Her hidden gems are rich beyond all dreaming,
From hidden mountain caves Thy light is streaming;
O wondrous land… O land of India!

And still the snowy Himalayas rise
In tranquil majesty before our eyes,
Beyond the plains… above the pines.

While through this ever-never changing land,
As silently as any sadhu band
That moves at night… the Ganges shines.

There we'll hear the song that only India can sing;
Softer than the plumage on Garuda Deva's wings!

High upon a minaret I stand
And gaze across the desert sand
Upon an old enchanted land.

There's a maharaja's caravan
Unfolding like a painted fan:
How small the little race of man.

See them all parade across the ages:
Armies, kings and saints from history's pages,
Played on one of nature's vastest stages.

The lonely plains fly off to greet the dawn,
While down below the busy life goes on,
And women crowd the old bazaars.

Where turbaned Sikhs and beggars line the streets;
And holy men in silent calm retreats
Pray through the night, and watch the stars.

All are in the song that only India can sing –
India, the Jewel of the East!

Where Souls Dream God

From start to finish, India is a land of surprises, of contrasts and extremes. Life becomes prosaic with too much business, too many dull certainties, so in India one feels that life is a great adventure; an experience of mystery and surprise... Though I have had the advantage of some Western education, yet I feel that in India alone I found the true solution to the mysteries of life.

Paramahansa Yogananda, *Journey to Self-Realization*

The words to the *Song of India* which are transcribed on the preceding pages were taken from an old Mario Lanza recording, slightly adjusted by this author to reflect the spiritual glory of the Motherland. Before departing for my fifth pilgrimage to India in the fall of 2004, my heart was aflame with longing to be back in that holy land. I would often sit on our bed in the morning and sing this song. Thrills would run through my body and tears would flow. At some point in the course of my life the realization had come to me that Spiritual India is more a state of consciousness than it is a physical reality. Drinking a hot cup of chai in my stainless steel cup on a cold morning can put me in the Himalayas! The physical reality of India can be trying at times, yet the spirit rejoices to be in this great land "Where souls dream God."

I have long been drawn to the holy land of India. As with many of us, perhaps, India held an indefinable attraction. In my early teens, my father gave me a fascinating book: *Man Eaters of the Kumoan*, by Jim Corbett. I hadn't the slightest idea where "Kumoan" was, but I devoured those stories as readily as the blood thirsty tigers devoured the local hill people! I thrilled with anticipation as local hero, Jim Corbett, stalked the man-eating tigers and leopards that plagued the Himalayan hill country of his time. Little did I know that one day I would be walking those same hills, visiting the same tree in which Jim Corbett stayed for days with little sleep, awaiting the "Man-eating Leopard of Rudraprayag." To this day that tree is clearly marked as an historical landmark. Yet far from the thought of chasing tigers, I would be on the trail of *tirthas* and saints: a pilgrimage tradition that marks India as unique amongst all the nations of the world.

Sages say that there are really only two types of people: the wise who are seeking God, and those still caught in the web of delusion who are not. A fortunate few have their eyes of wisdom wide open. They see God and His goodness everywhere and in everything. The rest of us perceive a world of darkness and anxiety. We face a life fraught with many fears and apprehensions, frustrations and incompleteness.

Perhaps you have heard this well-known saying: "Two men looked out from the jailhouse bars: One saw the mud and one saw the stars." This analogy could hardly be more appropriate than when it is applied to the country we call India. Those of us who love that country are not blind to the mundane realities of poverty, corruption and social injustice. Such is the way of the world in the age in which we live. India is certainly not exempt from the often agonizing state of modern times. In its efforts to copy the materialistic ways of Western society, India has, in some superficial ways, become alienated from her ancient spiritual heritage. Yet, as we have seen, there is another India: Spiritual India. There is an ongoing resurgence of spirituality in India today, and her message of love for God and humanity is spreading in all lands. Hear Yoganandaji's prediction, once again from his poem, *My India*:

The Western brothers by matter's might have conquered my land; Blow, blow aloud her conch shells all! India now invades with love, to conquer their souls… But with newfound boundless love I behold my India expanding into the world. Hail, mother of religions, lotus, scenic beauty, and sages! Thy wide doors are open, welcoming God's true sons through all ages.

So we find it to be. This great country is not only for those who are blessed to have been born within her geographical boundaries. Today many *swamis, sadhus* and *sadhakas* from the West and throughout the world live in India where they find the environment highly conducive to spiritual practice. Many others make pilgrimages to this holy land. A few of their stories are told in this book. Yet these wonderful stories are but a drop in the ocean. Perhaps this book will be the first of many such collections. Indeed, this author hopes that this will, in fact, be the case. We encourage your contribution toward the next volume. (Please see "India Stories Project," page 357). Such stories will never end so long as "Souls dream God."

Spiritual India is the real India. Paramahansaji speaks of India as a personification of Divinity. I often think it remarkable that such a great master, himself a divine incarnation, would say with inexpressible reverence: "Where

Ganges, woods, Himalayan caves, and men dream God – I am hallowed; my body touched that sod."

Why might this one country amongst all the nations of the earth display such an unbroken lineage of sanctity? From time immemorial, India has specialized in the science of God-realization. Even in this modern period of world history – and perhaps especially in this day and age – we find genuine saints who have reached the pinnacle of spiritual attainment. The Western pilgrim begins to realize what a land of saints India truly is, for it seems that every holy site, every tree, mountain, river, stream or temple is associated with one or several great spiritual personages of the past or the present.

Once, while walking in the foothills of the Himalayas, my wife, Hilary, and I passed through a small village in search of a Shiva *mandir* located on a hilltop just outside the village. When we arrived, the morning *puja* was over. No one was present there in physical form. We entered the temple where we meditated for some time in what seemed like an otherworldly environment – partially in this world and partially on a transcendental plane. The light seemed of a softer texture than ordinary sunlight. Across the courtyard, shaded by a large tree under which were installed two small stone *lingams,* stood the shrine of a saint. His picture hung on the wall of a simple concrete *kutir.* Was it his presence or the location itself that made this place so special, so divine?

As Swami Mangalananda, an American *sannyasi,* so perceptibly told us: "India is, and will always be, a land of living saints. The rich spiritual tradition, and the esoteric knowledge of yoga and meditation that is inherent in the culture, allows evolved souls the opportunity and capacity for continued spiritual growth and attainment." From our own experience, we have found that to be true beyond a doubt.

Prior to my first visit I had read about India, seen films about India, watched movies set in India, had conversations with Indian nationals, and spoken with several Western devotees who had been to India on pilgrimage. The reality that I discovered when I arrived, however, made me realize that nothing could have prepared me for the veritable onslaught of feelings and emotions that literally sprayed forth like a fountain while I was in a land where, in one way or another, nearly everyone is a devotee of God. Dimly forgotten images, long hidden in the recesses of my mind, began to come to the surface. Some of these images I had never associated with India at all. Upon my arrival, riding through the streets of Mumbai at midnight, seeing the flickering oil lamps in the chai stands and the little shops along the roadside brought an indescribable thrill. Later, while staying in an ashram in the Himalayan foothills, upon seeing the simple plaid woolen blankets on the beds, such as those used by the local villagers, I could not hold back the tears. It seemed such an odd thing – yet there was an intimate familiarity! In little ways India was telling me: "You have come home."

It would seem as though India has been selected by the Great Power of the Universe to be the repository of Truth for mankind from age to age. Truth Absolute has become known in this world by the Sanskrit name of *Sanatana Dharma,* the "Eternal Religion." Sages have defined Truth as exact correspondence with Reality. Consequently, whatsoever is empirically true in any religion is, by its very definition, part of *Sanatana Dharma.* Too often we may think of religion as a set of beliefs *about* God and spirituality. Fortunately, this limiting conception is fading rapidly with the advent of our expanded understanding. Of course, people can believe virtually anything – and they do! The question is, "Is it true?" followed by a definitive corollary, "What is Truth?" A wonderful and amazing facet of Truth is that it can be perceived and realized in the 'laboratory' of our own individual consciousness through spiritual development. Truth will be inwardly revealed to each one of us in the course of our own divine awakening.

Countless Truth seekers through the ages have plumbed the depths and ascended the heights of the inner world. They have testified to the existence of God. They have uncovered the spiritual laws which govern the universal order. These seekers have become finders. We call them *rishis,* sages, saints and masters. Those divine ones who have attained complete oneness with God in a previous life and have answered the call of the Divine to return to earth for the upliftment of mankind and the perfection of their disciples are known as *avatars.* Their testimonies have become the scriptures of the world; their teachings the hope of humanity. This is *Sanatana Dharma.* Rather than "religion," let us say, "The Eternal Way of Truth."

There are two main tributaries merging into the vast ocean of *Sanatana Dharma. Sankhya* is the philosophical river, *Yoga* its practical aspect. *Sankhya* tells us the purpose of life; *Yoga* the way to achieve it. *Sankhya* tells us what Spirit is, what God is, what Nature is, what the soul is, what we are as human beings and what our relationship is to all of these. Of greater significance than this esoteric knowledge, *Sankhya* philosophy answers the grandest and most profound questions confronting each and every one: "What is the purpose of my life?" "Why am I here?" Here all forms of intellectuality become reduced to their utmost simplicity. The heart opens in unimagined splendor! It is here that the priceless gem of genuine spirituality is born. This truth is echoed in the teachings of all great masters, yet Paramahansa Yogananda expresses it profoundly and directly when he says: "Man has come on earth solely to learn to know God; he is here for no other reason. This is the true message of the Lord," (*Man's Eternal Quest*).

The understanding that the only purpose of life is to be reunited with God; that all beings will eventually find their way back to Him, is a foundational belief of Hinduism. Indeed, it is the bedrock of Indian society. Thus we find that spirituality is all pervasive in India. Small *mandirs* are found by the roadside and in the home. Taxi drivers as well as truck and bus drivers, worship the Lord installed as a sacred image on the altar of their dashboard before beginning work for the day. Shopkeepers do likewise. God is perceived to be everywhere and in everything – enshrined in the temple of all nature.

All rivers are holy rivers, all mountains holy mountains, stately trees, sacred trees. Ubiquitous as the sacred symbol of the Formless Infinite, round or oblong stones known as *Shiva Lingams*, are worshipped everywhere. God is known to be both immanent and transcendent, the world permeated by the living presence of Divinity. We too can perceive God everywhere once we have discovered the Lord residing in the temple of our own hearts. This is the testimony of the sages. It is their promise to each and every soul.

Due to this intrinsic understanding of the purpose of life, another prominent feature of Hindu society is a deep respect and reverence for holy men and women. Indeed, those who have renounced the attractions of the world to concentrate on spiritual attainment and selfless service to humanity deserve our respect and admiration. Paramahansa Yogananda writes, "In India, hundreds of young men are crazy for God, as hundreds here (in America) are crazy for money and power," (*The Divine Romance*). The age-old tradition of renouncing the world to seek God alone and to serve Him in others has led to a subculture of literally thousands – perhaps millions – of individuals who have chosen to live the monastic life in one form or another. Some are affiliated with large organizations, various religious *akharas* or *sampradayas.* Many are *swamis* or *sannyasis* belonging to one of the eight branches of the Swami Order established by the great philosopher-reformer-saint, Sri Swami Shankara (Adi Shankaracharya). All *swamis* take three basic vows: celibacy, non-possessiveness, and acceptance of mankind as one's larger family. *Swamis* usually wear *garua* colored clothing, signifying their affiliation with the ancient Swami Order. Other *sadhus* and *sadhavis* may be independent monks or nuns with no organizational affiliation. Many are penniless wanderers who subsist solely on alms. They may dress in white, or with a *kaupin* only. In the case of an estimated 50,000 *Naga Babas,* no clothing at all!

Naga Baba
Kedarnath, October, 2007

Two Swamis
Kumbha Mela, Prayag Raj, 2001

Sadhus
Kumbha Mela, Prayag Raj, 2001

Happy Swamis
Grand Procession, Makar Sankranti Day
Kumbha Mela, Prayag Raj, 2001

"Little Shiva"
Kumbha Mela, Prayag Raj, 2001

Sadhu
Nainital, February, 2001

Kali Murti
Rishikesh, October, 2004

Sadhu
Garwal Himalayas, October, 2004

Swami in Omkareshwar
Narmada Jayanti, January, 2009

A Mahatma
Kumbha Mela, Prayag Raj, 2001

9 Tenants of Sanatana Dharma

1) There is one, all pervasive Supreme Being who is both immanent and transcendent.
2) The universe undergoes endless cycles of creation, preservation and dissolution.
3) All souls are evolving toward union with God and will ultimately find *Moksha*: freedom from the cycle of rebirth and oneness with Spirit. Not a single soul will be eternally deprived of this destiny.
4) The law of karma, by which each individual creates his or her own destiny by their thoughts, words and deeds.
5) The soul reincarnates through many births until all karmas have been resolved.
6) Divine beings exist in unseen worlds, and that worship and rituals, as well as personal devotion create a communion with these *devas* and gods.
7) A spiritually awakened master or *Satguru* is essential to know the Absolute. Just as a lamp is lit by another lamp, a true Guru lights the flame of God-consciousness in the disciple. Also required are the disciple's good conduct, purification, self-inquiry and meditation.
8) All life is sacred, to be loved, revered and protected, and so practice *ahimsa*, or non-injury.
9) No particular religion teaches the only way to salvation above all others. All genuine religious paths are facets of God's pure love, deserving tolerance and understanding.

Respect for spiritual practices and the high ideals of *Sanatana Dharma* extend far beyond a reverence for holy men and women. The path of spiritual marriage (*grihasta ashrama*) is considered to be on par with that of renunciation when the *dharmas* pertaining to that path are faithfully observed. The path of the *grihasta* lies in spiritualizing all of the various relationships and experiences which one may encounter in life. The epic poem, *Ramayana,* demonstrates how to bring the lofty ideals of spiritual living into whatever station of life one may be called. When the now famous television production of the *Ramayana*, produced by director Ramanand Sagar, was shown in seventy-six weekly episodes, most government offices around the country would close during that one-hour time period. In cities, towns and even rural villages, everyone would gather around the only television in the village, often in the schoolmaster's home, to watch this great spiritual drama unfold. Such is the innate tendency toward spirituality which is to be found in the people of India.

I had visited the ancient cave temples on Elephanta Island in the Mumbai harbor during my first pilgrimage in 1992. On my second visit there in 1995 I immediately sought out the inner shrine room which is raised above the floor of the cave. There is enshrined a large *Shiva Lingam* made entirely of natural stone. Choosing an especially dark corner of the already dark chamber, I sat for meditation. The sacred enclosure encompasses an area of only about fifteen feet across with five feet in the middle being taken up by the *Lingam* and the stone platform on which it stands. The *Lingam* is encircled by a narrow walkway leading to and from entrances at each end of the shrine. Pilgrims and visitors enter the chamber, light incense as an offering, *pranam* and perhaps touch the *Lingam* in reverence and then depart.

Sitting in a dark recess of a corner of that stone chamber I thought myself to be hardly noticeable to visitors. Soon a small group of four young teenage boys entered the enclosure. They were having fun, talking in a playful sort of way. When they became aware of my presence, however, they immediately fell silent. Circumambulating the holy *Lingam,* they walked over to where I was seated, reverently touched their hands to the ground in front of me, offered their *pranams* and quietly departed. What a moving demonstration of the respect the Indian people generally have for anyone who is seeking God and spiritual upliftment. I was humbled and grateful to be shown such an example of purity and humility as expressed by these young boys. How can one not help but wish that the youth in our Western countries might emulate their example!

During all our pilgrimages to India one of our greatest delights has been interacting with the children. For those of us coming from America, their purity, simplicity and guilelessness would scarcely be believed. In this and in many other ways, the moral, ethical and spiritual standards of traditional Indian society could set the standard for the upliftment and transformation of our global family. This is one of the timeless yet immanently timely messages of the sages.

Due to my affinity for India, most people I know assumed that had I been there even before I made my first trip. When I was younger I secretly dreamed of living the life of a *sadhu* – even, in my fancy, a *sanyassi* – staying in temples and ashrams, or just sleeping by the side of the road with only a piece of cloth or a blanket for warmth. How well I remember one Easter vacation in Laguna Beach, California. I was a young teenager, staying with my best friend, Hal, and my mother, for a week at the beach. Hal and I awoke early one morning and decided to go for a walk on the beach alone. It was a chilly, foggy morning as we walked along. No one was in sight. We went by what appeared to be an old piece of canvas lying on the sand. Walking up to it, I kicked it with my foot. To my great surprise and teenage embarrassment, someone was actually sleeping there, rolled up in that old, rough piece of cloth. Hastily, we scurried away! At the same time, a thrill went through my body. From that day on – and I don't remember for how long, although it was certainly more than a year – I refused to sleep in my bed. I rolled up in a blanket and slept on the floor. Later on in my life, after reading about the wandering monks and pilgrims of India, it made sense, though my parents, I'm sure, must have thought I was crazy.

As an aspiring yogi, the life of a *sadhu* seemed romantic and appealing. In reality, it is a hard life, and one not suited to me in this incarnation. I was born in the West to learn certain lessons, and I can say that there has been no lack of them! Nevertheless, my heart is rooted in the spirit and soul of India.

It was on Sunday, February 9th, 1992, that I first arrived there. After briefly landing at the Kolkata (Calcutta) airport en route, we touched down at midnight in Mumbai, then still known by its British name of Bombay. India at last! My heart and mind were spinning. I could hardly believe it. Then we drove through the city in the middle of the night. The smells hit you first – or is it the humidity? Feelings, images, long sleeping memories – all were beginning to awaken. The roadside fires, the smoke, the dimly lit shops, the chai stands, the wayside restaurants. If ever there had been any doubt as to whether or not I had lived here in another life, there was none now.

The next morning our group of pilgrims bussed back through the city to the Gateway of India, an imposing arch overlooking the harbor. Nearby we found two eclectic looking snake charmers sitting on the crowded street corner with their cobras. Boarding a small boat, we set off for the Elephanta Caves. The excursion was fascinating. The long and broad steps leading up to the hilltop cave complex are lined with makeshift shops. It was here that I made my first purchases. For the sum of five rupees I bought a key chain to which was affixed the shape of a heart, colored in the likeness of the national flag of India. On it was written the words, "I Love India." I am still carrying that key chain today.

Enjoyable as visiting the ancient cave temple was, it was the return trip by boat that was most memorable. There were literally hundreds of people crowded onto a narrow stone pier barely four feet wide. The tide had come in while we were in the caves. The top of the peer was just at water level, and in some places the water was actually splashing over the pier, making it wet and slippery. We had to take a small boat out to our larger boat and climb over the rails from boat to boat. To make things even more interesting, one boat, obviously swamped with far too many passengers, began to flounder. Everyone was hastily attempting to get off that boat and onto any other that happened to be in the vicinity. After that drama, things settled down. All were safe.

The predominant feeling on the return trip, I remember, was one of deep peace and gratitude. The occasional chilling splash of water which hit us from the wake felt like a blessing coming directly from the Lord Himself. A friend and I began to chant: *Shiva Shiva Shambo Shankara, Hara Hara Hara*

Mahadevara / Gangajata Dhara Gauri Manohara, Parthi Puri Parameshwara, ("God the Father, Supreme Spirit, the Most Auspicious One; the Great Renewer, You alone are the Supreme Ruler of this world and the Supreme Lord within and beyond all creation"). This drew the attention of a number of beautiful young children who joined us. At first they were just listening in a shy and curious way, yet soon were joining in. There was much fun and laughter. We were teaching them English while they did their best to teach us Hindi. One of the ladies in our group photographed them with a video camera and showed it to them on playback. All were jumping and giggling, "Auntie, show me! Auntie, show me!"

The ride back across the city at night was quite overwhelming. It was my first experience of the sensory overload that seems to define the larger cities of modern India. People, cars, trucks, three-wheel taxies, bicycles, and cows were everywhere! The city seemed to be alive with a constant party atmosphere. Oddly enough, after only one day, I was starting to feel a part of it all. There was an intangible feeling of harmony, an unmistakable undercurrent of joy, as it were, which seemed to permeate the very atmosphere.

The city, with all its commotion, stretched on and on. We passed large elaborate weddings in progress, with their multicolored lights, streamers, fireworks, Western-style bands, and live Indian music. On the flipside were the beggars. Some were severely disfigured, deformed or blind; the bone-thin, dirty old women; the little urchin children grabbing you by the hand and crying "*Bakshish! Bakshish!*" They have expertly learned how to cry in just the right way, aimed straight at the heart of the sympathetic. One might suppose that they have received early theatrical training. Quite likely they have! Some are very enterprising, wiping off the windows of the taxis in the hope of getting a reward. We have entered a different world.

The next evening we hired a taxi to take us to one of the largest of the several *Yogoda Satsanga Society* meditation groups in the city for *kirtan*, meditation and dinner. Once again we had to cross the city. There were four of us in our taxi. We had great fun chanting *bhajans* all the way. We were in a joyous mood, singing and chanting. In retrospect it seems we may have distracted our driver, for he got quite lost a number of times! He was chanting along with us, you see, all the while getting more and more excited. Finally it seemed that he could no longer contain himself. He suddenly turned to us with a huge smile on his face that was even more expressive than his words, as he exclaimed, "Nothing like this has happened to me! This is the happiest day of my life! I am Hindu also!" We broke up with laughter, while at the same time our eyes were brimming with tears. It was so moving. He was so sincere. It was so perfect.

On my second day in India, I wrote in my journal: "Thinking of God, chanting inwardly, doing *japa* and meditating seem to come naturally here. I fall effortlessly into a meditative state whenever I close my eyes. I would hardly have believed it. You may have heard that it is like this here in this holy land, yet it doesn't really impact a person until you are experiencing it yourself. Everything seems like ordered chaos – just right somehow – permeated with aliveness and consciousness."

Darshan of the Shankaracharya

Known as the "Golden City of a Thousand Temples," Kanchipuram is the home of one of the *Shankaracharyas* of South India. At the time of our visit in 1992, the Shankaracharya *Math*, Kamakoti Peetham, was presided over by His Holiness Sri Sri Sri Chandrashekarendra Saraswati, the 66th *Shankaracharya* of his lineage. Revered throughout India as the "Sage of Kanchi," he was 97 years of age at the time. Having met Paramahansa Yogananda, he had written a glowing tribute to the Master: "A great shining light in this world, such a soul comes on earth only rarely, when there is a great need among men." 1992 was the year in which the birth centennial of Paramahansaji was being celebrated in India. Swami Sharanananda, of *Yogoda Satsanga Society*, had recently returned from a visit with the Shankaracharya, hoping that he might provide some further words about Paramahansaji that could be incorporated in the centennial tributes. Swamiji told us that he had brought a few of Paramahansa Yogananda's books with him as gifts for the *Shankaracharya*. One of them was *"Man's Eternal Quest."* On its cover is a beautiful photograph of the Master. Swamiji told us that the *Shankaracharya* had closed his eyes, gently stroking the picture with the palm of his hand for several minutes. He then proclaimed, "Everything in this book represents the highest truth. Nothing can be added to it." He later sent a beautiful tribute to be used in the *YSS* Centennial commemoration.

Arriving in Kanchipuram, we visited several ancient temples built around the 8th Century. These included the Kailash Temple and the imposing main Shiva temple called "Ekambareshwar," with its towering *goparam*. There we received *darshan* of the 108 black stone Shiva lingams installed within. After making the traditional offerings and receiving *tilak* and *prasad* from the *pujaris*, we exited to receive a special blessing from the temple elephant who placed his trunk on top of our heads in benediction. Once outside we were shown a huge mango tree said to be 3,500 years old that produces four different types of mangoes on the same tree!

On the spur of the moment our guide suggested that we proceed to Kamakoti Peetham, the Shankaracharya Math, in the hope of receiving *darshan* of the Shankaracharya, Sri Chandrashekarendra Swamigal, himself. His Holiness carries the title of *Jagadguru*, "Guru of the World," or alternately, "Guru of the Universe," for, indeed, Hinduism teaches that, "He who knows God becomes God." Our quest was rewarded in a remarkable way.

Arriving at the Math we were stunned to see a line of literally thousands of pilgrims and devotees winding around the building and on down the street! Suddenly, however, we had a wonderful and completely unexpected surprise. Someone, and to this day I am not certain who it may have been that took it upon themselves to be so kind and gracious, guided our small party around the long line of waiting devotees right up to the *darshan* room! Those who had queued up in line were passing ever so quickly before the door of a small room in which the saint was seated. After a brief glimpse of His Holiness they were quickly ushered on by and out the exit, receiving a small banana as *prasad* on the way out.

In contradistinction, our party was directed to climb over the ropes into an area that was occupied by the temple musicians and directly in the line of view of the *Shankaracharya.* There we were able to gaze in upon the holy man for as long as we wished. How was it possible? Who was responsible for this incomprehensible blessing? Why were we thus honored while the Indian pilgrims, many having come from far distant locations, were able to remain for only a few brief moments? My head was spinning. I didn't know whether to feel blessed or guilty. Nevertheless, I did know that I wanted to absorb as much as I possibly could while in the presence of such a great soul. I was looking intently into his eyes. The atmosphere seemed surreal. We were sitting next to the group of temple musicians who were playing absolutely thrilling yet raucous music on drums beaten with sticks, huge *kartals*, a *sruti box,* and two blasting *nadaswaram* trumpets! Wow!

While sitting and meditating, I was deeply connecting with the saint through his eyes. I remembered how my Guru said that he used to purify his body by rolling in the dust where such great ones had walked. It was a blessed experience indeed, and a deep sense of gratitude filled my heart.

The 97 year old pontiff ate little, living an extremely simple and austere life. One might assume that such a highly respected public religious personality, who is often likened to the "Pope of the

Hindus," would live in an outwardly aesthetic, well-kept and appointed dwelling. On the contrary, *Kamakoti Peetham* is an ancient-appearing structure nearly indistinguishable from the shops and other buildings along the dirt road that passes through Kanchipuram. Such is the wonder of India – and we may add, Her glory as well. In Paramahansaji's words: "India may not have material skyscrapers and all the sometimes spiritually enervating comforts of modern life – she has her faults, as all nations have – but India shelters many unassuming Christlike spiritual 'skyscrapers' who could teach the Western brothers and sisters how to glean the fullest spiritual joy out of any condition of life," (*Journey to Self-Realization*)).

Sri Chandrashekarendra Saraswati Paramacharya Swamigal attained *mahasamadhi* in 1994, just prior to his 100th birthday.

Three Saints, Three Religions

When we make up our minds to go on a spiritual pilgrimage, so many miracles often occur that one cannot help but wonder as to the Guiding Force that is directing our destiny. Following the path of a *satguru*, devotees naturally relate these synergistic and serendipitous occurrences to the guidance of the *guru* – and rightly so.

In previous years, Polestar Tours had made it a part of their itinerary to visit Mother Theresa when they were in Calcutta. In February, 1995, however, we had heard news reports that Mother was still in Rome recovering from a recent heart attack. It was still undecided weather or not our group would visit her Mother House on this trip.

We had heard about a large underground shopping mall not far from the Oberoi Grand Hotel where we were staying. Some of us were curious and it seemed like an interesting adventure, so we decided to check it out. As we roamed amongst the shops, we happened to notice two nuns belonging to Mother Theresa's Missionaries of Charity, clad as they were, in the blue-bordered white saris that are characteristic of their Order. We introduced ourselves and the kind sisters informed us that Mother Theresa had just returned to Caluctta. They warmly invited us to come to the Mother House, saying that there was a good chance that she would greet us.

Hearing the news, our tour guides, Drs. Thomas and Victoria Parker, arranged for us to go the very next day. After a short period of meditation in the upstairs communion hall, Mother Theresa soon entered, kneeling in the back of the hall and joining the angelic voices of the resident nuns in their mid-day prayers. In such a holy environment, who would not feel the Divine presence?

After the conclusion of the worship service, she met with our group on the balcony just outside the communion hall. Mother always seemed to delight in meeting the SRF devotees, and this occasion was no different. She spent quite some time with us all, answering questions, passing out prayer cards, and blessing us. I remember how her feet were gnarled.

Her frail body gave the appearance of having gone through many trials, yet her silent strength amply demonstrated that she was beyond identification with her body. An unmistakable aura of luminosity emanated from her, radiating a feeling of peace and love. We all felt blessed, and very fortunate to be in the presence of such a saintly soul.

After the pilgrimage tour concluded that year, a few of us stayed on for a week or so in the holy city of Rishikesh. No sooner had we checked into the Ganga Kinare Hotel than our guide met me outside the entrance to my room. From 'out of the blue' he asked, "Would you like to see the Dalai Lama tomorrow?" What a question! It seems that His Holiness was dedicating a new Tibetan Buddhist temple in the nearby city of Dehradun. The hotel management, who were Buddhist, happened to be one of the sponsors of this momentous event. They were able to provide complimentary passes to their guests, and we were the lucky recipients!

The following morning found three of us, and Anil, our friend and guide, on a chartered bus headed for Dehradun. The newly constructed temple was truly spectacular. The atmosphere was festive. Many little shops had been set up along the roadside. Security was tight. We had to wait for quite some time, yet eventually were admitted and treated to a gourmet banquet. An outdoor pavilion had been set up to accommodate the hundreds of guests, which included a large contingent of Tibetan Buddhist monks and nuns.

After opening ceremonies, which included dancers in fantastically elaborate costumes and musicians playing traditional long ceremonial trumpets, the Dalai Lama was introduced. After a brief talk it was announced that His Holiness would be available on the following day at such and such a time to meet with those who were visiting from other countries. Unfortunately, our schedule did not allow us to return the next day.

One member of our group dearly loved the Dalai Lama. She boldly approached one of the officials and told him that we could not return tomorrow. "May we see the Dalai Lama *today*?" He responded that at exactly 1:33 PM, His Holiness would be leaving the temple. If we were waiting at the bottom of the temple steps when he departed, he would no doubt meet with us for a few minutes. That is exactly what happened. He appeared right on schedule, greeting us and blessing us with his kind, warm-hearted, all-embracing nature that is so typical of one who is established in divine consciousness. We presented him with the traditional white scarves which were then returned to us with his blessings.

During the time we spent at the Tibetan temple complex, while the guests were taking their meal, we met a woman *sanyassi* from America whose name was Swami Gurudevananda. She told us that she had come from the States to be with her *Guru*, H.H. Swami Chidananda Saraswati, successor to the great master, Swami Sivananda of Rishikesh, and president of The Divine Life Society. When she had arrived in Rishikesh, however, she was informed that Swami Chidananda was not at the ashram after all. He was traveling and they did not know when to expect his return. She felt heartbroken.

We had not paid a visit to Sivanandashram ourselves on this visit, and decided to do so the next day. Almost immediately upon our arrival, as we were walking into the *darshan* hall where the great master's *samadhi* is located, a young man – apparently an ashram resident – excitedly approached us from behind. He exclaimed, "Our master, Sri

Swami Chidanandaji, has just returned to the ashram for just three days! Would we like to meet him?" Can you believe it!

We accompanied our serendipitous guide to the main temple and were led inside. A wedding ceremony was in progress. The wedding party was seated to the left of the inner sanctum, as the officiating *pujari* was performing the ceremony. To the right was seated a group of holy men, including His Holiness, Sri Swami Chidananda Maharaj. In his company was a *sadhu* who appeared to be divinely intoxicated. He had a shaved head and appeared to be completely naked except for a blanket which lay across his lap. His eyes were closed as he rocked gently back and forth.

After some time we were invited to go up to Swami Chidanandaji for his blessing. He spoke briefly with some of our companions, although for my part, I took his blessing silently. What a remarkable scene it was!

Our divine *Gurudeva*, Sri Sri Paramahansa Yogananda, often called the organization which he founded in the West a "Church of All Religions." How appropriate, we thought, that in the course of just a few short weeks we had received the *darshan* and blessings of a Christian saint, a Buddhist saint and a Hindu saint –

without the slightest pre-arrangement on our part. It was demonstrated once again that when a devotee goes on pilgrimage with sincerity of heart, "anything can happen!"

The Eagle Miracle

After spending some time in India, time itself takes on a different sense of proportion, so it comes as no surprise that a person may begin to question 'reality'. So called "mundane events" become full of divine potentiality. In fact, the very phrase, "mundane reality," is a misnomer, for everything is permeated with the living presence of the Divine at all times. A sweet realization begins to dawn on us that every beggar, every shopkeeper, every passerby may, in fact, be a *siddha* in disguise. Whether it be in the form of a test or a blessing, each circumstance, every happenstance, appears to be orchestrated by a Higher Power. In a land where everything is filled with the living presence of God, life becomes a great mystery and an unparalleled adventure.

An American *swami* who has been living in India for a number of years told us, "In the West we just don't have the concept that physical objects such as rivers and mountains can be actual manifestations of God. The concept is hard to get across until you actually experience it. Arunachala, the holy mountain at Tiruvannamalai, the sacred river *Ganga,* and other such physical manifestations are truly God in form. There can be no doubt about this. I can't explain it, yet I have experienced it."

Once, while visiting the famous Shiva temple at Tarakeshwar in the countryside near Kolkata, I was standing, leaning slightly against the inner wall of the courtyard outside the entrance to an adjacent shrine. My eyes were closed in meditation and my consciousness was quite interiorized. Suddenly I was startled and brought to outer awareness by someone pushing their finger into my forehead. Opening my eyes, I peered down upon an elderly woman less than five feet tall. She had reached up to place a *tilak* between my eyebrows – and quite forcefully too! Gracefully she shuffled away without so much as asking for alms. Who *was she*?

What about the holy cow in Omkareshwar? She placed her entire head on top of my head while I was meditating by the *sangam*, as if in benediction. (See: "*Friday Morning in Omkareshwar,*" Page 77). The reader, of course, may think such thoughts to be absurd. Yet those of us who have been in India and have begun to attune ourselves with her unspoken mysteries find the dividing line between physical and metaphysical realities dissolving away. A new dimension opens into a life filled with potentiality and magic.

Studying the lives of the great masters, we often hear anecdotes as to how they may appear in different forms and guises to different people at different times. The extraordinary life of Neem Karoli Baba, for example, is replete with such incidents. Maharaj-ji, as he is known to his disciples and associates, might promise to attend a wedding or religious function, or to visit a certain devotee's home. The parties would then be highly disappointed when the Master seemingly failed to appear. Upon questioning, Maharaj-ji would often counter that indeed he had been there. He would then relate such and such an incident, saying, "Do you not remember the old beggar that came to the wedding and you threw him out!" or, "Did you not see the parrot sitting on the window ledge?" He could accurately relate all the events which had taken place. It sets the mind to wondering... or, it stops the mind from wandering. The choice is ours!

On the 10th of July, 1984, fourteen years after acquiring the property, a *murti* of Sri Hanuman-ji was installed in the then just completed temple at the Neem Karoli Baba Ashram in Rishikesh. The *ashram* is located in the Virbhadra portion of the city, 6 kilometers south of Rishikesh on the road to Haridwar. In April, 1985, Hanuman *Jayanti* was being celebrated there for the first time. It was a colorful day filled with great festivity. Devotees chanted the *Hanuman Chalisa* and recited *Sundarkand* from *Ramacharitamanas.* The atmosphere became supercharged with devotional intensity. When the *Ramayana* recitation was about to conclude, a large monkey walked right in through the main gate. Passing by the crowd of devotees, it entered the temple. Lifting the cloth covering the *prasad,* it helped itself to some sanctified refreshments. Leaving the temple, its body suddenly became small enough to slip through the barbed wire perimeter fence. There it danced about joyfully! That monkey then proceeded directly to a hut which had been built for Baba Neem Karoli and went inside. The hut had only one door and no windows. Many devotees naturally felt that this was none other than Hanuman himself. Others thought it was actually Maharaj-ji in the guise of a monkey. Someone was finally courageous enough to look inside. The monkey, of course, had vanished. Everyone felt that this was Maharaj-ji's *lila.* A report on this remarkable incident was published in the Indian daily newspaper, *The Hindustan*, dated April 16th, 1985.

Sant Tulsidas, who lived in the 15th Century, was a poet, saint and author of *Ramacharitamanas* and *Sri Hanuman Chalisa.* He obtained the *darshan* of Sri Ramachandra and Sri Lakshman in a remarkable manner. Tulsidas was residing in the holy city of Varanasi (Banaras). After his morning bath in the holy waters of the *Ganga*, it was his wont to carry water from the river to nourish a sacred fig tree which grew close to his *kutir*. One day, much to his surprise, an astral being emerged from the tree and informed Tulsidas that his acts of caring devotion had freed him from long imprisonment within that tree. In gratitude he would like to offer the saint a boon. Tulsidas replied that he wanted nothing other than the *darshan* of Sri Ram, Himself. The *deva* replied: "Everyday at Hanuman *Ghat,* a saint comes to narrate the holy *Ramayana.* Lord Hanuman always assumes the form of an old leper and comes to listen to that timeless, nectarian story. He is the first to arrive, leaving only after everyone else has departed from the place. Hold his feet tightly. Don't let him go! Acknowledge that you know who he is. He will certainly bestow on you the grace, blessings and *darshan* of Sri Ramachandra." And so it happened as the benevolent spirit had declared.

The Hindu scriptures affirm: "The knower of *Brahman* becomes *Brahman.*" A *siddha*, being one with God, has all the powers and attributes of the Divine Sovereign including omnipresence, omniscience and omnipotence. Such a being is everywhere at the same time, knows everything in the past, present and future, and can do anything without limitation. Can we comprehend it? Do we even believe it? Deep within the temple of our hearts, in the joy-filled tranquility of our souls, we recognize the truth and say, "Yes!" Such is the destiny of each one of us.

In answer to the age-old question, "Is God personal or impersonal?" One master remarked, "God is both personal and impersonal. In the ultimate sense, God is impersonal. Yet when you realize the impersonal God, you will find that

He is more personal than the personal God." Paradoxical? Not really. In fact, how could it be otherwise? He is our very own Self. What could be more personal than that?

The *Vedas* declare, *Ekam Sat* – "Only One exists" – followed by its corollary, *Tat Twam Asi* – "We are that One." It should come as no surprise that the masters who have realized God are able to shape-shift into any form they choose to bless and uplift their devotees – or just for the sake of play.

When staying at the *Yogoda Satsanga Society* ashram near the village of Dwarahat in the Himalayan foothills, it is only a short drive to the trail leading to the cave of the great *Mahavatar Babaji.* This is the cave in which the deathless master was staying at the time of his meeting with *Lahiri Mahasaya,* India's *Yogavatar,* "Incarnation of Yoga." Their predestined meeting in 1861 resulted in the *Kriya Yoga* dispensation for the modern world which is spreading in all lands.

Rounding a turn in the twisting mountain road midway between the ashram and the trail – assuming the day is clear and the Himalayas are in the mood for giving *darshan* – the snow-capped peaks literally explode into view. The panorama is so striking that the inevitable impulse is to pull over and take in this awe-inspiring sight. That was our experience!

As we were standing by the roadside during our pilgrimage in 1995, watching the bright mountain peaks framed by a valley of green hills, an eagle suddenly appeared in the distance. Flying three large and complete circles around the mountain peak between the hills, it was gone as suddenly as it had appeared. In what seemed like an instant, an eagle then appeared in the sky directly above where we were standing. If it was the same eagle that we had just observed in the distance, it would have had to traverse the distance to us with astounding rapidity. Flying three low circles in the sky directly above us it once again disappeared from view. No one saw where it went. It just seemed to disappear without a trace. I was able to photograph it during its encircling flight.

Amazed as we were, the 'icing' was yet to come. We continued our drive for another thirty minutes or so until we reached the beginning of the trail that wanders behind quaint and picturesque mountain farms and into the woods. It is a walk of about two hours at a leisurely pace, and the last portion is a fairly steep uphill climb. As we were making the final ascent to the open area just below the famous cave, an identical eagle suddenly appeared in the bright blue sky directly above Babaji's Cave. Flying three complete circles over the holy site, that eagle too was gone! We did not see it again.

As you may well imagine, the depth of feeling that coursed through my being as I watched in amazement as the eagle appeared above Babaji's Cave can hardly be described. To bring into linguistic expression who I thought that may have been, or what its appearance might have meant, is best left to the reader's imagination. After all, this is India, where mundane reality and Divine Reality intermix and commingle in such a way as to surprise and delight the astonished devotee.

Hari-ki-Pairi Ghat

A conundrum presents itself to those of us who are deeply attracted to and feel in tune with the great spiritual culture of India. Being from the West, with our light skin and incomplete knowledge of the language, rituals and culture, it is difficult to fully fit-in to the land we so dearly love. This can be heart wrenching at times. I remember riding in a rickshaw through the crowded streets of Varanasi one afternoon on my first trip to India. We were in the midst of a dizzying array of all manner of motor transport, bicycles and pedestrian traffic. There he was: a Westerner approaching us from the opposite direction in another rickshaw. Without having time to edit my thoughts, what ran through my mind went something like this: "What is he doing here? He doesn't belong here." As though I did!

There is a profound upside to this phenomenon, however. We turn again to Paramahansaji's words in his poem, *My India*:

The Western brothers by matter's might
have conquered my land;
Blow, blow aloud, her conch shells all!
India now invades with love,

To conquer their souls…
with newfound boundless love
I behold the borderland of my India
Expanding into the world…

This is what we are seeing in the West today. The great master, Sri Ramakrishna Paramahamsa once remarked, "Religions will come and go, but Hinduism is eternal." Yogananda proclaimed, "Destroy all books on yoga, and those truths will be revealed anew, for Truth is eternal." *Sanatana Dharma* is not just an Indian religion. It is a world religion, kept safe in India during the dark ages of materialism. Now, like a blossoming lotus, its fragrance of *Satyam* (Truth), *Shivam* (Auspiciousness), and *Sundaram* (Beauty), is spreading in all lands through the awakening consciousness of devotees everywhere.

World religions authority, Huston Smith, recalls that in the 1950's the eminent British historian, Dr. Arnold Toynbee, predicted that in the 21st Century, "India the conquered would conquer her conquerors." In an interview in the *San Diego Union-Tribune*, April 7th, 1990, Smith said, "What he meant was that basic Indian insights would find their way into our Western culture, and, because of their metaphysical and psychological profundity, our way of thinking in the West would be influenced by Indian thought just as Indian technology has been influenced by ours."

Reflecting on the course of world affairs that began with the discovery of atomic energy, Dr. Toynbee observed: "It is already becoming clear that a chapter which had a Western beginning will have to have an Indian ending if it is not to end in the self-destruction of the human race… At this supremely dangerous moment in human history, the only way of salvation for mankind is the Indian way – Emperor Asoka's and Mahatma Gandhi's principle of nonviolence and Sri Ramakrishna's testimony to the harmony of religions. Here we have an attitude and spirit that can make it possible for the human race to grow together into a single family – and, in the Atomic Age this is the only alternative to destroying ourselves."

How many *swamis, sadhus* and *sadhakas* we have met in India who are from the Western countries, not to mention the rapidly growing Hindu subculture here in America. Where we live in Encinitas, for example, we often have to choose which *kirtan,* meditation or *satsang* we would like to attend on any given day of the week. Although *Sanatana Dharma* is spreading from coast to coast, it seems to many of us who live in Encinitas that our coastal town is the closest thing to a 'holy city' in America at this time. It is the 'place to play' for most of the traveling *kirtan wallahs* who go from city to city singing the holy Names of God. Bhagavan Das, the well-known American *sadhu,* teacher and *kirtan* singer who was brought to the attention of many through Ram Dass' classic book *Be Here Now*, told us that Encinitas is one of the *108 Shakti Peeths,* or centers of Divine Mother energy in the world. He noted that if this were India, temples and ashrams would be built all up and down the coast. Perhaps it will be so one day.

It is estimated that as many as two thousand followers of Paramahansa Yogananda live in or around the Encinitas area. This is the location of the hermitage where the great master spent so much of his time and penned his spiritual classic, *Autobiography of a Yogi*, a book that has catalyzed the transformation of countless lives. Much of the Master's commentary on the New Testament, which he titled, *The*

Second Coming of Christ, was written here in Encinitas. It was here also, on the grounds of his hermitage, that Saint Francis appeared to him, inspiring him to write his great poem, *God, God, God.*

Encinitas is also host to a large Ammachi *satsang,* featuring wonderful kirtans, and sharing the teachings of Sri Amritanandamayi Devi. We have a Baba Hari Dass *satsang,* a Satya Sai Baba group, and devotees from many different paths within the comprehensive framework of Hindu Devotional Mysticism. My wife and I also host many *kirtan* and devotional music concerts in our area. We feel that the true purpose of music is to uplift the consciousness, leading to actual communion with the Divine. Several years ago we founded the Encinitas Kirtan Circle which meets weekly at several different close-by locations. The Kirtan Circle is open to all who love to chant the Names of the Divine Beloved.

Although we may never completely fit into the fabric of colloquial Indian culture, we do find ourselves to be part of a larger and awe-inspiring vision, as the eternal truths of *Sanatana Dharma* emerge world-wide.

"Hail, mother of religions, lotus, scenic beauty, and sages! / Thy wide doors are open, / Welcoming God's true sons through all ages…" continues Paramahansaji in his great poem. And so we return again and again – as often as we can – to our beloved India, this "ever-changing, never-changing land" where souls dream God.

It is always a thrill to attend the *Ganga Arati* at Hari-ki-Pairi *Ghat* in Haridwar. When we are in India we never miss the opportunity. Numerous *arati* ceremonies are conducted up and down the holy river, most prominently in Haridwar, Varanasi and Rishikesh. Yet the Ganga *Arati* at Haridwar is preeminent. Every evening, at *sandhya,* an hour or so before sunset, thousands of pilgrims begin to assemble at the *ghat.* The *Hanuman Chalisa* and other devotional *bhajans* and prayers are sung over loud speakers while the *shakti* builds in devotional intensity. Just as darkness descends, numerous *pujaris* emerge from the ancient *Ganga Mandir* holding huge flaming ghee lamps that look like campfires being held in the palms of their hands. While the *Ganga Arati* hymn is being broadcast over the assembly and thousands of enthusiastic *bhaktas* are singing along, the priests artfully swing their flaming lamps down to touch the surface of the river in a divinely choreographed dance of devotional delight. Families and individuals of all ages offer small leaf boats filled with flower petals illumined by ghee lights, to a river which is none other than the living form of the Goddess. The *diyas* move rapidly along the surface of the living waters like bright soul-flames dancing on waves of bliss. The entire atmosphere is surcharged with a thrill of joy! The Divine Presence is tangible. It may not be adequately described in words yet it can certainly be felt.

It so happened that in March of 1998 we were fortunate to be able to spend a few days at the *Kumbha Mela* which had convened at Haridwar that year. Along with an Indian doctor, who was also a guest at the *Yogoda Satsanga Society* camp, we decided to walk to Hari-ki-Pairi Ghat one evening to attend the *Arati.* Knowing that the crowds would be enormous during the *Mela*, we arrived two hours early. Taking seats on the platform behind those who had already arrived, we were sitting about thirty feet from the water's edge. Soon a steady stream of pilgrims began pouring into the congregational area directly across the *ghat* from the *Ganga Mandir.*

Pilgrims Awaiting Ganga Arati
Hari-ki-Pairi Ghat, Haridwar
Kumbha Mela, 1998

Sitting directly in front of me was a pleasant looking gentleman who appeared to be in his forties. He was messaging the hand of an angelic looking *swami* who was seated next to him to his right. With long white hair and beard, he seemed ageless; a hoary reminder of the *rishis* of yore. How sweetly, I thought, did this disciple honor his *guru*. I felt immediately drawn to the saint. Without his knowledge, I reached out my right hand to reverently touch his ochre cloth. Inwardly I *pranamed*.

We had been listening to the thrilling chanting which was being projected over the loudspeakers, and my consciousness was partially withdrawn in a semi-meditative state. Suddenly, one of our favorite devotional hymns, the *Hanuman Chalisa*, began to be sung over the public address system. My wife and I were transported. This chant of forty verses in praise of Lord Hanuman, composed by the previously mentioned saint, Sant Tulsidas, has been made popular in the West by Krishna Das and other disciples of Sri Neem Karoli Baba. Maharaj-ji encouraged his devotees to learn and recite this great prayer, declaring that it was imbued with tremendous spiritual power. Tulsidas, himself, says in his *Chalisa*, "Whosoever recites this verse one hundred time will be freed from bondage and attain everlasting life. Whosoever even hears this *Chalisa* being sung will be perfected, as Shiva is the witness." My wife and I had learned this beautiful chant and greatly enjoy singing it, so when the *Chalisa* began we were joyfully singing along.

Then an amazing thing happened. When the disciple sitting in front of me heard my exuberant singing of the *Chalisa,* he stopped massaging his guru's hand. Reaching behind his body, yet without looking at me, he began to message my feet! The effect his action had on me was a strange mixture of shock, surprise, embarrassment, unworthiness, pleasure and joy! As soon as I became conscious of what he was doing and why, I made every mental effort to choose the latter two reactions! Waves of energy were coursing up through my entire body with a feeling of rapturous pleasure. For as long as that chant continued – probably seven or eight minutes – this person, who was completely unknown to me, sat carefully and tenderly messaging my feet. As soon as the chant was over, he returned to his previous expression of love and affection for his guru. Never once did he glance back at me.

After the *arati* had concluded and the lights were turned on, everyone stood to make their way toward the river for a physical touch of Her grace, or to move toward the exit, as was each person's wont. It was then that I bent down to touch the feet of this extraordinary person who had been the channel of a most unusual experience. He quickly caught me and held me up so that I could not do so. We then *pranamed* to one another. The sweetness and the love that were conveyed through his eyes is indescribable. After a brief moment of soul recognition we parted, yet that experience remains vivid in my memory today, even as I write.

Up to this point we had not been able to get close to the holy river Ganga. We had purchased our leaf-boats that we would launch downstream with prayers for our families and friends, and the fervent desire that all devotees might draw closer to God. Now we were longing for the touch of the chilly yet vibrant water. Working our way through the loosely assembled crowd, we saw a tall young man with a little girl on his shoulders. She appeared to be his daughter and could not have been more than three years old. She was very tiny, with a pretty frilly dress. Remarkably, she was directing this man who was serving as her vehicle as they moved from person to person through the crowd. She would approach someone and ask in flawless English, "What is your name?" "Where do you come from?" Then she would reach out her little hand, touch that person softly on the head and say, "God bless you!" She would then move on to the next person. We took our turn. Though I didn't fully comprehend what was taking place, I did feel that I was in the presence of a truly unique and beautiful soul. I often imagine that the person

Ganga Arati
Haridwar, September, 2006

Arati Mata tumari, jo jana nita gaata, Maiya jo jana nita gaata / Dasa vahi sahaja me / Mukti ko pata / Om... Jai Gange Mata!

"Mother, this Arati is for You. Those who sing this song everyday are Your devotees and thus find mukti. Om...Victory to Mother Ganga!"

who originated the saying, "wonders never cease," must have been referring to this eternally wondrous land of India!

There are numerous examples of child saints and *bala yogis* in India. Swami Jnanananda Giri, a Kriya Yoga adept from Switzerland, has been living continuously in India since 1952. He tells of meeting a number of such child yogis during his life as a wandering monk. In his spiritual autobiography, *The Transcendent Journey*, Swamiji writes of one young boy whose name was Mukunda. Mukunda's mother used to visit the ashram in which Jnananandaji was residing. When the child first started visiting the ashram, he was only one and a half years of age. He would allow himself to be dressed in an orange dhoti only. Otherwise he would wear nothing at all. He would often smear his body with ash and then sit with the other devotees.

When Mukunda was about two and a half, he would accompany Swami Jnanananda and another saint, reverently referred to as Bapu, to the seashore for their evening meditation. Some of the devotees found it incredulous that such a young child could meditate. In order to test him they asked, "What does Mukunda do in the evening by the sea? On what does he meditate?" To this the child simply replied, "When Mukunda is in meditation, Mukunda talks to the ocean." They asked, "What does the ocean tell you?" The little yogi smiled and replied, "The ocean says: 'OM!' "

Some well-meaning devotees occasionally brought toys for Mukunda. All of these, even a toy car, were unceremoniously placed into a mortar and pestle by the child and ground into powder. One day a lady arrived from Brindaban. She had brought a nice slate writing board and chalk as a gift for Mukunda, thinking that he may learn to write. She told him that it had come from a great distance. To this the child replied, "Mukunda does not require anything from a far distance. What he requires is very close at hand!"

Mukunda would always shun the company of children his own age. When asked why he refused to play with the other children, he would simply reply, "Mukunda talks only with the great ones!"

A saint who became quite well known in the West in the late 1980's and early 1990's was Shiva Bala Yogi. After a spontaneous spiritual experience at the age of fourteen in which Lord Shiva appeared to him and became his *guru*, he remained immersed in *samadhi* twenty-three hours a day for the next ten years.

In his inspiring book, *Modern Saints and Mystics,* Major-General A.N. Sharma tells of meeting a number of young girls, many in the holy town of Brindavan, who were as though modern day *gopikas,* intoxicated by the love of Lord Krishna, serving him in others, and waiting for the Lord to come to them. One of these was Sri Santoshji, a *'gopi'* of rare attainment. From her early years she was found to be intoxicated with divine love. She remained silent for many years, rarely even so much as opening her eyes. Shifting to Brindaban, she spent all of her time in meditation, prayer and devotional singing. Santoshji had no other interest in this world than to meet her Lord Krishna, and to serve Him in His devotees. Being in her presence one would feel automatically uplifted, quickly forgetting the world and its troubles.

The lives of other girl-child saints, names such as Sri Sarlaji, Ushaji, Mata Krishnaji, Kumari Vimal and Sri Dharm Devi can be read in Dr. Sharma's remarkable book, published by the Divine Life Society, Rishikesh. Swami (Papa) Ramdas, himself one of the pre-eminent spiritual savants of this century, tells the story of Dharm Devi from his own experience:

"During Ramdas' visit to Lahore, he came across a remarkable girl. She was found to be fully intoxicated with divine love. Her shining face suffused with smiles of spiritual ecstasy and the spontaneous flow of words replete with wisdom from her lips bear witness to a rare manifestation of the Divine Spirit in one so young and innocent. Ramdas felt immensely happy in her blessed company on three occasions. Her talks are so fresh, brilliant and elevating. When Ramdas saw the girl, he made up his mind to present to the readers of *The Vision,* a short life sketch of the girl.

"Sri Dharm Devi did not, at her birth, manifest any unusual signs prophetic of her later spiritual greatness. When she came to the age of three, she evinced a whole-hearted love for Lord Krishna. She would embrace whatever happened to be before her as the image of Krishna. She declared that she was inspired by Krishna, who had sent her into the world to preach the gospel of Divine love for dispelling ignorance and the consequent misery. In her childhood her only play was about Krishna and Radha, such as *Rasalila,* the Divine play of hide and seek. At the age of five she had for the first time the experience of *Prem Samadhi,* or love trance, which lasted for about ten hours. Her father used to have talks with her on the love and knowledge of God, and she was intelligently discussing these subjects.

"At present she remains in a continued state of divine intoxication, always thinking of her Lord Krishna. Sometimes she has addressed large audiences on spiritual subjects. Interested persons go to see her and when questioned she replies intelligently and with amazing promptness. Sri Dharm Devi is small in stature and build for her age. There is an abundance of playfulness in her movements. She is totally free from shyness. Her face is always aglow with a strange luster. Her eyes are mostly closed, and they have a contemplative look in them. When she is emphasizing a point by appropriate gestures, she keeps her eyes open for a time and we see in them an unusual brilliance mingled with tenderness. The replies to questions put to her pour out of her mouth in a pleasant spontaneity. You are dazzled by them, for they are so full of wit and wisdom. Further, she speaks with confidence and authority. She is simple in her ways and humble in spirit. She displays love for the society of saints. She is manifestly intoxicated with love for Krishna…

"One of the friends in our group requested Dharm Devi to initiate him into her method of meditation. She took him to an adjoining empty room. Soon we heard a sweet and enthralling strain coming from the room. The girl was reciting in a high and measured tune, 'Radhe Shyam'. The friend who was taken for initiation admitted that he was greatly impressed.

"Another sight which produced a touch of enchantment on Ramdas was this: Dharm Devi was asked to call Krishna by her favorite manner – "Mere Prabhu" (Literally, "My Lord"). She warned us that she could not call him thrice, for if she did so she would go into *samadhi* for several hours, but she would call him only twice. We agreed. With a charming smile, eyes nearly closed and face uplifted, the words, 'Mere Prabhu, mere Prabhu,' issued from her beautiful lips with all the sweetness and rapture of love. We were thrilled."

Certainly, to behold Him as all and in all is the greatest vision. **– Sri Dharm Devi**

Diwali at Indore

In the midst of noise and revelry, the Diwali lamp burns as a silent reminder that enlightenment and radiance are the goals of human life.

Srimati Vimla Patil – *Celebrations: Festive Days Of India*

Each year, in the month of Kartik (mid-October to mid-November by the lunar calendar), on the darkest night of the new moon (*amavasya*), the sound of firecrackers and the flash of skyrockets announce the celebration of Diwali. It is the most universally popular festival in a land of festivals and holy days. Homes are decorated, sweets are distributed, and countless *diyas* (oil lamps) are lit to create a world of fancy and delight. Of all the festival days celebrated in India, Diwali is the most glamorous. Though rooted in Hindu mythology, Diwali, or Deepavali, as it is also known, is enjoyed by people of every religion. The magic and radiance of this holy time of year impart an atmosphere of happiness and joy in outward expression and a calm tranquility within. Having experienced *Diwali* in India for the first time in the fall of 2004, we compared it to the exuberance of the Fourth of July, the joy of Christmas and the freshness of New Years all rolled into one!

We were assisting Darshan Tours leader, Gangadas Bell, in taking a small group of Western *yatris* to two of the *Char Dhams,* the four famous pilgrimage destinations in the High Himalayas. We were going to Kedarnath and Badrinath, the former being the most revered temple dedicated to God in the form of Shiva in the Himalayas, and the latter the most sacred Vishnu shrine. Both temples date unto antiquity. Many wonderful legends are associated with each. Badrinath, or Badrinarayan, is intimately connected with Mahavatar Babaji, the deathless master first revealed to Western readers by Paramahansa Yogananda in *Autobiography of a Yogi*: "The Northern Himalayan crags near Badrinarayan are still blessed by the living presence of Babaji, guru of Lahiri Mahasaya."

After the tour was over, my wife and I were looking forward to spending some time at a holy location for a retreat. We had thought of returning to the Himalayan foothills, which we love; perhaps Almora or Nainital. Several years ago, however, I had been captivated while reading about the sacred island of Omkareshwar in the scintillating book, *India Unveiled,* by Robert Arnett. I had inwardly resolved to visit there one day. It was in Omkareshwar, after all, that *Adi Shankaracharya* met and received initiation from his great *guru*, Sri Govinda Jati. After that meeting he very quickly attained the highest state of God-realization. Omkareshwar is also the location of one of the twelve *Jyotir Lingam* temples, well known throughout India and the world as centers of great spiritual power.

Swami Nirmalananda, of the Atma Jyoti Ashram, informed us that an American *sannyasi,* Swami Mangalananda, had been residing for several years at the Sri Anandamayi Ma Ashram in Omkareshwar. He suggested that we contact him. Both Swamis Nirmalananda and Mangalananda are direct disciples of Sri Ma Anandamayi (Anandamoy Ma), the great woman saint of this century about whom Paramahansaji has so eloquently written in his autobiography.

Swami Mangalananda cordially invited us to come to the ashram for a retreat, promising to show us around the area and to introduce us to several saints. One of these was *Brahmarishi* Barfani Dada, who is reputed to be more than 300 years old. His name literally means "Ice Brother," for it is said that he had spent more than 100 years in the high, snowy regions of the Himalayas, including 30 years with Mahavatar Babaji near Mount Kailash. I had to wonder how many people have gotten an invitation like that!

Hilary and I took a pleasant 18 hour overnight train ride from Delhi through Bhopal to the city of Indore in the Central India state of Madhya Pradesh. Procuring a three-wheel taxi rickshaw, we soon arrived at the ashram of Sri Anandamayi Ma, which was founded by *Mahant* Sri Swami Kedarnath-ji Maharaj, an eminent disciple of Ma. Swami Mangalanandaji, who had been out of the ashram at the time of our arrival, came to our room that evening. He became an instant friend and soul companion.

Swamiji had just finished his manuscript for a new book on the life of Sri Anandamayi Ma, entitled *OM MA: Anandamayi Ma, a Brief Life Sketch* (later published in India as *A Goddess Among Us*). He asked if we would like to read it. Although the book had been written at the request of Baba Kedarnath, we were the first to read the completed manuscript. We found it to be very moving and informative. On more than one occasion Hilary and I found ourselves wiping away the tears as we read aloud to one another.

As divine synchronicity would have it, the night following our arrival was the beginning of the annual festival of *Diwali*. We were moonstruck, although there was no moon! Fireworks, skyrockets, bombs and crackers were going off continuously all night long for three consecutive nights. Standing on the balcony of the ashram, we watched in amazement. Sleep was difficult. It sounded like we were in the midst of a war zone. The tranquility of the ashram, however, made the perfect counterbalance, replete as it was with beautifully colored, intricate *rangoli* patterns set in front of the *Devi Mandir* – all surrounded by the warm and attractive glow of the *diyas.*

On *Diwali* night we made our way to the nearby ashram of *Brahmarishi* Barfani Dada. The master, whose birthday was also being celebrated, was giving *darshan* on a covered veranda. Devotees were gathered together singing *bhajans,* while visitors and well wishers came forward to present devotional offerings to the saint. Barfani Dada, however, appeared completely unconcerned about everything that was going on around him. At times he would be talking on a land phone in one hand and a mobile phone in the other, as people called to offer "Happy Birthday" and "Joyous *Diwali*" felicitations.

The open courtyard was lined with streamers and brightly colored lights, reminiscent of our Christmas lights in the West. Huge firecrackers, which sounded like bombs, would be detonated from time to time right in the midst of the ashram complex, shaking us to the core. It took some getting used to. (Actually, we never really did!)

After receiving the blessings of Barfani Maharaj and taking holy *prasad,* we visited the beautiful temple on the ashram grounds and then returned to the Anandamayi Ma Ashram which had so quickly become 'home' to us.

For days thereafter, wherever we went, including a day trip to the holy city of Ujjain, we would see remnants of the holy days of *Diwali.* All the domestic animals were thoroughly decorated with colorful woodblock prints, painted horns, tinsel garlands and colorful streamers. The pink polka-dot cows regally crowned with bright blue horns will ever remain etched in our memories!

Whatever may be the outer celebratory expression, or the diverse legends associated with it in different parts of India,

Diwali symbolizes the triumph of light over darkness. In her book, *Celebrations: Festive Days of India*, the author Srimati Vimla Patil so beautifully writes: "Each year on *Diwali*... one lamp lights another, and like a flame burning steadily on a windless night, brings a message of peace and harmony to the world."

Friday Morning in Omkareshwar

A few hours' drive south of the city of Indore, resting in the midst of the holy Narmada River, is the small island of Omkareshwar. An aerial view shows the island to be very much in the shape of the Sanskrit character for *OM* (ॐ). It is a rocky island with architectural ruins dating to the 11th Century. Omkareshwar is known primarily as a center of pilgrimage, for it is the site of one of the twelve great *Jyotir Lingams* which are held to be veritable embodiments of Lord Shiva. The picturesque temple is situated on a cliff overlooking the holy river.

Arriving by taxi, we crossed the wide and tranquil Narmada by ferry. Accompanied by Swami Mangalananda, we arrived at the Anandamayi Ma Ashram mid-afternoon. The ashram is also built on the rocky cliffs overlooking the river. Climbing a long flight of steps, we were greeted at the top by a beautiful shrine to Lord Hanuman. Hanumanji was painted a brilliantly shining orange paint, so typical of many Hindu icons. I humorously came to call this island 'Stair-kareshwar', as it seemed we were forever climbing staircases wherever we went!

After showing us around the ashram, Swamiji provided us with a room with the exalted name of 'Avadhutananda Kuti.'

It was the room in which Baba Kedarnath's own guru, Sri Swami Avadhutananda, used to stay. Swami Kedarnath, whom we had had the good fortune of meeting while we were staying at the Indore ashram, founded and oversees both of these two ashrams. We were delighted to hear that he would be arriving in Omkareshwar in just a few days.

"Baba," as Swami Kedarnath is affectionately known to his devotees and associates, is a true *mahatma*: a great soul. His appearance and bearing reminds one of the ancient *rishis*. Being in his presence leaves no doubt as to his sanctity. Evenings at the Omkareshwar Ashram were often spent with Baba and a few devotees on the veranda overlooking the holy Narmada River while the moon and stars danced above, their luminosity shimmering on the dark wavelets below. How timeless we felt; how blessed to be from America and yet able to partake in a scene and an experience that can only be described as quintessential India! How many times through the ages, we might wonder, have devotees sat at the feet of one of the great ones like this, listening to his holy words of wisdom, steeped in a peace indescribable.

During our stay at the Omkareshwar Ashram, another saint was temporarily residing across the river at the beautiful Annapurna Ashram, built in classical South Indian style. He was traveling to the holy sites of all twelve *Jyotir Lingams,* researching their history and meditating upon them for a forthcoming publication. He related to Swami Mangalananda that the Omkareshwar *Lingam* was 50,000 years old and that from the moment the *Lingam* arose from the earth, two mantras have been continuously emanating from it, one radiating blessing and upliftment; the other for the expulsion of evil.

It was announced that on the following day a *bandhara* would be celebrated in the ashram. The occasion was to honor and bid farewell to one of the resident *sadhus* who was embarking upon the Narmada *Parikrama.* This arduous *sadhana,* which involves walking around the entire circumference of the sacred Narmada River while living entirely out of doors, takes, on the average, about two years to complete. Pilgrims often begin the *Parikrama* at Omkareshwar, walking toward the ocean while keeping the river on their right. At the mouth of the Narmada in Gujarat they cross over and walk back up the other side to the source of the river at Amarkantak, then back down to Omkareshwar. The *yatris* cannot carry any money. They must depend entirely upon the grace of *Narmada Maiyya* to feed and shelter them.

During my stay at the *Mahakumbha Mela* at *Prayag Raj* in 2001, I met a realized master whose name was Tapaswi Baba (Kalyandas Babaji) who had completed this *Parikrama* several times.

On the day of the *bandhara,* our beautiful ashram on the cliff-side was filled with *swamis* and *sadhus.* There was much kirtan followed by a wonderful feast in which we were invited to participate. Later, Baba spoke informally with the visiting holy men. Other than Swami Mangalananda and a young *sadhu* from Israel who is now known as Brahmachari Omananda, we were the only Westerners present. The hot *rotis,* cooked on a low clay oven by a *brahmachari* from the ashram, then tossed on the coals for a finishing touch; the steaming *puris,* served at the ashram only on special occasions, and the subtly spiced *sabji* dishes cannot be adequately described. Sitting on the concrete floor of the dining hall on worn cotton mats, eating this simple, heavenly meal with our fingers, felt like yet another level of 'coming home'.

Swami Mangalanandaji told us that each Friday morning he would go on *parikrama* around the entire island of Omkareshwar. Following the pilgrim trail around the island's perimeter, he would worship and meditate at the various shrines along the way. He liked to visit several saints and ashrams along the *parikrama* route, and would conclude at the Omkareshwar Temple for *darshan* of the *Jyotir Lingam.* This famous temple is visited daily by pilgrims from all over India. He invited us to join him the next Friday.

Swamiji informed us that once, while he was proceeding on his Friday morning walk, he had been very meticulous in stopping and performing worship at all of the many shrines along the route. As he was descending the stairs leading down toward the main temple, he met a large cobra coming up the stairs toward him. He stood still and watched as the cobra crossed the stairway and perched on the adjoining cement buttress, raising its head as if to give him *darshan.* The snake then crawled off into the brush. Swamiji told us that he had felt greatly blessed, taking the cobra to be a direct manifestation of Lord Shiva.

We awoke early Friday morning and met Swamiji at his room just off a small balcony overlooking the river. Leaving the ashram as the darkness was beginning to fade into the morning light, we made our way to the *sangam* for meditation. The circumfluent Narmada flows around the tiny island. Where the river rejoins itself at the southern tip is referred to as the *sangam* and is considered especially holy. It is an ideal place for meditation.

Swami Kedarnath

Swami Kedarnath Distributing Prasad
Sri Anandamayi Ma Ashram, Indore
November, 2004 (Diwali)

Sri Anandamayi Tapo Bhumi, Omkareshwar

As we were walking down a fairly steep embankment toward the riverside, I slipped and fell, slightly cutting my knee on a rock. I simply ignored it and looked for a good place to sit for meditation. Choosing a flat area next to the river, I had no sooner closed my eyes and lifted my gaze than I felt a very heavy weight pressing down on top of my head. I was stunned and surprised, to say the least. What was this! Without moving my head, I opened my eyes and looked up. A huge black head was pressing down on mine – a big, beautiful mother cow!

My mind went into a spin. A few minutes prior, while arriving at this location, we had not so much as noticed her presence. Where had she come from? It seemed as if she had appeared out of that proverbial 'nowhere' to place the full weight of her head on top of mine! I drew the attention of my wife, Hilary, and Swamiji. They were amazed! As long as I sat there, so long did *Gomataji* (Mother Cow) remain! I took more than 800 photographs on this particular pilgrimage, while my wife took only two, yet she took the best one! (See page 90). This was truly a blessing. As we got up to leave, I noticed that my leg felt fine. Upon inspection I could not so much as find the location of the cut which had occurred only thirty minutes earlier. My body, mind and consciousness felt renewed and refreshed as we continued our walk around the island.

Soon we arrived at an attractive *mandir* next to the pilgrim trail wherein lay a huge *murti* of Lord Hanuman. The reclining image was perhaps twenty-five feet in length and '*bahot sundar*' ("very beautiful!") The story is told that at this very location, Bhima, of *Mahabharata* fame, the younger brother of Arjuna, was on pilgrimage walking *parikrama* around Omkareshwar when he saw Hanumanji asleep by the side of the pilgrim trail. His long tail was crossing the path. It seems that Bhima still had a bit of an "I problem" at the time, thinking himself to be the strongest man alive and virtually invincible. Not wishing to show any sign of disrespect to the venerable Hanuman by stepping over his tail, Bhima kindly requested Sri Hanumanji if he would be so kind as to move it aside so he could pass. Hanuman replied that he was very tired. Would Bhima please move it for him? Try as he might, the 'strongest man alive' was unable to budge Anjaneya's tail by so much as an inch! Bhima's pride was, of course, humbled.

Honoring Sri Hanumanji, and accepting his lesson graciously, Bhima begged forgiveness and continued on his way. It all happened here!

A short distance from this temple we came upon a very humble hermitage. A few modest thatched huts were surrounded by well-kept vegetable and flower gardens tended by a lone elderly lady. Swamiji informed us that this was Om Shanti Ashram, the home of an exalted woman *sadhvi* whose name was Bhole Maiyya (literally, "Simple Mother.") Would we like to meet her? Need he ask?

Sri Bhole Maiyya soon approached from within one of the simple huts. The deep peace emanating from her was palpable. Although we remained there for only a short time while she and Swamiji exchanged greetings in Hindi, we were very much impressed by her simplicity and aura of sanctity. We felt blessed to be in her presence. Her words to Swamiji were that all were welcome there, in her "abode of peace".

Swamiji further explained to us that Bhole Maiyya and a few of her associates had to walk down to the Narmada River and hand-carry water back up to the top of the hill in order to water their beautiful garden areas, and also for drinking and cooking purposes. She told him that she would need 1000 rupees to have a pipe and pump installed that would carry water to their simple ashram. That is approximately twenty US dollars yet beyond the means of that simple ashram. We felt privileged to be able to contribute toward this project. Swamiji presented her with the money after we had left the island. She was most grateful. He later informed us that the water delivery system had been completed.

We saw our next destination coming up from a distance: the Vedic Gayatri Mandir and Brahmachari Vidyalaya. Here young priests are trained by a remarkable personage, Acharya

Sri Subash Chandra. Upon our arrival he sang Sanskrit *slokas* for us with such power, intensity and grace that we were literally transfixed. Subash Chandraji then invited us into the small ashram building to meet his guru, the venerable Brahmachari Raghunathji Maharaj, a highly respected saint who never leaves this humble rural hermitage. Although he spoke only in Hindi, we were fortunate to have Swamiji with us as translator. Since my wife and I have chosen the adventurous and at times challenging *sadhana* of spiritual marriage, I asked Maharaj-ji if he would give us some advice that might assist us on our path. He spoke a few words in Hindi and then indicated that Sri Subash Chandraji would teach us certain *slokas* which, if learned and recited daily for 30 days, would bless us in our marriage. He further assured us that chanting these sacred verses would be a blessing to our environment, our families, and indeed, to anyone who might hear them being sung. I recall being excited to take up the challenge.

During our stay in Omkareshwar, we made two subsequent visits to the Vedic Gayatri Mandir and Acharya Subash Chandraji, transcribing no less than three pages of exquisite Sanskrit *slokas* and recording them on cassette. Up to this point we have yet to fulfill that particular *sadhana* in its entirety. Stay tuned. We're working on it!

The prayers are entitled, *Veda Sara Shiva Stavaha*, and begin:

Pashunam Patim Papanasham Pareshyam
Gajendrasya Krutyam Vasanam Varenyam
Jatajuta Madhye Spuradangavarim
Mahadeva Mekam Smarami Smararim

Continuing on through an impressive array of ancient hilltop ruins dating from the 11th Century, we were surprised to see, once again, Sri Subash Chandraji! He walked briskly up to where we were standing on the hillside near the ruins. Greeting us warmly, he began singing in full voice – and what a voice it was! – to the sky, the earth, the trees… yet most of all, to the Great Spirit Who infuses them all. We were amazed. He departed with a blessing, leaving us to wonder, "What was that all about!"

Descending the long flight of stone steps leading down to the riverside at the north end of the island, we reached the famous Omkareshwar Temple. After *darshan* of the *Jyotir Lingam*, we went into the underground cavern where *Adi Shankaracharya* had received initiation from his guru.

The story is told that on the banks of the holy Narmada, as a young boy who had already renounced the world, Shankara met a great and renowned saint whose name was Gaudapad. Asking to be become his disciple, the saint deferred, directing him to his foremost disciple, Govinda Jati, who accepted him and initiated him into meditation and yoga *sadhana*. In a remarkably short period of time, the young Shankara achieved complete Self-realization: union of the *atman* and *Paramatman* (soul and Spirit) – oneness with God.

Lord Buddha declared that life in this world is rooted in suffering. He taught the means to end suffering forever through the Eightfold Path of right conduct and meditation. Shankara, on the other hand, emphasized the positive approach to the purpose of life, declaring that the true nature of the Self is *Satchidananda*: "Ever-existing, ever-conscious, ever-new joy or bliss." The conception of God as unalloyed, unconditioned joy, attainable by anyone willing to purify his or her heart and mind, found acceptance wherever the saint traveled. Sri Shankaracharya's extensive and insightful commentaries on many of India's greatest scriptures is legendary, and he is recognized as one of the greatest minds of all time.

Many years before the present-day ashram had been constructed in her name by H.H. Sri Swami Kedarnath, Sri Anandamayi Ma, herself, had spent ten days on the island of Omkareshwar. Our final destination of a most amazing morning was a visit to the upstairs room in the guesthouse where Ma had stayed. It is located very close to the Omkareshwar Temple in the bazaar area. Completing a memorable *parikrama*, we returned to the ashram in time for the mid-day meal.

Adi Shankaracharya

Swami Mangalananda with Temple Ruins
Omkareshwar, November 2004

Holy Cow!
Omkareshwar Parikrama
November, 2004

Shiva Lingam Abhishek
Omkareshwar Parikrama

Sri Bhole Maiyya
Om Shanti Ashram, Omkareshwar

Sri Brahmachari Raghunath-ji Maharaj
Vedic Gayatri Mandir, Omkareshwar

Sri Subash Chandra
Vedic Gayatri Mandir, Omkareshwar

India Rising

Paramahansa Yogananda often remarked that the spirituality of India combined with the material efficiency of America would lead the world into a higher age of peace and prosperity. Having just returned from India (February, 2009), our sixth visit since 1992, we have seen the Westernization of India over the years. In the cities especially, we see that Western modes of dress have been adopted. Many people are chasing after the ephemeral dream of material prosperity. Technology has skyrocketed and the middle class is growing rapidly. We hear complaints about the younger generation. Some say that they are not interested in preserving their cultural heritage and religious values. We see what appears on the surface to be a decomposing sense of morality and modesty, especially as reflected in pop culture, films and music. Yet this is far from the whole story.

Visiting Akshardham in New Delhi on our recent pilgrimage was a real eye-opener. The Swami Narayan Organization (BAPS) has created a 'wonder-of-the-world' class temple and cultural complex to showcase the high and glorious achievements of India through the ages, focusing on Her adherence to *dharma* and the great spiritual legacy of Her sages and *rishis*. Built only a few years ago on 110 acres by the Yamuna River, it is located on the outskirts of the capital. Akshardham is a wonder and an inspiration to behold. Its glorious central temple, enshrining exquisitely beautiful *murtis* of the founder, Swami Narayan, Radha Krishna, Sita Ram, and Shiva Mahadeva, clearly demonstrates that the detailed craftsmanship of Indian artisans of the past is still very much alive today. Built as a spiritual theme park, as it were, there are currently three wonderful exhibits. The first tells the story of Swami Narayan, his life and his mission, through a series of animated figures set in different thematic sets. Moving from diorama to diorama, the salient points of his incarnation intimately unfold before us.

The second attraction is the amazing film, "Neelakant Yatra," which was shown in IMAX theaters in America and worldwide under the title, "Mystic India." It is a strikingly beautiful production. At Akshardham, a special theater was constructed to show the movie to visitors, and it is replayed many times each day. The film is a very inspiring cinematic presentation narrating the life story of Neelakant, the young boy sadhu who later became known to the world as Swami Narayan. Neelakant left his home in a small rural village at a young age, wandering all over India and far into the high Himalayas. Following the course of his travels provides an ideal backdrop on which to showcase the art, culture and music of this great and wondrous land, revealing its splendor, its majesty and its magic.

To view the third exhibit, the visitor boards a small boat and sets off down the 'Ganga', moving through various scenes of India's past. We meet the great scientists, law-makers, traders, doctors, saints and sages from the dawn of India's great historic civilization. Upon exiting the exhibit, we are met by a dramatic display graphically emphasizing the importance of *ahimsa* and vegetarianism, an important theme in the teachings of Swami Narayan. Thousands of people visit everyday. Akshardham provides a glimpse into our future as more and more people begin to adhere to the great ethical concepts of *Sanatana Dharma* such as *ahimsa* (non-injury) and *satya* (truthfulness). The Swami Narayan organization has more than 700 *sannyasins* who serve their country and the world by instilling moral and ethical values, and spiritual ideals, through their example of dedicated service to humanity and love for God.

While in Rishikesh we visited the Parmarth Niketan Ashram, founded by H.H. Pujya Swami Chidanand Muniji. Here orphaned children, both boys and girls, are living in the *gurukul* and receiving spiritual and educational training. The same is true at the Sri Anandamayi Ma Ashram in Omkareshwar, where spiritual ideals are being implanted into the hearts and souls of hundreds of bright and talented, yet very poor children.

Our own Guru's organization, *Yogoda Satsanga Society of India*, and its many educational institutions, is growing in leaps and bounds. There are now centers and meditations groups throughout India. A second *kendra* has now been opened in Delhi, and a large retreat center has been constructed at Noida, on the outskirts of the city. A new retreat is also being developed in the jungle on the Ganga in West Bengal near a village called Teilery.

We have mentioned only a few of the numerous spiritual organizations that are working tirelessly to preserve the great and elevated cultural, religious and spiritual legacy of India for the future generations and for the world. Modern saints and spiritual leaders such as Satya Sai Baba, Ammachi, Sri Sri Ravi Shankar, Sakthi Amma; the monks of the Ramakrishna Mission, the Sri Aurobindo Ashram, and many others show that there is real hope for India to continue to light the way for humankind on its journey to a higher life in Spirit.

Sri Swami Avdheshananda Giri, who was chosen by *Hinduism Today* magazine as "Hindu of the Year" in 2008 says: "…our task is to lead and organize thousands and thousands of *sannyasins* associated with the *Juna Akhara* all over India, who are serving the people. Our work, the sum of all our efforts, is to create *samskaras*, deep impressions in people's minds… We want to shape the devotee's character."

(Please read the interview with Sri Swami Avdheshananda in Appendix II, page 341. You will find it thrilling!)

Let us listen to these words of Swami Ramdas, one of the truly great spiritual luminaries of modern times:

Soon, India will rise in all her glory. Then she will be not only spiritually great, but will have material wealth also in plenty. India has a great destiny to fulfill in the world. Her chief heritage is spiritual power and glory. Her children have only to be awakened and made conscious of this rich inheritance. Our Rishis and Avatars have left their indelible impress upon us all. They belong to all ages and climes. Our outlook also must be universal.

Thou taught'st me first to love
The sky, the stars, the God above;
So my first homage – as 'tis meet –
I lay, O India, at thy feet!

From **"My Native Land,"**
By Paramahansa Yogananda

Akshardham Temple, New Delhi

STORIES

These stories are not systematized or arranged in any way. They are offered as a scintillating collection of gems by those Western devotees who love India and the spiritual glory for which She stands.

If the reader would like to contribute his or her own stories for a proposed subsequent volume, please see the ***India Stories Project*** section of this book.

Stories	**Page**

Paramahansaji wrote the following poem in 1934 after fourteen years in America. His mind was turning lovingly to his beloved India, to his revered guru, Swami Sri Yukteswar, and other dear ones from whom he had been so long absent. This writing preceded his year-long return visit in 1935 – 1936.

If I Visit India

Paramahansa Yogananda

After four and ten years, when I behold thee, my India,
I shall roll in the dust at thy feet;
And I shall relive the scenes where childhood laughed, wept,
and dreamed.
I shall weep for familiar flowers of faces that have been
plucked from the vase of my gaze.
I shall stand, as of yore, with folded hands under the temple
dome of sheoli leaves,
Where the tree willingly dropped blossoms on the altar
of the grass,
And my tears commingled with the dew in fragrant devotion
To wash the feet of Light emerging from the dawn.
I shall go where before I was not allowed to go
Because I was a little boy.
I shall touch the sod where sleep faded footprints of my
beloved Gurus and parents.
I shall see the dear faces made sad by my busy forgetfulness
and by despair, thinking ne'er to see me again;
They will gleam with joy to behold my living form amongst
them once more.
I shall return to those places where I wept for God
And waited long for Him –
Expectant, doubt-filled, sorrow-filled, anguish-filled,
despair-filled –

Only to laugh and wildly dance in ecstasy of unexpected
Meetings
When I least anticipated His Presence.
Ah, those dreams – beloved dreams, forgotten darling
dreams –
I shall dream again in the sweet company of India.
Together, India and I played, wept, and laughed.
Together again, we shall play, weep, and laugh;
And pray and dance in ecstasy.
I shall behold every little dark, forgotten niche
Where memory will rekindle the faded light of candles of
experiences.
I shall behold the same sky and moon,
And embrace the same breeze laden with the fragrant living
God
Blossomed into Being in the garden of devotion of the great
Masters.

And if I see India once more,
I shall blush to hear again from her lips
Of my first love,
Of my love for the Most Beloved of all.

©Self-Realization Fellowship
Used by permission

O India, How I Love You!

Sri Daya Mata

O India, how I love you! What mysterious force in you calls forth my love? You are not always clean outwardly, your climate is not the best, your heat is unbearable, your rains are miserably uncomfortable, your creature comforts are nil as compared with the West; but you have a towering spiritual strength, and there is the tenderness of the Mother in you as you welcome all visitors to your shores. Your imperishable greatness has been best expressed in the lives of your saints – Sri Rama, Sri Krishna, Buddha, Chaitanya, Babaji, Lahiri Mahasaya, Sri Yukteswarji, and our own divine guru Yoganandaji, as well as Ramakrishna Paramahansa, Maharishi Ramana, Aurobindo Ghosh, Swami Sivananda, Ananda Moyi Ma, and countless others who have found soul freedom through devotion to your lofty ideals.

© Self-Realization Fellowship
Used by permission

The Holy Man of the Kumbh

By Gangadas Bell

I would like to share a story from my first trip to India in 1989. We visited one of the Kumbha Melas, the ancient religious fairs, held since antiquity at Allahabad, or Prayag Raj, as it is called by Hindus. This Kumbha Mela was attended by as many as 20 millions pilgrims over its six-week duration. There were thousands of swamis, *naga babas*, yogis, saints and holy men of all kinds.

I was very sick with the Asian flu in late December. I had to ask my parents to come over and help me pack my bags for India. I was so weak I could not even get out of bed. My parents, of course, thought I was crazy to even think about going to India in that condition. Some Westerners are worried about getting sick in India. I guess I had to go there to get well! Fortunately, I was traveling with a devotee who was also a nurse. She got me on the plane and helped me to be comfortable during the flight. I remember her giving me a picture of Mahavatar Babaji, the deathless master described by Paramahansa Yogananda in the *Autobiography of a Yogi,* and asking me to pray to him. A great nurse indeed! This was truly amazing in and of itself since my first visit to a Self-Realization Fellowship temple was for a Mahavatar Babaji Commemoration Service at the Fullerton Temple in California. Catherine, my nurse and traveling companion, had had a remarkable spiritual experience with Babaji during a similar service at Fullerton Temple, so we both felt a deep connection with the *Mahavatar.*

I was still very ill when we arrived in India, but finally did recover before heading up into the Himalayan Foothills for a visit to Babaji's Cave, the cave on Dronagiri Mountain where

Babaji initiated Lahiri Mahasaya into *Kriya Yoga* in 1861. The two hour hike to the cave was spent mostly in chanting to Babaji. Shortly thereafter we set off for the Kumbha Mela. Upon arriving we found that all the roads were closed due to the immense crowds of pilgrims. Leaving the bus, we had a long walk to the Yogoda Satsanga Society camp in the *mela* grounds – a walk of three or four hours in the hot sun. After enjoying *satsang*, meditation and a delicious lunch, many of the devotees wanted to return to our hotel. They were not, however, looking forward to the long walk. I suggested that we all chant the name of Babaji together as we walked along. Even though the weather was still hot, the walk became a joy instead of a burden.

Two days later we returned to the *mela*. Once again, we all took up the chanting of Babaji's name as a group. The long walk took on a different perspective, and we were enjoying it immensely. As our group was nearing the *YSS* camp, approaching from a side lane, we turned onto the road on which the camp was located. Catherine was in front leading the way. We saw a beautiful, tall and youthful looking saint who appeared to be in his late twenties, ahead of us by about 100 yards. He was directly in front of the *YSS* camp, surrounded by a small group of disciples – six as I recall – all clothed in ochre. Interestingly, the saint himself was dressed in yellow. All of his disciples were much older than their guru. As soon as Catherine turned the corner and the saint saw her, he stood up and raised both his hands toward her with his palms outstretched in a gesture of blessing. He began walking toward us with a radiant, beaming smile. Catherine just crumpled and staggered toward him with her hands folded in a gesture of *pranam*. He passed by and looked at her. He approached our group, coming within three feet of us. He gazed at me, all the while beaming his radiant smile as I looked straight into his eyes. It is impossible to describe what he looked like. He was truly a being of light. He was so beautiful! His eyes were just sparkling. He had a sparse beard and light brown hair of a copperish tone. His robe was pale yellow. The guru and his disciples rounded a corner and we lost sight of them.

I ran up to Catherine and helped her into the tent at the *YSS* camp. Coincidentally, Brahmacharini Mirabai, a wonderful *bhajan* singer from *YSS*, was chanting. I assisted Catherine to sit down at the back of the tent. She was obviously in an ecstatic state. I left her alone for about an hour while the chanting was in progress. When I returned all she could say was, "I have to find him! I have to go and find him!" Needless to say, that was simply not possible in a crowd of 10 million. Naturally, we were reluctant to jump to the conclusion that this may actually have been Mahavatar Babaji so we started referring to him as "the holy man of the Kumbh." Still, the resemblance was so striking that it was difficult not to think in that direction.

One of the most interesting after effects of this remarkable experience was that throughout the rest of our time at the Kumbha Mela, and indeed while in India, we would often pray to "the holy man of the Kumbh." We would invariably receive a response as little thrills of energy running through our bodies.

Leaping ahead now by sixteen years, to my trip in the fall of 2005: We had just visited Haridwar and Rishikesh and were camping on the Ganga near Kodyala, just south of Devaprayag. From there we proceeded up to Gangotri, near the source of the Ganga, and then on to Badrinath, one of the holiest pilgrimage destinations in the high Himalayas.

The Badrinath Temple, or the 'Temple of Badrinarayan,' as it is also called, is mentioned by Paramahansa Yogananda as the location where Mahavatar Babaji now resides: "The Northern Himalayan crags near Badrinarayan are still blessed by the living presence of Babaji, Guru of Lahiri Mahasaya," (*Autobiography of a Yogi,* Chapter 33.) This temple has a deep and ancient connection with the deathless master.

A few devotees and I would have our daily morning and evening meditations together. We would always pray to Babaji, tuning in with him, and would have the sweetest experiences. The night before leaving Badrinath village we were returning from having *darshan* at the temple. I was walking with a woman and her daughter who were from Israel. The girl wanted to look in some shops, so we walked down a narrow and dimly lit lane. While she was shopping, her mother and I were standing outside gazing up at the silhouettes of the imposing Himalayan peaks which surround Badrinath Valley. Two very high peaks were rising just above us. Suddenly, in the sky between the peaks, a small orange-colored light appeared that grew rapidly in size to that of a full moon! Just as suddenly – after about 10 seconds – it shrank back down and took on the appearance of a small star. Slowly it moved behind the mountain. We were looking at each other saying, "What was that!" We were stunned, not knowing what we may have seen.

Badrinath Temple

When I returned to the States I wrote about this incident to one of the *YSS sanyassis* who responded that we were truly blessed. He felt that this was actually Babaji. He went on to say that Babaji had been known to appear to other devotees in just this same way.

Sundaram (the author) tells that when he and his wife, Hilary, went for the *darshan* of a saint who is reputed to be several hundred years old by the name of *Brahmarishi* Barfani Dada in Indore in 2004, they were informed that he had spent 30 years with Babaji near holy Mount Kailash. More recently, it seems, Barfani Dada had taken a few of his close disciples on a pilgrimage to Kailash. He woke them up in the middle of the night and told them to come with him to the edge of Lake Manosaravar. There they beheld several bright lights coming over the top of the mountain and plunging directly into the sacred lake. These were followed by a very bright orange light which also plunged into Manosaravar. Barfani Dada then said that the orange light was Mahavatar Babaji.

Brahmarishi Barfani Dada
Barfani Dham, Indore
Diwali, 2004

Gangadas (Craig Bell) is the founder of Master's Darshan Tours and Mystic Tours of India. He is a member of Self-Realization Fellowship and a disciple of Paramahansa Yogananda. Gangadas resides in Encinitas, California.

India Pilgrimage, 2006

By Gangadas Bell

Question: What attracted you to go to India in the first place?

Gangadas: I was attending the Self-Realization Fellowship Convocation in Los Angeles in the summer of 1988 when my roommate brought a brochure to our room and told me, "I'm going to India!" I said, "I want to go too!" so I filled out my application with Polestar Tours, offered by Drs. Thomas and Victoria Parker, long-time SRF devotees who had been taking devotees to India since the mid-1970s. Just before leaving for India in January, 1989, I got a bad case of the flu. I was still determined to go, and after a week in India I recovered. My impression at the time was that India was very heart-centered. It was very easy to feel the presence of God there. Whether we were in a train station, an airport, or wherever we went, there was an underlying feeling of *shanti* (divine peace) which permeated the country. That experience was wonderful, and India kept calling me back again and again.

Every year the Parkers, who had been taking groups to India for many years, would say that this was going to be their last trip. In 1998 they decided not to organize a tour, so I decided to take a group as an experiment. We had ten wonderful people and everything went extremely well. Even though Polestar Tours resumed the following year, I also took a group in 2001, which included the Kumbha Mela, and every year since 2004. The Parkers and I now work together to ensure that everyone who wishes to do so may visit this great holy land and receive support and guidance from experienced and spiritually oriented guides.

During our pilgrimage in the fall of 2006, we had a group of nine for the mountains and nine again for the plains. The plains portion includes most of Gurudeva, Paramahansa Yogananda's, ashrams and many locations described in the *Autobiography of a Yogi*, including Varanasi (Banaras), Puri, Kolkata (Calcutta), Serampore and Ranchi. The mountain portion includes Haridwar, Rishikesh, camping by the Ganga, at least one of the *Char Dhams* (four highly revered holy temples: Gangotri, Yamunotri, Kedarnath and Badrinath), and the *YSS* Ashram at Dwarahat, including a pilgrimage to the cave of Mahavatar Babaji.

We arrived in Haridwar on the final night of *Navaratri*, the huge fall festival of nine nights dedicated to the Divine Mother. All the hotels were filled and we were all very tired. We decided to camp along the Ganga, but then we had a flat tire. Our driver went across the street to a hotel just to see if, by any chance, there might be a room available. He came back excitedly saying that there were nine open rooms! We enjoyed staying at that hotel so much we spent the next night there as well.

In Haridwar we went to the Sri Anandamayi Ma Ashram in Kankal where her *Samadhi* is located and her body is enshrined. That afternoon we visited Swami Keshabananda's Ashram where a portion of Yogavatar Lahiri Mahasaya's ashes are enshrined. In the evening we went to the famous Ganga Arati at Hari-ki-pairi Ghat, the most elaborate worship of Sri Ganga Devi, whose living presence is manifesting in the form of the river Ganga. On this night we counted an amazing thirty-two *pujaris* waving huge flaming ghee lamps as the *arati* song, "Om Jai Gange Mata!" was being played over loud speakers. Thousands of assembled pilgrims and devotees were singing along, their hearts filled with reverence, awe and devotion. Can you imagine? The effect is indescribable!

Our group arrived later than we should have, and the *ghat* was absolutely packed with people. There was no place for us even to squeeze in. I apologized to the group and told them there was no way we could even get close to the *arati*. Just as I said those words, a man approached and asked us to remove our shoes. He then led us to a shoe stand where he and another kind gentleman guided us down the steps and

Ganga Arati, Hari-ki-Pari Ghat, Haridwar

through the crowd, leaving us right in front where the priests would be performing the *arati.* They never asked for money or anything. We were completely blown away!

Betty, one of our pilgrims, told us afterwards that she could have gone home right then, after only one day in India, and been completely satisfied. It was so overwhelming! As if that were not enough, when we came back up to the road we were met by a large procession of elephants and carts carrying the Deities. *Sadhus* were dancing all around us. What an experience!

The next night we attended the Ganga Arati ceremony at the Parmarth Niketan Ashram in Rishikesh. Again it was spectacular. The spiritual energy was so high. At Parmarth hundreds of young *brahmachari* boys from the ashram, many of whom are orphans, chant wonderful kirtans to Radha and Krishna, Sita Ram, and the *Hanuman Chalisa.* Then the *Mahant*, Sri Swami Chidanand Muniji, comes out and leads chanting in his beautiful voice. We all started singing to God and it just went on and on. We were 'gone.' This was our second day in India!

From Rishikesh we went to our beautiful beach camp about two hours' drive up river. On the way we stopped at Vashishta's Cave (Vashisht Guha), one of our favorite places to meditate in all of India. One of the guides on our tour, Amita, had heard us talking about this holy cave on a previous trip, so she and her daughter went there just a few months prior. It is very dark in the cave, with just an oil lamp at the end of the inner chamber, so it takes a while for your eyes to become accustomed to the dark. Nearing the sanctuary they were surprised to see an old, long-bearded *sadhu* chanting mantras which reverberated throughout the cave. Incense filled the enclosure. Not wanting to disturb the *sadhu*, they came back out. Seeing Swami Shantananda Puri, who, along with Swami Chaitanyananda, is in charge of the cave and adjoining ashram, they inquired about the *mahatma* in the cave. He assured them that there was no one in the cave. They said, "Oh yes there is. We just saw him!" His simple reply was, "That often happens." When they went back in, of course, no one was there.

The cave is said to extend many kilometers beyond the point where visitors can go, having been blocked off. It is well known that *siddhas* reside in the innermost regions of the cave constantly immersed in divine communion. From time to time visitors see them in the accessible portion of the Guha. Many people have had visions there of H.H. Sri Swami Purushottamananda-ji, the God-realized master who occupied the cave for many years and who established the present-day ashram.

After leaving Vashisht Guha we spent five days at the river camp, which was simply wonderful. It is a pristine location with a riverside meadow, beautiful waterfall and white sandy beach. When you meditate there on a rock outcropping you feel as though Ma Ganga is flowing right through you. At first some members of our group were asking, "What are we going to do in camp for five days?" Later, those same people we asking, "Why do we have to leave!"

After visiting the high Himalayan shrine of Kedarnath, the holiest temple to Lord Shiva in the Himalayas, and Badrinath, the Vishnu temple near where Mahavatar Babaji still resides, we came back down to the 5000 foot level and the *YSS* ashram near the village of Dwarahat. There Swami Nirvanananda Giri and Brahmachari Vasudevananda had a wonderful surprise in store for us. We were visiting during the holy days of Diwali, India's joyous 'Festival of Lights.'

The morning of Diwali began with a *satsang* for the children of the *YSS* school followed by a delightful dance and music performance. Afterwards, Swami Nirvanananda asked our group to 'lay the lights'; in other words, to set out the hundreds of small candles that would be lit later that evening. As we were laying the lights around the ashram, a thunderstorm came up and it started to rain, so we had to go back out and pick them all up again. Then we went into the *Dhyana Mandir* for a *kirtan* with Brahmachari Vasudevananda. By the time the *kirtan* was over the skies had cleared, so once again we set out the lights. That night after our evening meditation, we lit all the lights for Diwali. It was spectacular! I can't tell you what a thrill that was! The entire ashram was illumined with hundreds of twinkling lights dancing in the dark night. Our dear Swami Nirvananandaji was so happy to share this with us. It was one of the very special highlights of our pilgrimage.

Every time we go to India the experience is different. You never know what it will be like. Yet if you go with the right attitude, every trip is wonderfully rich and filled with so many blessings.

During the *satsang* that we had with our revered Swami Shantananda Giri of *YSS* at Ranchi, who is the senior swami in *YSS*, I ventured this question: "Swamiji, some people who come on the tours with us love India so much. They can hardly stand being away from India. Others come and have a hard time being here. Why is it so?" He answered, "The people who have a hard time don't find God and Guru in every moment. When you find God and Guru in every moment, you can't help but enjoy India." **Jai Gurudev!**

Diwali, 2006
Yogoda Satsanga Society Ashram, Dwarahat

ॐ

My Little Boys

Hilary La Pierre

During our pilgrimage to India in the fall of 2004, we decided to visit Sarnath located on the outskirts of the holy city of Varanasi (Banaras). It was here that the Lord Buddha began his world-transforming mission by presenting his first sermon after attaining enlightenment to his first five disciples. From here, in what is often referred to as the 'Deer Park,' the *Dharma* began to spread. Sarnath was a significant center of Buddhist activities and monasteries for hundreds of years. Its museum has a wonderful display of Buddhist and Buddhist/Hindu artifacts which span the centuries.

Close to the museum is the ornate temple with a large and exquisite *murti* of the Lord Buddha plated in pure gold. The walls are covered with beautiful frescos depicting scenes from the life of the Compassionate One. Enshrined in the main altar is a fragment of bone reputed to be from the Buddha himself. While in the temple we were allowed the singular privilege of meditating in the inner sanctum just behind the main altar.

Not far away is a tree grown from a sapling of the famous Bodhi Tree in Bodh Gaya under which the Master attained *Nirvana*. This is the location where he presented his teachings for the first time. The site is commemorated by a life-like statue of the Buddha, his hands held gracefully in a traditional teaching *mudra,* giving spiritual instructions to his first five monks. Some distance away stands the huge Dharmekh *Stupa*, a characteristically Buddhist monument made of brick and stone. Circumambulating this *Stupa*, pilgrims from all lands walk in prayer and contemplation.

After leaving the temple I made my way alone toward the massive *Stupa* a quarter of a mile away down a straight walkway lined with trees. Two little beggar boys accosted me. They seemed to be about five to seven years old, and were, of course, asking for money – or whatever they might be able to get from the lady from America. They were barefooted and pretty ragged looking little guys, yet very cute. They began pulling at me, putting their fingers to their mouths to indicate that they were hungry. Having just been meditating with the Buddha, who is so full of love and compassion, rather than becoming irritated or angry I just smiled. Joining my hands together at my heart in *namaskar*, I began to sing the *Gayatri Mantra*. We continued to walk slowly, one on each side. I was watching them out of the corner of my eye. They put their hands together in *anjali mudra* and began to sing along. We kept walking and chanting for at least ten minutes, until we approached the gate leading to the *Stupa* where our friends were waiting for us.

Everyone was smiling with delight at the beauty of this scene and joined in, as did my husband, Sundaram, who had been following some distance behind. We were all singing the great *Gayatri Mantra* together. Inwardly, I was doing a 'double take' at the irony of the scene as us Westerners led these Indian children in connecting with their own spiritual culture. Whether it was the power of the *mantra*, the peace of my own heart, or the sacredness of the location I don't know, yet the result was a feeling of sweetness: a touching communion of heart and soul.

Later, while we were staying at the Anandamayi Ma Ashram in Omkareshwar, there were nine young *brahmachari* boys who lived in the ashram. They really captured my heart. Their ages ranged from nine to eleven. Some were orphans while others were from very poor families who were unable to care for them.

What delightful children! They were up at the crack of dawn to visit the temple and to receive a blessing before beginning their daily regimen of Sanskrit prayers, hatha yoga asanas, and academic studies. They were expected to attend evening *arati,* and a few were excellent musicians, especially playing the *mrdgangam.* Sometimes they were so sleepy they could hardly stay awake. My heart really went out to them. One was so tired at night that during *arati* he laid his head on my lap. It must have been my motherly instinct that made me wish that I could take them home with me!

During our stay in the ashram, a day trip had been planned, traveling up the Narmada by boat to Darvi Kund. There the river plunges over spectacular and powerful waterfalls. This is the location where many of the *Narmadeshwar Shiva Lingams* are collected. During the monsoon season, when the river rises and the waterfalls are not so crushing, divers collect the sacred stones. Shops in Omkareshwar are filled with every imaginable size *lingam.*

On this trip a few of the young boys from the ashram were invited to come along. Gurumit, (now Swami Gurusharanananda), and Swami Mangalananda, brought a harmonium. One of the boys played the *dholak*, and we all chanted on the boat. Arriving at Darvi Kund, we bathed and swam in the deep pools. The men and boys were busy diving to the bottom in search of small *lingams*.

After a dip in the clear and refreshing water, I was sitting on the rocks next to a pool enjoying the fun. Several little boys would dive to the bottom and bring up all sorts of beautiful stones. They would swim over and lay them next to me. Another young boy, who wasn't even part of our group, walked over and showed me something very special that he had found. It was a white stone about two inches long that was definitely in the oblong shape of a *lingam*. He pointed out to me that there was an image of the Sanskrit symbol for "OM" clearly visible on the stone. I was amazed! He laid it down next to me and left. I never saw him again, yet that precious *lingam* is still enshrined on an altar in the kitchen of our home.

Hilary La Pierre, a member of Self-Realization Fellowship, is delighted to be the wife of the author. She enjoys practicing and teaching the many aspects of yoga, while embracing the great adventure of life! Namaste.

The Hidden Yogis

Krishna Das

Without K.C., whom I called "Baba," and Mrs. Tewari, "Ma," I wouldn't be alive today. They adopted me after Maharaj-ji, Neem Karoli Baba, left his body. I became a member of the family, and had all the privileges and responsibilities of an eldest son. They fed me and soothed my spirit that was suffering so much after the disappearance of Maharaj-ji's body.

Over the years we did pilgrimages all around India – this tiny little Indian woman holding the hand of this huge American as she navigated up the hill called Hanuman Dhara in Chitrakut, or slowly descended to the *ghats* in Benares for a bath in the Ganga. To see her smile was an amazing thing. The compassion, sweetness, and tenderness of her nature radiated like the sun breaking through the clouds, and made my world OK again for a little while. Her love saved me time and time again from the black holes of my weird Western emotions. She fed me until I was ready to explode with food that tasted as if it came from heaven.

Ma's physical suffering was intense for many years. I am happy for her that she now has been released from the abode of pain that was her body. Once she was writhing in agony from neuropathy caused by diabetes. I said, "Ma, are you alright? Can I do anything?" She smiled weakly and said, "Don't worry. Machine broke, inside OK."

Baba was my best friend. No matter how messed up and depressed I was, he always rescued me with love and the bottom line. I told him everything about my life, and he never judged me or got upset at my shortcomings and failures. He enjoyed pushing my buttons and making me furious. I would yell at him and argue, with no holds barred. When I finally calmed down, I would see he was usually right. One time he said something to me that ticked me off. As my anger rose, he said, with much joy and anticipation, "You will fire upon me now?" His favorite response to my reactions to things he told me was, "My boy, is there something wrong with your brain?" Then he would proceed to straighten out the twisted circuitry of that brain.

He was a hidden yogi who had been doing meditation and *tapasya* since his childhood. Wherever we traveled, he received the respect of the *sadhus* and *babas*. Every morning he sat up in bed at around 4 AM and stayed there, lost to the world, for hours. When others began to wake and move around the house, he would take the *mala* that Maharaj-ji had bought for him and do *japa* throughout the day. There were many mornings when I woke up next to him only to see him sitting there like a living *murti* of Shiva.

He had been one of the devotees that Maharaj-ji put into *samadhi* with a touch or a look. On his last day at his Kainchi ashram, Maharaj-ji put Tewari into a very deep *samadhi* and told him to take care of the Westerners. When they were alone together in the back room, Maharaj-ji reached into his *dhoti*, pulled out a huge wad of money and threw it at Tewari saying that he should go to America and teach meditation. Tewari started to cry bitterly and said to Maharaj-ji, "Do you think I come here for money?" So Maharaj-ji took the money back. Then Tewari rallied and started to abuse Maharaj-ji: "Now I see what kind of *baba* you are, hoarding money like that! I'm going to tell everyone!" Maharaj-ji just laughed and said, "What money?" Then he reached into his *dhoti* again and pulled out a bunch of little pieces of paper saying, "I am getting old and losing my memory, so I keep the names and addresses of the devotees on these scraps of paper." The money was gone.

Another time Tewari came from Nainital to Kainchi and started abusing Maharaj-ji. "Why did you bring me here? I was happy in Nainital and had no intention of coming here, but you dragged me." Maharaj-ji yelled back, "I have nothing to do with it. I drag no one here, but you and I have been together for 83 lifetimes. It just has to happen!"

In April 1997, the three of us traveled to Rishikesh by train from Delhi. It was an overnight trip. I helped Ma and Baba get comfortable and tucked in for the night in their lower berths. Then I climbed up onto one of the upper ones. We had traveled all through India together and I always looked forward to a good sleep on the trains with them. This night was different. I looked at these two old people and was filled with a joy and happiness that was so intense I fought sleep for many hours just so I wouldn't lose the feeling. There was no place in the universe I would rather have been than on that train with these wonderful beings, traveling from anywhere to anywhere. I felt so blessed. I felt complete and full. It was the last time we traveled together.

One morning after this Baba got up early in the morning as usual. He asked Ma what time it was. She said, "3:30." Baba got out of bed and walked to the door. He stopped outside the bathroom and stood absolutely still. Ma asked him what was wrong. He did not reply. He then fell stiffly. He was taken to the hospital and was in a coma for three days after which he opened his eyes. When asked how he was feeling, Baba replied, "Perfectly alright." He then closed his eyes and died.

All during this time, the people in the hospital had prevented Ma from seeing Baba. She was totally distraught when she was told that he had left the body and cried out, "I could have saved him with my mantra!" When Ma did *puja* with this mantra, the ghee lamps that usually only burned for a half hour or so, would stay lit all through the night, or as long as she sat there doing her prayers.

Ma always had told Baba that she wanted to die first, as all Hindu women prefer to die before their husbands. One time Baba replied, "Well, no matter which one of us goes first, not more than 18 months will separate us." Ma left her body exactly 18 months to the day after Baba.

There are no words to describe the beauty and love that these extraordinary beings embodied. They were in the world, but at the same time, they were completely in God.

Devotion is a disease that we catch from those already infected with it. From Siddhi Ma, Dada, K.K. Sah, the Tewaris, and many of the other old devotees of Maharaj-ji, I was exposed to this wonderful 'illness.' I pray that it is terminal.

Krishna Das is a well known 'kirtan wallah' who travels the world singing to his Guru, awakening all who will listen to the transforming power of the Holy Names of God.

The Bus Story

Krishna Das

Ram Dass was not supposed to tell people about where Maharaj-ji (Neem Karoli Baba) was. When I told him I wanted to be with Maharaj-ji he told me, "Well, I can't send you there, but I'll give you the address of someone you could write to. So he gave me K.K. Sah's address in Nainital. So I wrote a letter and introduced myself as a student of Ram Dass, and said I would like to come and see Maharaj-ji. I got a letter back from K.K. saying that Maharaj-ji was not in the hills at this time, (K.K. lives up in the mountains), but that when he returned he would show him my letter and get back to me.

So I got a letter back maybe a month or two later. It said, "Sri Maharaj-ji has returned to the hills after his winter on the plains. After two weeks I was able to go to see him at the temple in Kainchi. As you know, Maharaj-ji does not encourage devotees to come to him, but his doors are always open. So if you are traveling in India, you are free to come for his *darshan*." I'm out of here. He's there and I'm going to be there soon!

Many years later – many years later – when he thought I could handle it, K.K. told me what happened that day that he took the letter to Maharaj-ji. There were actually three letters: mine and two from other devotees. K.K. walked into the room and Maharaj-ji was sitting on his *tahket*. A *tahket* is like a cot.

Now you've got to understand, the set up is perfect. K.K. grew up in Maharaj-ji's lap from the time he was a baby. And his way of relating to Maharaj-ji – his type of devotion – was like a spoiled child and its father. He didn't treat him like a great saint. He wasn't scared of him. He felt no distance. He'd grown up in his lap. The fact that he was now fifty years old had nothing to do with it. He still felt the same way. He was that free with him.

So he walks in the room, sits down and puts the letters on the cot where Maharaj-ji is sitting. Maharaj-ji is talking to the other people in the room. K.K. begins to peel an apple and cut it up in slices so he could feed it to Maharaj-ji. Maharaj-ji only had three teeth and you had to cut things up small if you wanted him to eat them. As he was feeding Maharaj-ji the apple Maharaj-ji noticed the letters and said, "What's this?" K.K. said, "Letters from Ram Dass' students. They want to come to see you." Maharaj-ji says, "Nahi! Tell them not to come! What do I have to do with this!" And then he goes back to talking to the other people in the room.

K.K. being K.K., he began to pout. He looked at Maharaj-ji and would not feed him the apple anymore. Maharaj-ji pushed his forehead up and said really sweetly, "Kailash," because "Kailash" was his nickname. So he said, "Kailash, kabat? What's the matter?" K.K. would not talk to him, wouldn't look at him, and wouldn't feed him the apple. Finally Maharaj-ji threw his hands up in desperation and said, "Alright, tell them what you want. Tell them what you want!"

Now K.K., being a good devotee, wouldn't lie about what Maharaj-ji said. Yet if you remember the text of the letter: "Maharaj-ji does not encourage devotees to come to him, but his doors are always open. So if you are here in India traveling, you can come and see him." Do you believe it? My whole life was dangling on a piece of apple!

It's perfect, of course. It could have been somebody else. It could have been a different devotee who could have written me a letter right away saying. "Maharaj-ji says not to come." I wouldn't be here today. He appeared to be uninvolved and uninterested in what was happening, and yet behind the scenes, the Great Puppet-master was pulling all the strings.

So we get to India and we go up there. K.K. happened to be at Kainchi that day, at the temple. We walked into the room and I had these apples, because I was told, "You bring apples." So I got these apples and had polished them up. I come into the room and bow down. There's Maharaj-ji in his blanket, you know. I put the apples down on the cot and by the time I had bowed down and sat up he'd taken the apples and is throwing them to other people in the room. So it's like, "What did he do? He doesn't like my apples!" I'm here a minute and I already messed up! He immediately caught that, so he looked at me and said, "What did I do? Did I do right? Did I? Did I do right? What did I do?" He was asking me about throwing the apples to the other people. So I gave him an answer – a wise answer. I said, "Anything you do is right, Maharaj-ji." "Ahhh! What did I do? Did I do right?" So I said, "I don't know." Then he leans over to me and he says, "When you have God, you don't need anything." I wanted him to keep my apples. I thought they were *my* apples. I just stared at him blankly. He looked at me again, and said it again: "When you have God, you don't need anything." Then he looked at me really close and said, "When you have God, you have no desires." Ohhh!

We were sitting there awhile and he was talking to us. He turns to K.K. and says, "What do you want?" I found this out later. K.K. says to him, "Do something for these boys." So Maharaj-ji says, "They're from good families. When the time comes, when the time comes." Then he fed us and told K.K. to take us back to town.

We stayed at the hotel owned by his family. Maharaj-ji told us to come back in three days. We came back in three days and he saw us for about a minute and a half and then told us to come back in four days. We came back in four days and he saw us for about a minute and a half. Meanwhile, I'm thinking, "What am I in India for? I'm in India to be with him and he keeps sending us away."

Other Westerners started to arrive. There were eight or nine. Over the month or two that this was going on, we went to see him every few days and he would tell us to come back in a week. A week! It was an eternity. So we'd go back to town and we'd walk around the lake. And we'd walk around the lake again. Then we'd walk around the other way… again. And we'd sit around and read books.

Then he sent us traveling with Bhagavan Das. We wound up in Bodh Gaya. 1970 in Bodh Gaya was an amazing time. The Tibetans were pouring over the mountains into India for the very first time in large numbers. It was incredible! We visited very high lamas – these beautiful lamas who had just come out of Tibet. It was amazing. One lama we visited was Kunu Rinpoche. He was the teacher of the Dalai Lama's teachers. He was a really old man – just beautiful!

Then we stared doing these meditation courses. Ram Dass showed up. He had come back to India and couldn't find Maharaj-ji, so he came down to Bodh Gaya where we were. We did these ten day Buddhist meditation courses, one after the other. Basically it was the Tibetan bowl and *mala* oiling club. That's what it turned out to be. We'd sit up on the roof and pour oil onto our *malas* and our bowls… and we meditated.

One of the guys had driven a beautiful Mercedes tour bus overland from Europe to India. He was leaving to go back to

Delhi and offered us a ride. We thought, "Ok, we'll go back to Delhi. Then we'll go to find Maharaj-ji from there."

We all got on the bus – I think thirty or thirty-five of us. Now, one of the guys in the group had been to Allahabad where there's this big festival every year of wandering monks and *sadhus* that come from all over India. And pilgrims also come from all over to take a bath in the conjunction of these three rivers. It's supposed to be a very special holy place.

So he had been there and said, "We've got to go there. It's just a little bit out of the way. You won't believe it. There are millions of these *sadhus* with long matted hair, and everything is unbelievable."

So all the way from Bodh Gaya to Allahabad we were arguing about whether we should stop or weather we should go straight to Delhi – because we were anxious to find Maharaj-ji. Ram Dass was kind of the elder – not kind of, he was the elder – the boss. But he made a big show about being democratic about it all, you know, so we had big discussions. Everybody was saying, "I think we should," or "I think we shouldn't." We took votes. We talked about it again. We took more votes. It was totally insane; much ado about nothing. Anyway, it was decided that we would take a quick trip there, take a look, and then get back on the road, so we could get back to Dehli and not have to stop on the way for the night.

So we pulled into the grounds where this *mela* was held – it's called a *Kumbha Mela*, or a *Magh Mela* – where there had been millions and millions of people – and there was nobody there! The *mela* was over and everybody had gone back to where they came. Nobody! There were miles of nothing where there had been people shoulder to shoulder just a few weeks before.

We were just about to head right back out to the highway when somebody said, "Well, there's a Hanuman temple over there in the corner." We had a special connection to Hanuman because everybody used to say that Maharaj-ji was actually Hanuman in a human body, so we felt close to Hanuman. We thought we'd go up the temple to have *darshan*. You see, that was our 'profession,' at that time: having or taking *darshan*. "*Darshan*" mean to "have the sight of a saint or a god." So that's what we did. We went to this temple, that temple; this *baba*, that *baba*. It was a tough life.

So the bus made this long arcing turn away from the river and toward the corner of the area there where the temple was located. There's a path along the side of the huge area which is like a sidewalk. Just as we pulled around and got up to the sidewalk and headed towards the temple, someone shouts, "There's Maharaj-ji!" And in fact, Maharaj-ji was walking in the opposite direction of the bus, away from the Hanuman temple, and there was a gentleman walking with him holding his arm. He wasn't even looking up. He wasn't looking at the bus. If we hadn't seen him the bus would have gone right past him. Yet as the bus approached, without looking up, he said to this gentleman, whose name was Dada, "They've come. Oh, they've come."

We stopped the bus and ran out. We all fell down crying. Ram Dass was crying; everybody was crying. We couldn't believe it! We were touching Maharaj-ji's feet. And he was saying. "They've come. This is good. This is good."

Then they get on this little cycle rickshaw and start cycling through the bazaar to Dada's house. And he asked the bus to follow. So here's this huge silver Mercedes bus with thirty-five Westerners on it following this tiny little cycle rickshaw with two elderly gentlemen, one with a blanket, going through the bazaar, weaving in and out of the tiny streets.

We pulled in front of this house, which turned out to be Dada's house. We were then asked to take our meals. It was explained to us that early that morning Maharaj-ji had told them to prepare food for thirty-five people, because we would be coming.

Now if the veil had been thin enough, that story alone – what more could you ask for? Look how 'real' we thought we were, making our decision. "Should we stop? Should we not?" and it got to be a pretty heavy discussion. "We should go!" People are yelling. "This is it. You don't get a chance to see these things…" Other people are saying, "Ah, it's just a bunch of this…" "We want to find Maharaj-ji. We want to find Maharaj-ji." "Well, we'll just go quickly and then we'll be on our way." Who was doing what? Who made that decision?

We think we're running our own lives. Oh yes, God does everything, but, you know, I decide if I'm stopping at the red light or not. I decide what to watch on TV. Where do you draw the line? Early in the morning he said to prepare food for thirty-five people. That was before we even knew what we were doing. We hadn't even made a decision yet.

And they fed us so much food. We ate everything on the plate because you know, in India people are poor, so it's considered very bad to leave food on the plate. But then they fill it up again and again. And then they brought dessert… and more dessert… and more… and Maharaj-ji kept saying, "Feed them! Feed them!"

The Bhakti Files

Jai Uttal

In the holy places of India – towns and villages permeated with devotion – magic is a daily occurrence. Perceptions shift like clouds moving across the sun. When the aroma of God's name wafts down a village street, we suddenly find ourselves walking in the ancient footsteps of Ram and Sita, or Hanuman, or Radha and Krishna. Throughout the day we hear bells ringing, mantras being uttered from every doorway, Kirtans bursting from the primitive loudspeakers. We smell incense and flower offerings. We catch glimpses of Gods and Goddesses around every corner. Doing pilgrimage to the sacred shrines is an invitation to the mystical breath of *Bhakti*.

The ancient village of Vrindaban, the town that was home to the young Lord Krishna and His beloved Radha, is one of these great sanctuaries, imbued with worship. The lines between the past and the present, the astral and the concrete, are very thin, and pilgrims come from all over India to partake of the nectar of *Rasa*, or divine emotion, that colors the town. When I first visited Vrindaban, I was absolutely stunned by the sheer quantity of living temples. It seemed that literally every other building was a holy shrine, and the sound of God's names reverberated from wall to wall, street to street, crumbling alley to archaic temple.

On day in Vrindaban, I was walking along Parikrama Road, a path that circumambulates the village. Devotees walk this dusty path (approximately five miles) as an act of worship, feeling that they are Radha, circling the body of her lover, Krishna. Walking around Parikrama, you see ancient India – priests chanting the Vedas, pilgrims weeping, *sadhus* gathered around their *dhunis* swaying to the driving rhythms of a Kirtan chant, peacocks, cows, and on and on. I used to take this walk every morning before dawn, timing it so I could have my first chai of the day watching the blood red sun rise over the Yamuna River. As the sun climbed into the sky, my heart never failed to melt at the passionate cries of "Radhe" or "Hare Krishna" that echoed through the misty morning air.

On this particular day, as I was walking away from the river, I heard a horrific racket. A young *sadhu* covered with white paste and wearing a simple cloth around his waist was sitting on a small stone wall banging cymbals together and screaming, "Radhe Shyam, Radhe Shyam, Radhe Shyam," at the top of his lungs. Instantly my *shanti* was shattered. The cymbals seemed louder than the rock concerts I'd left back home in the States, and his raspy voice was like sandpaper to the inside of my brain. Where was the blissful India that I loved? I hurried my steps and tried to get past him without being noticed. Just then an old, old man in orange robes bent with age, sporting long dreadlocks, stepped out of the little hut adjacent to the path. The young *sadhu* became silent as his ancient guru offered me tea and cookies. We sat and sipped the steaming chai, watching the brilliant emerald parrots fly from tree to tree, sinking into a deep, heavenly meditation, listening to the distant strains of Kirtan floating on the gentle wind. What peace.

As all things must pass, the chai was finished, the cookies were gone, and the old man dismissed me with a soft smile. I *pranamed* – touched his ancient, cracked feet – and continued my walk. At that moment the racket began anew. CLANG, CLANG, CLANG, CLANG! The horrible cymbals and the hoarse, screaming voice! Oh God, how quickly my inner peace disappeared. But as I turned around for a last pained look, the magic descended. This old man, who seemed barely able to walk, was dancing in the doorway of his hut. Suddenly his crooked body was filled with the grace and beauty of a young maiden. His delicate swaying hips, his beatific smile, his long flowing hair – the old *sadhu* was transformed into Radha, the Goddess of Love. And to complete the mysterious change in awareness, the young *sadhu's* Kirtan was now the sound of angels singing. His terrible cymbals had transformed into a divine orchestra of tinkling bells and chimes. My heart stopped beating, tears sprung from my eyes. Here was Radha Rani, dancing her love for Krishna, amidst the gardens of Vrindaban.

When it seemed the world would end in an ecstasy of love, the old man simply stepped inside, leaving me to the heat, the dust, and the *sadhu's* cacophonous song. But my mind was quiet, and my heart was full as I continued down the path. I had been given yet another reminder to see beyond the surface reality into what is hidden, to trust the perceptions of the heart before those of the judging mind. I had been given a few drops from the ocean of *Bhakti.*

Jai Uttal is a bhakti yogi, a foremost exponent of kirtan, and a leader in the genre of sacred world music. Jai is a devotee of Neem Karoli Baba (Maharaj-ji).

The above story is reprinted from the notes accompanying his highly acclaimed CD, "Kirtan: The Art and Practice of Ecstatic Chant," (Sounds True, 2003).

Rameshwaram

Jai Uttal

About fifteen years ago, over twenty years after Maharaj-ji had left his body, I was in South India visiting my spiritual mother, Siddhi Ma, who was taking care of Maharaj-ji's ashrams since his death. Though she herself is a being of great saintliness, she prefers to stay somewhat hidden from the public eye. One morning Ma said to me through an interpreter, "Hurry up, Jai. Pack a small bag. We're going to Rameshwaram!" Rameshwaram is an island off the southern tip of India. Though very small, it is considered an extremely powerful place of pilgrimage, as it was here that Lord Ramachandra worshipped Lord Shiva after destroying the demon armies and the evil ten-headed king, Ravana. It was also from these soft sandy shores that the great monkey Hanuman made His death-defying leap across the ocean to bring Rama's ring to His beloved Sita, imprisoned in Ravana's blood-stained gardens. AND it was a sixteen-hour train ride in a third class non-AC cattle car sleeping on a hard, vermin infested bench! Oh well, my mother asked me to come and I was honored.

In those days I had been re-reading the Ramayana and finding many deep truths and spiritual messages in the ancient words of Tulsidas. Earlier, when I had actually been sitting at the feet of my Guru, I had basked in the living reality of the story. Now I found myself relating to it almost psychologically, as a glorious tale of archetypes, a grand enlightened mythology, but surely not literally 'true'. All this changed very rapidly when we landed on the shores of the holy island. First Ma took me and my fellow travelers –

mostly Indians, with perhaps two other Westerners – to an old broken down ruin a little ways outside of the town. Seagulls were swooping down around the rubble looking for treats as a few elderly pilgrims made their rounds, reciting prayers and turning *japa* beads. "This was Bibhishan's palace," Ma said with a slight glance in my direction. My inner world trembled and I knew that something strange was beginning to happen to me. Bibhishan, Ravana's brother, a demon who loved God with all his heart and soul, and who stopped Ravana from killing Hanuman, was coroneted by Rama Himself as the new King of Lanka. He was one of Sri Ramachandra's eternal companions. The energy in those old stones was palpable.

Next Ma took us to a dirty pool of old brackish water and, sitting down on the *ghat* she said that this was where Lakshman, Rama's brother, used to bathe. She added that Maharaj-ji, who was once called Lakshman Das, used to take his baths here as well. Then we went to the forest where Mother Sita worshipped the snake goddess; then to the point high up in the hills where Rama made His battle plans. Finally we arrived at a very large indentation in the ground carefully tended by a seemingly ageless *pujari* who was lighting incense and singing prayers. "What's this about," I wondered. Ma seemed to hear my thoughts. "This is Hanuman's own footprint! You know, the force of His leap was so great that the very mountain upon which we are standing was smashed into the earth. All the animals, even the mighty elephants, fled for their lives, and all the trees and plants and flowers were pulled across the sea behind Him like the tail of a giant comet!" My heart was pounding in my chest. Archetype? Myth? No, I thought, this was true history, a divine *lila* that occurred for the salvation of all. I felt it and knew it with my whole being. Tears sprung from my eyes.

Truly, this was one of the most wonder-filled and awe inspiring journeys of my whole life. But I must be honest and say that that inner knowledge, that TOTAL belief, seems to wax and wane inside of me. Sometimes as I sing I SOOOOO much feel the presence of Radha and Krishna, or Shiva, or Hanuman, and at other times my songs are taking me deep into the caverns of my own heart, my soul. And you know what? It really doesn't matter that much to me at all. I understand that my mind is a limited mechanism and that the spirit within only can comprehend the miraculous realm of the spirit. Well, Maharaj-ji told us to sing God's Name and to feed people. Couldn't be more simple, could it?

Bhagavati Mai

Jai Uttal

About twenty years ago I was in India, visiting my Guru's ashram in the Himalayas. After a few very quiet weeks I got the inspiration to make a pilgrimage to Badrinath, way up in the mountains, thirteen miles from the Tibetan border. Badrinath is one of the four main pilgrimage places established by Adi Shankara in the ninth Century. As I was packing the car, making sure I had enough blankets, sweaters and hats to not freeze to death on the journey, my Indian mother, Siddhi Ma, came running up to me with a package. "Here Jai, please take this blanket and this thermos of milk to Bhagavati Mai, a great woman *sadhu* who makes her home up in Badrinath on the banks of the Alakananda river. When I asked how I would find her, Ma simply smiled and said, "Maharaj-ji will guide you."

Twelve hours of driving over tiny curving roads, overlooking thousand-foot drops into the vast, rocky cliffs below, *japa mala* turning 'RAM RAM RAM RAM RAM RAM", taxi driver falling asleep at the wheel, making wrong turns…. OH MY GOD!!! Would I make it there alive???? Well, it turned out that the driver's drowsy wrong turns actually saved us from a snowy avalanche and a slow, freezing death! Wow, was someone looking out for me? After a sleepless night in an icy and extremely rustic guesthouse, we hit the road again. As the morning sun rose above the great Himalayas, we arrived in holy Badrinath.

After settling into my hotel room, I began the daunting task of finding out where I could find Bhagavati Mai. After all, I had an important package to deliver. One by one, the people who I asked simply pointed their fingers to the jagged cliffs above the raging waters of the Alakananda. There, in the distance, was a figure sitting in stillness, wrapped up in a very high-tech looking 'space blanket' (remember them?), reading from a large golden-brown book, which was propped up on the rocks. Every few minutes another *sadhu* would step up to this figure and gingerly turn the page of the book. As the day grew warmer, that same *sadhu* gradually removed layer after layer of blankets, finally revealing an elderly but statuesque woman with short gray hair wearing what appeared to be a used burlap sack as her only garment. As unassuming in appearance as this woman was, her energy seemed to permeate the village, sitting in total stillness, without moving, ALL DAY LONG!!!! From a distance I began to feel my mind and my heart become more and more inwardly focused. Her PRESENCE was like a soul magnet, awakening the deep heart-call of all who walked within the shadow of those rocky ledges.

After many long hours, the sun began to set. Now began the breathtaking scene that became permanently imprinted in my consciousness. With the help of her attendants, Bhagavati Mai stood up and lit a very large *arati* lamp, with gigantic flames shooting up into the night sky. Dusk happens very quickly in the mountains and very soon just the traces of a blood-red sun were dancing between the fingers of fire as Bhagavati Mai slowly turned in circles offering her reverence and light to all the mountains, rivers, Gods and Goddesses of the Himalayan range. This is where words fail me: The colors, the high-pitched sound of her voice, the chill of the night winds, the whirling flames from her lamp, the awe inspiring spiritual energy of this great being. Now this was a ceremony! Cecil B. de Mille couldn't have even dreamed of anything more spectacular.

I stood by the side of the road, and as she passed I extended my hand and gave her Ma's package. Bhagavati Mai looked into my eyes; rather she looked THROUGH my eyes, and kept singing in her strange alien-like voice. Perhaps she was singing the *Srimad Bhagavatam*, for this is what she had been reading all day out on her hard and lofty perch. Then she was gone into the night.

The next day I rather timidly went to visit this *sadhu* in her ashram, an old run down little shack on the side of the road. She welcomed me like a long lost son and wept at the wondrous gift I had brought – a blanket and some milk. Then, through her tears, she cried that the gates of the great temple of Badrinath would be locked until her dearest friend, Siddhi Ma, came to visit. We sang and sang for the rest of that day and night, eating *halwa* and drinking strong chai – calling to the spirits of eternal love and liberation.

With Anandamayi Ma

Vinay Griest

I was in London in 1978 and decided to hitchhike to India. I was young and open. Many interesting and wonderful adventures happened during this pilgrimage. I arrived in Rome, for example, and there were literally throngs of people at the Vatican. I asked someone what was going on and he told me that the cardinals were electing a new Pope. Everyone was awaiting the outcome. When I asked how long the process took, he replied that it had already been three days. I then asked how they would know when a decision had been reached. He said that they would release white puffs of smoke from the chimney. I looked up at the chimney and there was the smoke, so I said, "Like that?" And he said, "Yes! That's it!" A few minutes later out came the newly elected Pope John Paul II, and I was there to hear his first address.

Traveling through Greece, Turkey, Iran and Afghanistan, I came into India from Pakistan. I arrived first at Amritsar, which is the center of the Sikh religion. This was perfect for me, as my first spiritual practices had been through the 3HO (Healthy, Happy, Holy Organization), founded by the Sikh guru, Yogi Bhajan. I was really inspired while visiting the Golden Temple, the holiest shrine in the Sikh religion. From there I wasn't sure where to go since I didn't have any preconceived plans. I had heard that Hardwar was a holy city, so I decided to go there. I took the train to Hardwar, came out of the station and bought some bananas. I was just casually walking down the street when I felt a sudden jerk which startled me. A monkey had run up from behind, grabbed the bananas, jumped up on a rooftop just out of my reach, and was sitting there laughing at me – eating my bananas and throwing the skins down at me. Welcome to the holy city!

I didn't quite know what to do, as I was in a town where I knew no one. Then, an elderly gentleman, who I think witnessed the whole episode with the monkey, came up to me and said that he was a retired teacher. He asked me what I was doing, so I told him that I had come to visit saints and holy places in India. I also mentioned that I needed a place to stay. He responded that there wasn't any room at the *dharmasala* where he lived, but he was walking down to Kankhal to the ashram of the great woman saint, Sri Anandamayi Ma. Would I like to join him? I had heard about her from reading *Autobiography of a Yogi*, by Paramahansa Yogananda. She was one of the saints I had hoped to meet, so of course, I said, 'Yes!"

As we walked along he gave me many instructions about living life in India, some of which were quite explicit and won't be repeated here! The Kankhal ashram is just next to the Ganga, so we were more or less walking along the river as we went. My new-found friend thought that I could stay at the Anandamayi Ashram, but that turned out not to be the case. Ma was not there at the time; she was traveling, and there was 'no room in the inn.'

Next door, however, there was a very sacred and ancient Shiva temple. It had been built on the site where Sati, who later incarnated as Parvati, had self-immolated when her father, Daksha, had disgraced her husband, Lord Shiva, according to the *Puranic* legend. The *lingam* enshrined there is so old and worn that it doesn't even look like a *lingam* now. The temple itself is considered to be one of the most sacred Shiva temples in India. I was given a semi-open room on a rooftop adjacent to that temple. Although there were some large and somewhat aggressive monkeys staying on the rooftop, somehow I managed to get into and out of my room.

I enjoyed attending *arati* at the temple and visiting with some of the 'ashramites.' That night, though, I had a very interesting and vivid dream. Anandamayi Ma had called me on the phone saying, "Come to me. Come to me now." Not surprisingly, when I woke up the next morning the dream was all I could think about. It was very realistic. I enquired as to where Ma was and found that she was in Bombay. I was told that she would be there for three days and no one knew where she would be going next. When I asked how long it would take me to get there, they said, "24 hours," so off I went!

When I got to Bombay, which did, in fact, take a full 24 hours by train, again I didn't know anyone. I met some Hare Krishna devotees and stayed at their temple. From there I went to see Ma for the first time. She was staying at a large estate with beautiful gardens. It wasn't extremely crowded. Still there was quite a long queue line for *darshan*. When we got to Ma we just knelt before her. We didn't touch her. As soon as I bowed to her I felt like I had put my head in a vacuum cleaner. That's all I can say. There was just nothing there. When I came up, it took a few seconds to regain my composure. Then my mind started working again. It was all very strange, yet indescribably beautiful to be in her presence. Ma was unlike anyone I had ever met. The sparkle of divinity absolutely flowed from her. There could be absolutely no doubt that here was a God-realized being.

I don't recall where she went next but I started to follow her around the country for the next three months. We went to Pune and many other places, including Brindavan. It was wonderful being with her in Brindavan since it was a small ashram and only a few other devotees were present. I met many of her close disciples, including Swami Nirmalananda, an American disciple who later founded the Atma Jyoti Ashram in the Borrego desert in California, (now relocated near Albuquerque, New Mexico).

The time with Ma passed quickly. Her complete identification with the Self changed the attitude and thoughts of everyone around her. Being with her it was easy and natural to live in the eternal present, where God's *kheyal*, as Ma would say, is the only reality.

The time came too soon when it became obvious that I would have to leave India. My funds were running out – that is, what little I had had to begin with. I was back at the Kankhal ashram where Ma was staying, and the great festival of *Shivaratri* was approaching. Ma had set up many *homa kunds* in the *darshan* hall, and *pujaris* would be making offerings during the *yajnas,* worshipping many *Shiva lingams.* At that time the caste system was still being very much enforced, and as Westerners we were not allowed into the hall. However, outside the awning, where we could still see inside, Ma had told the Indian devotees to set up an altar with a Shiva *lingam* just for the Westerners. It was equipped with all the accouterments for the *puja.* There were four of us and we had no idea what to do with all those things. There were trays of all types of offerings: leaves, flowers, fruits, sandalwood powder, incense and so on. We did the best we could, playing with all the sacred 'toys.' We didn't know the mantras or the order of worship, but we were sincere in our devotion – and we had a lot of fun, too.

We continued in that way all night long, and we could see Ma inside while she watched over the *puja* as it progressed through the night. At one point Ma suddenly came outside and walked over to our messy offerings. I was nervous, knowing that I had not done the offerings properly. She bent over and carefully examined our flower-covered *lingam*. She looked at us, laughed knowingly and lovingly, and then returned to her seat in the pavilion. The Brahmins seemed envious of the special attention and blessings Ma had given us Westerners. After that experience our offerings became even more concentrated and powerful.

Near the end of that long night a most remarkable thing happened. Suddenly, like a flash of lightning, Ma stood up and turned into Shiva – literally! Her appearance became that of an ascetic man; it was shocking. She stood up in that amazing *bhav*, holding a *trishula* and radiating incredible divine power. Ma had become Shiva!

That was one of the most amazing things about Anandamayi Ma. She did not have a fixed identity at all. This was near the end of her life and there were times when looking at her I thought she was literally ready to leave her body. In fact, I remember once saying to myself: "Ma is dying. I'm actually watching her die." One time while I was thinking this way, something caught my attention. I looked over and saw a young girl skipping across the courtyard. It was Ma. She would transform herself just like that. She seemed completely free and spontaneous with no sense of self-consciousness. Unlike anyone I have every met before or since, I knew I was in the presence of a being who was completely free, who was an absolutely pure channel for God.

That was the way she lived her life. She would just get up and walk to the train station. Everyone would ask where she was going, but no one knew. We would all just follow. Since she was so well known and revered the conductors would accommodate her graciously. The rest of us had to make our own way to her next destination. That is the way it was when we went with her to Brindavan. And we never knew how long she would be staying. Usually it was not more than a few days. She was always moving around, making herself available to devotees all over India.

Sometimes she would remain at Kankhal for longer periods. She seemed to have a preference for that ashram. Today her *Samadhi* shrine is located there (the place where her body is enshrined), although she left her body at her ashram in nearby Dehradun. Ma would be available to everyone most of the day as she sat or reclined on her *takhet*. Occasionally she would ask someone to sing a *bhajan* or *kirtan*, or she might spontaneously begin singing herself. The chants she sang were usually simple *Harinam kirtan*. The atmosphere around her was very relaxed and informal. Sometimes she would just stand up and walk out. It was all quite unpredictable. She didn't follow a set program. You always had the sense that she was completely free.

Ma would immediately distribute any gifts that were presented to her, and many devotees would be looking to receive those sorts of things as her *prasad*. Shortly after I first met Ma and had time to sit with her, I prayed very sincerely: "Ma, I don't need material things from you. I don't need your personal attention. I just want to connect with you inside. Please show me God. I only want spiritual gifts from you." So during those three months with her she never so much as acknowledged my presence, even when I was sitting with her and just a few other devotees. Now, however, it was time for me to leave India and return to the States. I was sitting with a

Western devotee whose name was Ram, and I was telling him that I had to leave. He replied, "Really? Well, have you had a personal interview with Ma?" I replied that I hadn't. Ram answered, "Well, why not! You need to talk to her." During all my time there I didn't feel I needed her personal attention. My original prayer to her was sincere. I really did feel a deep inner connection with her. She had set me on my path – a path to seek God that was to remain throughout my life. I had given her my heart. Yet now, with Ram's scolding, and since I was about to leave India, I started to regret never having had any personal contact with her. Anyway, Ram insisted that he would arrange an interview for me. Ma, however, was getting ready to leave. She walked out of the hall and got into a car that was waiting for her. Ram was talking to one of the swamis. He then signaled for me to come over to the car. She just looked at me, so I said, "Ma, what should I do with my life?" I was completely sincere. I was completely willing to stay in India at one of her ashrams, as Ram was doing, if it was her wish. I had implicit faith in her guidance without reservation. There were no doubts. She just smiled and said something in Bengali which was translated as, "Go back to your Guru." This really impressed me, as I had never told her anything about the spiritual relationship I had with Baba Hari Dass before coming to India. That touched me deeply. Tears came to my eyes and I felt deep love for Babaji (Baba Hari Dass) welling up within me. What followed was so amazing and made such an impression on my mind that it will always remain vivid in my memory.

The car started moving when suddenly Ma fell forward as far as she could with her arms stretched out in front of her in a gesture of *pranam*. Then I saw a man, dressed in ochre, lying in the dirt by the side of the road with his arms stretched out toward Ma's car. The car came to a halt and this went on for the longest time. It became obvious that neither Ma nor the Swami in the dirt wanted to rise first. It seemed that to get up first would indicate a feeling of superiority which neither wanted to exhibit, so they both remained like that. Many types of people came to see Ma, of course. She received them all with great love and respect. Yet I had never seen such an expression of reverence from her until that day, as she was pulling away in the car. A whole crowd had gathered around. The Swami would not get up. Ma also would not rise. It was so touching to watch this play going on. I soon found out that this was Swami Chidananda, president of the Divine Life Society and spiritual successor to the great Swami Sivananda, who had come from Rishikesh to pay his respects to Ma. Up until that time I hadn't realized what an exalted being he was, but I learned quickly just by watching Ma's response. He had arrived just as she was leaving. Somehow the stalemate was resolved and Ma's car finally pulled away. That was the last time I saw her. I don't know how to describe it, yet being with Ma made me realize that God is real – and available to us at any time.

Vinay Griest resides in Encinitas, California, and is a disciple of the silent yogi, Baba Hari Dass.

Tirupati

Vinay Griest

I was visiting South India in the fall of 2001 with a friend, Ranji Rao, an Indian national who has been living in the States now for many years. He was unable to make the pilgrimage to Tirupati, however, so I decided to visit one of the holiest and most revered sites in South India on my own. While not well known in the West, Tirupati is, for many Indians, the holiest place on the planet. After all, they say, this is where Lord Vishnu is physically present for the duration of this Age.

One devotee explained to me that the Lord in the temple at Tirupati, who goes by the name of Venkateshwara, is not counted as one of the Ten Incarnations of Lord Vishnu, such as Krishna or Rama, because in this case, He did not take an embodied incarnation. Here, it is told, is the actual form of the Lord, along with His consort Sri Lakshmi Devi, dwelling on His left side near His heart. Another devotee told me that Tirupati was the third most visited religious shrine in the world, after the Vatican and Mecca. Whatever the truth of these assertions, I felt compelled to go.

The next morning at 4:30 AM, I wait outside a travel agency for the pilgrimage bus. After boarding, we wind our way through every back alley in Chennai, it seems, picking up pilgrims and finally setting off for Tirupati around 6:30. At 10:30 we arrive at the transfer station near the foot of the sacred mountain to buy our 'special darshan' tickets. The earliest *darshan* time still available is for admission at 4:00 PM. Sighing, I realize that this is going to be a long day. I am glad that I can easily afford the 40 rupee (one dollar) fee for 'special darshan,' since the earliest 'free darshan' ticket is for an 8:00 PM admission! The transfer bus takes us up and along the newly paved road winding through the lush and unspoiled forest. One by one we ride over the Seven Sacred Hills, each having its own special significance and spiritual meaning. Dropping us off at the temple grounds, the driver tells us, "Shop now. Meet at the line at 3:30 PM. Don't be late!"

I set out for an adventure in what seems like a 'Spiritual Disneyland' – a Fantasy Land of shops, temples, street performers… and lots and lots of people. Since I was the only white face among them, I attracted a lot of attention wherever I went. After a month in South India, though, I was getting used to this. I was thinking that when I get back to America, I will most likely feel ignored when I walk down the street and nobody stares and checks me out!

The place and the people are so fascinating: families coming for blessings, or perhaps for the first cutting of their child's hair. Young couples, just married, want to be blessed with a happy married life, healthy children and prosperity. Old people, sick people, teen groups… they are all here – shopping, eating, and waiting for their time to enter directly into the presence of the Lord.

I decide to sit quietly in a small Varaha Temple (the third incarnation of Vishnu), where the chant, "Om Namo Venkateshwaraya" is being sung continuously. The small *mandir* has a very calm and pure feeling, so I sit there for a long time letting the mantra seep deeply into my consciousness.

Very soon it is 3:30 – too soon, in fact! I return to the line to see a crowd of approximately five thousand pilgrims ahead of me waiting to get in. I had seen long lines before but this was unbelievable! Would I ever get in? Walking the third of a mile or so past those who were already waiting, I handed over my 4 PM ticket and was led to one of dozens of holding rooms, each packed with hundreds of pilgrims. Inside it was a 'zoo.' Every person in the room seemed to be yelling, arguing or performing some type of crazy activity. "This is a pilgrimage?" was my thought!

At 6:30 they finally opened the gate. Everyone made a mad dash to get through the tiny steel door. After a month in India my hypothesis is that Indians just simply enjoy pushing. It seems to be a cultural pastime. Anyway, the so called 'line' is a mile long in a completely enclosed metal cage packed solid with people. A nice breeze does flow through the bars, though, which mercifully open to the outside. I soon discover that while the people certainly have no inhibitions regarding physical contact, they do not like it when my feet touch them. I try lifting one foot behind me a little off the floor and kind of scooting along.

The line moves slowly. I am still the only white face I have seen all day. We pass a checkpoint and a guard notices me and pulls me out of line. "Oh no," I think. I know that foreigners are often not allowed to enter some Hindu temples, especially in South India. This had happened to me on previous occasions as well but Ranji always explained in the Tamil language why I should be allowed to enter the temples. I do not know what he said, but I suspect he lied, telling them that I was a great Vedic scholar or something. Now I am on my own. All I can do is point at myself and say, "Hindu!" The guard and I then embark on a one word conversation: "Hindu?" the guard asks, in obvious disbelief. He stares at the red *tilak* marking on my forehead and at my *dhoti*. "Hindu?" he asks again. "Hindu," I reply with a smile. "Hindu?" He checks one more time. "Hindu!" I boldly declare with authority. After a few more "Hindu" exchanges he smiles and pushes me back into the river of pilgrims. Whew! The remarkable thing was that twenty minutes later we came to another checkpoint, which, due to the snaking path of the corridor is back near the first checkpoint. There another guard started to pull me out. The first guard, probably impressed by my eloquence and my vast knowledge of Hinduism, stepped over the bar and came to my aid. He vehemently took my side! I have no idea what he was saying. I think it must have been something about what a great Vedic scholar I was, yet to me it was simply divine grace. OM TAT SAT!

Maybe it was the holiness of the sacred mountain, or maybe it was the devotional intensity of the pilgrims, but after an hour or so I finally began to relax and let go. I became just another point of awareness in a sea of souls going to God. I was inexpressibly happy and calm. I was strongly feeling the Divine presence and not so much aware of who or what was being touched. I felt a pleasant pressure on all sides as we oozed, like human honey, along the corridor. On a ramp some of us began to fall backward. Acting as a huge interconnected being, dozens of collective arms automatically came to hold us up. It was an unexpected and wonderful surprise.

It must have been around 7:30 when we finally began to flow ever so slowly into the ancient stone temple itself. Now the excitement really began to increase. Moving through the huge bronze doors I realize that my consciousness has shifted completely. Various scenes now float past as we move forward: priests shaving the heads of entire families, including the women, as a sacrificial offering; giant balance scales with a person standing on one side and the other side filled with an equal weight of grain, honey and silver. Perhaps that devotee felt he was paying off a lifetime worth of sins.

As we approach the ornate silver door leading toward the inner sanctum, our collective mind seemed to shift again. Some devotees are praying intensely while others appear worried. Are they wondering, "What will God think of me?" Others cannot contain themselves as they near the goal of a lifetime: actual sight of the Lord! "You will only get a few seconds with God," one gentleman tells me fervently: "Make the best use of it that you can." What prayer shall I offer in the presence of Divinity? Really for me, it is an easy question to answer. I will simply ask that Ram's will be done. I know, of course, that I could ask for the healing of friends who are ill, for wealth, prosperity or happiness, yet I don't know what is best even for myself, let alone anyone else. I am just happy to have the opportunity to be in the presence of this Divine Form, and to donate whatever *punya* may accrue to whatever purpose He thinks best.

Excitement is popping and crackling as we ooze through the solid gold doors into the sanctum sanctorum. Here He is also known as BALAJI (another name for Lord Venkateshwara). As in all the pictures I had ever seen, His eyes are covered by a mask. They are too powerful to be looked at directly, you see.

Now we're being individually guided one by one in front of the *murti* of the Lord by a firm yet loving line of men and women helpers. All of us are in need of assistance, as we are without exception in extreme spiritual or emotional states. Some are praying frantically. Some appear to be inebriated with divine ecstasy, while still others have lost consciousness entirely. My white face once again attracts attention, this time from a woman helper who pulls me aside and kindly explains something to me in a language that I cannot understand. It doesn't matter; my attention is only on Balaji. Yet inwardly I am thanking this very kind lady who has provided me with a few extra moments in the presence of the Divine.

Suddenly I am outside again. The sea of pilgrims is dispersing and there is a welcome coolness. I am happy and blissful. I take *pradakshina* and receive *prasad* from a 'ladu counter,' one of the helpers who distribute *ladus*, the blessed food offering given out to each pilgrim. The power of the Deity, the high emotions that I have experienced, and all that has transpired on this amazing day have pulled me into a peaceful state free from thoughts. I sit in a quiet corner of the courtyard, leaning against an ancient stone pillar for a long time, letting the deep silence of meditation steal over me.

Two Short Stories

Govind Antonucci

While visiting an ashram in South India, I came across a magazine article about a young saint living nearby whose name was Swami Isha. He has a mesmerizing appearance, much like that of Jesus, so I decided to visit him for his *darshan* and blessing. Swamiji had been a wondering *sadhu* for a few years, yet now never left the house he lived in with his parents. His devotees were building a temple and a guesthouse immediately adjacent to the property.

Swamiji greeted me warmly and made me feel welcomed as a friend. He told his family that I did "good *sadhana*," and that I should always be welcome there. Consequently, I visited him on several occasions. One time I mentioned that most devotees I had met in India had an *Ishta Devata* – a form of God that they held most dear. I felt sad because I did not know which form of God was right for me, and I told him so. Swamiji replied that I did have one. I just didn't remember. He asked me to close my eyes and meditate. After a few minutes, I began to see a divine form. Unfortunately, I could not clearly make it out. Swamiji then asked me to hold out my hand. He placed his empty hand above mine, making a fist. When he opened his hand a Shiva *lingam* dropped from his hand into mine. Since that time I have felt especially close to Lord Shiva.

ॐ ॐ ॐ

On another occasion I was visiting the holy town of Ganeshpuri on the advice of a swami I had met. This town is where a great saint of modern times, Bhagavan Nityananda, finally settled after wandering all over India for many years. Nityananda's chief monastic disciple, Swami Muktananda Paramahansa's main ashram is also located there. It is reputed to be a place where many ancient *rishis* had lived and done spiritual practices. It is said that the hot springs which are there were divinely manifested for these sages to bathe in.

This was rural India. The daily *arati* in the temple was wonderful. Giant drums were beaten that could be heard for miles around. I became curious, wondering if any saints were living in that area now. Inquiring, I was told that there was a saint living on the top of a nearby mountain, so the next day I set off to visit him. Even the look from a true saint is said to carry a great blessing. I arrived late in the day and was able to watch the saint performing evening *arati*. I was feeling rather lost, as no one there spoke any English, but by that time it was too late to return to the town.

By watching the people who were there I discovered that there was a *dharmashala* where visitors could spend the night. Following what the others were doing, I spread some heavy sackcloth under me, put some more on top of myself, and settled in for a night's rest. My stomach, however, kept reminding me that I hadn't eaten anything that day. It brought to mind the story in the *Autobiography of a Yogi,* when Swami Dayananda in the Banaras ashram where Mukunda (the future Yogananda) was living as a youth mandated him never to ask for food or to succumb to the belief that sustenance comes from man rather than from God. So I resigned myself to my 'foodless fate.' "It's OK", I assured myself. "I've fasted before."

Just at that time I was roughly shaken by an old man who kept shouting, "Khaana, khaana!" I didn't know Hindi and I thought he must be crazy, so I rolled back over to try to get some sleep. This little old man, however, was very persistent. He made it known to me that I should follow him. I thought that maybe I was sleeping in the wrong place, so I got up and followed him down to another room. There I found a delicious meal waiting for me! God does look after us, even beyond our expectations. This is especially apparent in the holy land of India.

Govind is a devotee of Paramahansa Yogananda currently residing in the Bay Area of Northern California.

Navaratri in Omkareshwar

Swami Mangalananda

During these days of Navaratri, the nine day festival honoring the Divine Mother, every neighborhood in Omkareshwar sets up its own image of the Devi and has a nightly gathering. There is a traditional dance that is done with short sticks that are clicked together as people dance in concentric circles. The oldest boy from our school organized a group of some of our most talented girls, and we nightly visited a different neighborhood for dancing and festivities. It was great fun watching everyone in their most colorful clothes dancing with so much joy!

I had a great experience: An ashram in Omkareshwar was giving a *bandhara* for the entire island. They invited our children to present a two hour program of *bhajans* and dances. We spent several days preparing a fantastic program with new chants and dance movements. We spent most of the day of the event in rehearsal, dismissing the children in the late afternoon with instructions to return in a couple of hours dressed in their costumes, rested and ready. Shortly afterwards we received word that our program had been cancelled. They had been unable to prepare the stage and obtain a sound system. We didn't want to tell the children and break their high enthusiasm. I sat with Brahmachari Gurumit (now Swami Gurusharanananda), the foremost teacher of our school, thinking what we might be able to do. Gurumit, feeling very moody, took his harmonium and started singing the most beautiful bhajan: "Tum ne mujhe bulaaya, Sharavali Ma" – "You have called me, O merciful Divine Mother." Suddenly he got a spontaneous idea which he felt was a response directly from the 'Merciful Mother' Herself!

There is a famous Durga *mandir* outside of Omkareshwar which we had been planning to visit with the children for quite some time. Gurumit said, "If they won't hear the children in Omkareshwar, we will take them to the temple and perform for the Devi Herself." The children arrived – the dancers all dressed in their most colorful clothing – long dresses, jewelry and makeup – all looking like little angels. We herded everyone out the front gate of the ashram and paraded along the river, across the bridge and through the bazaar where we hired two large carriages into which we loaded all our musical instruments and more than thirty kids. We were off for the countryside, singing and shouting! After an hour's travel or so, over unbelievably bad roads, we arrived at the *mandir*, set in the midst of the forested countryside, perfectly still and quiet.

The resident *pujari* set up a loudspeaker system for us, and Gurumit broadcast an open invitation to all the local villagers. Our teachers, along with some of the older children, went through the streets to make the announcement: "There is going to be a concert tonight for the Devi. All are welcome." Soon we had a large audience of villagers as we performed our entire program in front of the shrine of the Merciful Mother. Everyone was on their feet dancing for the final *arati*. What a joy!

Upon our return to Omkareshwar, we stopped at the festival where we had originally been invited to perform. There our hungry troupe was fed a sumptuous feast. The ashramites were overflowing with apologies and asked us to please return and present our program later in the week. Through Ma's grace it was a thoroughly enjoyable experience for everyone. I always love so much the time spent with our beautiful children.

Swami Mangalananda is an American direct disciple of Sri Anandamayi Ma residing at her ashram in Omkareshwar. He is the author of ***OM MA: Anandamayi Ma, A Short Life Sketch,*** *(Published in India as* ***A Goddess Among Us.****)*

Swamis Mangalananda and Gurusharanananda with students and teachers of Sri Anandamayi Tripura Vidyapeeth, Omkareshwar

Yatra 2006

Swami Mangalananda

Haridas, an American friend residing at Anandashram in Kasaragod, Kerala, invited me to come with him on a holy *yatra* and kindly offered to pay my expenses. He and an Indian couple from Anandashram, which was founded by Swami Ramdas, were making a video about the wandering days of Papa (Swami Ramdas). They only had Puri and Dakshineswar left to film.

We started in Jagannath Puri, staying in Ma's (Anandamayi Ma's) ashram right on the seashore. There are just two *sadhus* living there these days. They are both engaged in *sadhana* and received us with great kindness. I liked the atmosphere in Puri. It has a tropical seafront climate. The spiritual vibrations are very intense due to the great and ancient temple of Lord Jagannath, "Lord of the Universe." Countless pilgrims and *sadhus* congregate there.

I knew that the Jagannath Temple of Lord Sri Krishna is famous for being the strictest in all of India for not allowing foreigners to enter, yet thought that I would give it a shot anyway. I donned my turban and *tilak* and we approached the front gates. Haridas didn't want to try himself, yet he thought that I might be able to get in due to my 'Hindu' appearance. Before starting I bowed to the ground at the entrance and prayed to the Lord to grant me a *darshan*, and I felt His blessing.

I walked confidently forward along with the crowd going through the gate but soon was grabbed by two of the many uniformed guards that watch the entrance. I spoke forcefully in Hindi, acting outraged: "What is the problem? I am going for *darshan*!" They weren't quite sure what to make of me, asking if I was a Hindu. I replied irately that yes, I was a Hindu and a *sannyasi.* They looked at each other and rather respectfully directed me to an open office next to the gate. There the man in charge asked me a few questions in Hindi, such as my name and the ashram I came from. Then he asked, "…and your father's name?" I thought for a minute that I could lie and say some Indian name and probably get in, but how could I then stand in front of the Deity on the basis of a lie? So I answered truthfully and stated my father's name, which, of course, immediately brought the satisfied response: "Ahaa... no entry! Only Indian-born Hindus!"

I was later to find, however, that the feeling of response to my prayer was not mistaken. Lord Jagannath did give me *darshan* in a most unexpected way. So Haridas and I walked the *parikrama* and felt Lord Jagannath's blessing. He alone knows the heart of His devotees.

I had read that the *Samadhi* Shrine of Swami Sri Yukteswar Giri, the great guru of Paramahansa Yogananda, was in Puri, so we made inquiries as to its whereabouts and were misdirected to an ashram on the outskirts of town. Before going there though, we first made a visit to the famous Surya (Sun-God) Temple at Konarak. This temple is very ancient, its grounds and precincts having been excavated rather recently and preserved as a national monument. It stands in the midst of well cared for gardens surrounded by green jungle, and is amazing to see. The entire temple is depicted as Surya Dev's chariot, with huge carved stone wheels. Bhagavan Surya-Narayan is on the front with stone horses leading the way. All the sides are carved in intricate figures and symbols. As we sat under the shade of a large banyan tree, I could sense the feeling of ancient eternal India. India, after all, isn't really a country so much as a spiritual plane of existence on which the external expressions of culture and religion are built upon. No matter how much the superficial aspects of *Bharat* may change, that underlying spiritual reality will always remain present.

Returning to the city, we did eventually find Sri Yukteswar-ji's Karar Ashram near the ocean. It was a blessing beyond belief to *pranam* at the holy shrine of this great, illumined master and *mahayogi*. I went back the next day also, just to meditate in front of his *Samadhi*.

Another day, on the advice from the *sadhus* in Ma's ashram, we found the ashram and *Samadhi* of the great Totapuri, the Vedanta guru of Sri Ramakrishna! I never knew this but he lived over 250 years, only leaving his body in the 1950's. Isn't that amazing! His ashram was in a quiet, secluded area outside of town, and the marble tomb has a life-like statue of the great saint sitting on top. I sat with one hand touching the tomb and meditated there a long time, really absorbing its power and divine vibrations

On our last afternoon in Puri, one of Ma's *sadhus* wanted to feed us the famous *Mahaprasad* that is distributed from the Jagannath Temple. It is reputed to be the holiest *prasad* in India and a medium of great spiritual power. Sri Ramakrishna used to keep some of it dried in his room and would eat a small amount every day. So that day we had cooked rice and *dal* which had been offered to Lord Jagannath. We ate it gratefully and with great joy.

Swami Mangalananda
with Pranab Ghoshal and Haridas
Kolkata, 2006

The next morning found us in Kolkata. I had been there almost exactly five years previously, directly upon my arrival in India. At that time I loved the Bengali people and all the holy places, but the noise, pollution and confusion of the city overwhelmed me. I had always associated these rather unpleasant memories with Kolkata, yet I suspected that my experience this time might be different. On the earlier visit I had been carrying everything I owned, and had no idea what the future held for me. I was amazed at how different this experience turned out to be. All the elements that had previously buffeted my awareness were still there, yet I am now so used to India and its living conditions that I was able to look past all of that and tune into the history, culture and spirituality of Kolkata – and to really appreciate it.

I had made arrangements to stay at the Yogoda Satsanga Society (YSS) Ashram in Dakshineswar, which is very near the famous Kali Temple where Sri Ramakrishna had lived, and which has been blessed by the presence of many great masters.

Yogoda Math was a wonderful place to stay. It is in a secluded section of the town, directly on the holy Ganga. Here the sacred river is called the 'Hugli.' It is wide, beautiful and close to Ganga Sagar where the river merges into the ocean. The ashram itself is beautiful and well kept, with a large flower garden and a temple dedicated to the SRF/YSS line of gurus. We attended the meditations and services every morning before going off on our excursions. I became friendly with three of the monks that ran the center at the time, including Swami Shuddhananda and Brahmachari Jnanananda. The main force behind the ashram seemed to be Brahmachari Achyutananda, who, I found, was being transferred to the SRF Mt. Washington headquarters in Los

Angeles for a period of three to five years. (I was later able to visit him there during a trip to the States in 2008. He has since returned to India). Achyutanandaji is extremely talented and capable, a good drummer, bhajan singer and representative of a true Indian *Kriyaban*. We became fast friends. One evening we sat and sang *bhajans* together. The last day of my stay I was invited to have breakfast with the monks in their dining quarters.

We spent a lot of time at the Dakshineswar Kali Temple. I would sit in Sri Ramakrishna's room and recall the various divine scenes that took place there. I would feel that they were still occurring on a subtle level. Pranab Ghoshal, one of the priests of the temple who comes to the Kali Puja Festival in Laguna Beach, California, each summer was so kind and loving to us. He took us directly into the inner shrine right in front of Sri Ma Kali. We also met Sri Haradan Chakraborti, the head priest who conducts the Kali Puja in Laguna. He specifically remembered me, despite the passage of many years and my greatly changed appearance.

On two of the days while we were there I spent some time with a 95 year-old *sannyasi* whose name is Swami Brahmananda. He is still living the life of a wandering monk. To my surprise, I discovered that he has been a devotee of our Anandamayi Ma since the 1960's! We all ate the holy *prasad* of Mother Kali together that day.

The next day we paid a visit to Belur Math, the headquarters of the Ramakrishna Mission. We were invited to take Thakur's (Sri Ramakrishna's) *prasad*, so for those three days we were spiritually empowered with food that held great blessings.

One morning we went to the Kalighat Temple in the city. Afterwards I went in search of the house of Mahendranath

Gupta, the illustrious author of *The Gospel of Sri Ramakrishna.* I wound my way through many back streets in a residential area, enjoying the feeling of 19th Century Calcutta seemingly unchanged. The city must have been a great place of culture and aesthetic beauty in those days. It still has a unique charm all its own. It is wonderful when a negative experience and the memory it has evoked can be replaced by a positive one. Now when I think of Kolkata I think of these rare moments, and I am ready to return there again and again.

Through a series of little miracles I eventually did find M's (Master Mahasaya's) house. I meditated in the very room where the great saint had lived, where he penned the '*Gospel,*' and where he left his body. Sri Ramakrishna, as well as many of his companions and disciples, had been there on many occasions.

Another time we meditated in the room where Sri Ramakrishna actually left his body – in the Cossipore Garden House. It is preserved beautifully as a shrine of great power and holiness.

The Bengali people are wonderfully devotional. Their *bhakti* can be seen in every temple and shrine. There would be times when I would simply be walking down the street and people would run over to me and *pranam*. One night, on a street corner, an old man actually leaned over and started massaging my legs!

One morning we drove to the town of Serampore (Sri Rampur), where Swami Sri Yukteswar-ji's ashram was located. There is a *YSS mandir* there dedicated to the Master and built on a portion of the old ashram property. We were also taken to an ashram of another line of gurus stemming from the great Lahiri Mahasaya. Sri Shyama Charan Lahiri Mahasaya had many enlightened disciples. The Sa*madhi* tombs at this ashram radiated great power. The successor there was a simple man dressed in white and bent with age. He was a yogi and a *Kriyaban*. At first I thought that he was just a very sweet soul. As time passed in his company, however, I started feeling real holiness emanating from him. By the time we left, I was convinced that I was in the presence of one of India's many undiscovered saints. I asked him to bless me as we were leaving. He placed his hands on my head and transmitted great power. Living behind many simple gates on back lanes are saints known only to God and a few others. They don't seek public recognition, preferring to live a simple divine life, radiating blessings wherever they go.

While we were in Serampore we visited a temple which was also dedicated to Lord Jagannath. It was magnificent. Its history was depicted in beautiful murals painted on the walls. It seems that more than 500 years ago a *sadhu* went to Puri for Jagannath *darshan*, just as we had done. He was also not allowed to enter the temple. Perhaps it was because he was from a lower caste. Whatever the reason may have been, he felt very dejected. Weeping, he climbed a hill where he fell asleep under a tree. Lord Jagannath appeared to him and commanded him to go to the end of the Ganga in Bengal and establish a temple there in His name. The Lord promised that He would come and live there also. The *sadhu* did just as he was instructed by the Lord. In later years, Sri Krishna Chaitanya Mahaprabhu sent one of his close disciples to this very *mandir* to renovate it. The *samadhi* shrines of both the founder and this later saint are here.

Haridas and I realized that this was the answer to our prayers in Puri. The attendants opened the inner shrine just for us, allowing us to stand directly in front of the *murti* of Lord Jagannath for *darshan*! I felt overwhelmed with love and gratitude, realizing that God truly does answer the sincere prayers of His devotees!

While in Kolkata I was also able to visit Swami Vamanananda, who for many years was practicing austerities in Omkareshwar and had been in charge of the Ramakrishna Mission center which is located next door to our ashram. We had become great friends during the first three years I had been in India. He arranged for me to visit the home of Balaram Bosh, where Sri Ramakrishna stayed whenever he came to Kolkata. So much happened in this home during the course of the great master's life, and many are documented in the '*Gospel*.' It is now kept as a sacred shrine.

Next we went to the home of Sri Ma Sarada Devi. This was a supremely holy experience. Here she spent many years of her life, and here she left her body. It is now a temple which holds such power and holiness. Her great disciple, Swami Saradananda's room is also kept intact next to the room of the Holy Mother. I also appreciated the old-world architecture and the beauty of the old-style homes which are so much a part of the Kolkata charm. Swami Vamananandaji and I took lunch together and greatly enjoyed each other's company.

That evening I went to visit the Anandamayi Ma Ashram, as I had never been there before. It is a very large ashram, beautifully placed right on the bank of the Ganga. When I went up to sit in Ma's room a devotee came to me to tell me that our beloved Swami Bhaskarananda was there for Durga Puja! I immediately walked up to the roof area where I found Gopal Das, Swamiji's faithful attendant, and a whole crowd of Ma's devotees, many of whom had been to our ashram in Indore. It was like a family reunion! I went in and found Swamiji. He was in *maun*, which he always keeps on Monday, but was very pleased to see me. He greeted me joyfully. I told him about our new *Sannyas* Order established by Swami Kedarnath. He listened carefully, nodding and smiling in consent. I asked him for his blessings on my own *sannyas,* and he joyfully blessed me with both hands. He then gave me *prasad.* He had Gopal Das fill both his hands full of dried fruits and nuts, pouring it all into my hands in blessing. It is always so wonderful to see Swamiji. We sat for a long time on the roof enjoying the sunset together.

Swami Bhaskaranandaji asked Gopal Das to call the Varanasi Ashram and arrange my stay there on the next two days. Truly Ma is doing everything, leading me in even small matters. I left the next day for Varanasi (Banaras). I didn't have a direct train and was supposed to get off in the early morning at a particular station. When I awoke, I realized that I had missed my stop. The next stop was Allahabad. When I got down I thought, "Alright Ma, why have you brought me here?" I then remembered that Bhitika Mukerji, Ma's biographer and lifetime devotee lives here. She wrote the introduction to one of Baba's (Swami Kedarnath) books, and I had spoken with her on the phone in that regard. I had always wanted to meet her since she spent so much time with our Ma, literally growing up with Her and traveling with Her for many, many years. Bhitika used to play games with Bholanath, Bhaiji and Ma, when she was just a girl. Her autobiography, *My Days with Anandamayi Ma*, is really very beautiful and well worth reading. I found that I still had her phone number in my address book and so I called. I explained my situation and asked if I could come out for a few minutes to pay my respects. She graciously invited me to come, so I took a rickshaw to her home. She lives in her ancestral estate where Ma came and stayed whenever She was in the area. Ma stayed there dozens of times over the years.

Bhitika Mukerji was sitting in her living room and looking very dignified. She received me kindly. We talked for over an hour and got along beautifully. She told me many stories about Ma, and in turn was very interested in our ashram and the work we are doing in Ma's name with our school. Her whole life was in teaching and academia, so I invited her to Omkareshwar. At first she declined, saying that she was too old to travel. I reminded her that she had only to fly to Indore. We would pick her up and take good care of her. The idea seemed to appeal to her and she said she may come next year. I told her how the children would love to hear stories about Ma from her own experience.

I felt inspired to tell Bhitika about our plans to travel to Europe, since she had spent much time traveling and studying there, especially in England. I asked if she thought it was a practical idea. She enthusiastically encouraged me, saying that it would help to bring a unity among the devotees there and in our ashrams in India.

After leaving, I took the bus back to Varanasi, about three hours away. I went directly to our ashram where a nice room awaited me in the guesthouse. I spent two days in great joy in the ancient and holy 'City of Shiva,' and felt great blessings. I went repeatedly to the most famous of all temples, the Shiva temple of Kashi Vishwanath. This is often revered as the holiest temple in India. I had wonderful *darshans* and blessings there. I also found the home and separate temple dedicated to Yogiraj Lahiri Mahasaya, where he sat in lotus posture twenty-four hours a day immersed in *Samadhi* as people would come for his blessings, advice and guidance, or for initiation into *Kriya Yoga*.

Every morning I would meditate on the banks of Mother Ganga and watch the sunrise directly across the river, turning the waters crimson and gold. The boats plied slowly along as they have done for centuries. Timeless tranquility. Endless blessedness.

Eternal India!

CHALO MANA GANGA TEER

Swami Nirvanananda

Now I stop here on the banks of the Ganges;
Finally I stop here on the banks of the Ganges,
Meditating silently as the mist is rising.
The sun is pale on the water as the tole appears,
Watching silently as the great river slowly flows,
Gathering garlands of flowers
From the mountains to the sea.

Suddenly I am leaving all my thinking and sensations;
My deepest feelings and emotions.
A boat appears at dusk and disappears
Between the River and the sky.

Now I stop here on the banks of the Ganges;
Finally I sit here on the banks of the Ganges,
Contemplating Your profile shining in the stars:
Your crown among the stars.

India Yatra – First, but Not the Last!

Narayan Redondo

I had heard so many amazing stories about devotees' pilgrimages to India that I was aching to go. Even before I left the States I considered India to be my real home. Many devotees probably feel that way. *Bharat Mataji* was calling me to come home, and home it was. Time, ego, and worry were nowhere to be found in my world as I joined the group of pilgrims led by Gangadas. I made a promise to myself when I stepped off the plane that I would surrender to everything on my path – everything that came to me while I was in India.

That, by the way, would be my first advice to anyone who is thinking about going. Just surrender and go with it. If you are with a good tour group you are set. It is so accommodating and comfortable that all one need do is relax and soak in the love and peace that surrounds you. I did a pretty good job of it, yet there were a few times when I wasn't surrendering and I got 'taken down,' you might say, by strong vibrations that I had never felt before. That taught me a great lesson that I will cling to forever: keep the Heart open at *all* times. Here are a few of my experiences.

Throughout the entire pilgrimage I was floating on cloud after cloud. We went from holy city to holy city, visiting our beloved Guru's places. I had some idea of what I was in for, of course, so I was soaking it up. Master (Paramahansa Yogananda) is so present in India. I felt he was with me all the time, just as if he were in the other room doing his work while we were staying in the beautiful *YSS* ashrams. It wasn't until we arrived in Varanasi (Banares) and visited the Vishwanath Mandir (Shiva Temple) at Banares Hindu University that I was hit by a surprise that came, I knew, from not surrendering completely. We made our way into the temple, ringing the first bell then the next and the next. I was beginning to feel light headed.

As we progressed to the center of the temple we entered the inner shrine of the Shiva Lingam and were presented by the priest with garlands blessed by Lord Shiva. At that time I began sweating profusely, shaking and feeling very queasy. I had to hang on to the wall and to another devotee who was accompanying us. The rest of the time in the temple I was barely able to remain standing. It felt as though I were being held down by some invisible force. That is the only way I can describe it. As we stepped out of the temple gates I felt fine again immediately. It was so obvious since I had just left the temple grounds that were permeated with the divine vibrations of Lord Shiva. That was just the beginning!

After some time we arrived in Dakshineswar, on the Ganga outside of Kolkata, where Ma Kali appeared to Master as told in the *Autobiography of a Yogi*, (Chapter 22, *The Heart of a Stone Image*). As had happened in Varanasi, as soon as I stepped through the temple doors and entered the majestic grounds, the vibrations started hitting me from all sides, or so it seemed. The vibrations of temples that have been used for worship for so many years are permeated with a force field from God. I was struck again in a similar manner as in Varanasi, yet with even greater intensity. For the rest of the day I was out of it. Then a firecracker exploded by our door in the ashram in the middle of the night and I felt fine. It was as though nothing had happened at all.

The last experience of this nature, before I actually began to live up to my own inner vow of surrender, came when we were sitting in *satsang* with a highly realized *sannyasi*, Swami Shantananda Giri of *YSS*. As he spoke about Master's teachings, and about God and his own spiritual development, his eyes began to take hold of me. Again I started 'going down.' This time, however, I was able to fight it off long enough not to get sick. I began to realize what was happening to me. On some level I had been resisting these holy vibrations – the actual living presence of God.

My mind and heart hadn't fully grasped the reality that God is indeed omnipresent. Spirit really is everywhere! The only way to realize that is to be open and to constantly keep the mind and heart centered on God. Not only in meditation, or when we feel devotional. We need to see that at all times. God has to be in every place we visit and in every person we relate with. He must be in every thought, every word, and every action. God permeates everything; I was actually able to see Him working. From that time on I started having the most beautiful spiritual experiences I have ever had. I began surrendering not only to India, as I had promised myself, but also to *That* which most people think of as invisible. Without those blessed experiences I would not have been able to understand Swami Shantanandaji's words to us on our final day in India: "When you get that feeling of love for something whether it be like Ramakrishna falling into bliss when he saw a crane fly by, or the feeling of perfection in meditation; whether it's for a second or a minute, know that that is the vibration of God giving you a stroke of His or Her presence. Only from there can you expand it and keep on expanding it. That is when you will know God."

Narayan Redondo, an SRF member and devotee of Paramahansa Yogananda, resides in San Diego with his wife, Mariamma, and their son, River.

Holy River Narmada

Swamini Umamaiya Udasin

My beloved master has left his body. I have come to India to see his *Samadhi* place and to do the *sadhana* which has been given. Daily I will practice seven hours *japa* and three hours *dhyana.* Yet where? With the temperature already over 100 degrees Fahrenheit in early April, I can't imagine being able to sit for *sadhana* inside a shuttered *kutir* with a tin roof!

On intuition I accept the kind offer of an old man who says he knows just the place for my *sadhana* and will take me to Nareshwar on the Holy River Narmada by bus tomorrow.

"A river or a hill, a tree or a cloud, -- indeed any object of beauty, may raise one to contemplation of the Supreme Being and to silent worship of Him. In particular, sacred rivers, temples or images, which for generations have been the objects of devotion and worship, possess this power in a special degree, in virtue of the sacred thoughts they have witnessed and absorbed, just as garments retain perfumes," (Rajagopalachari's Ramayana).

I sit under a tree on a hill overlooking the Holy Narmada – a splendid scene – and beg You, Beloved Master,. to let me stay here in this vast and sacred place, by this holy River for my *sadhana.* The old man has the same inspiration and is, at this very moment, in the ashram office making inquiries on my behalf. And so it is arranged. Blessed grace!

Somehow I feel that I too may be cleansed and purified by this Holy River. I know, however, that Uma must do *tapas* to gain Lord Shiva! And so I set myself a schedule, including *mauna*: 4:00 AM to 8:00 AM by the River for *pranayama*, prayer and meditation, then to my room for chai at 8:30; *japa* beside the River again from 9:00 until noon, then lunchtime in the dining hall. After that, best of all things, at the hottest time of day when everyone else is resting, more *japa* from 1:00 till 4:00 PM while actually sitting in the River with the water up to my neck and

my *mala* floating on the surface. Chai again in my room at 4:30. From 5:00 until 8:00 in the evening I again sit by the River for *dhyana, asanas, pranayama* and chanting of the Guru Gita. At 8:30 I have warm milk in my room. After that, if I wish, I can join one of two *satsangs* going on at the ashram every evening.

What a River! What freedom, grace and upliftment I feel here! All along the water level as far as the eye can see are clean white sandy beaches which are really part of the river bed, visible due to the low water of the pre-monsoon season. Up on the real river bank – cliffs a hundred feet high – are trees to sit under in the shade. The wind always blows. The river is clear and clean with a white sandy bottom, and the water is pleasantly cool.

Before bathing I ask You to give me an open and faithful heart so that I might receive full benefit from this sacred bath. What joy! It is the first time in India that I have been in a place with such expansive space, beautiful scenery and the opportunity to be alone – to sit, to walk, to perform *asanas*. There is natural beauty and holy vibrations in all directions!

I find myself smiling for so many reasons as I walk to the River today! I can walk out of my room and off the ashram compound down the hundred steps to the River's edge, toes spreading in the sand and wind blowing at my back and trudge happily far away from all the pilgrims. Sometimes I walk for forty-five minutes until I find a solitary spot that suits me just right for bathing, swimming and reciting *japa* in the River. Then, after some time, sitting on my mat, clothes drenched and cool, I chant the Guru Gita and meditate. Any concern that I might have had about the difficulty of reciting *japa* for seven hours a day has gone. The *japa* recitation became exceedingly sweet after just a few days. In his book, *Japa Yoga*, Swami Sivananda remarks, "Sweeter than all sweet things, more auspicious than all good things, purer than all pure things, is the Name of the Lord."

I speak to no one but Bapuji (Umamaiya's Guru) when I am by the River, yet to Him I talk incessantly. I chant my heart out until my voice becomes hoarse. I cry and cry. I beg Him to appear right here on this river bank and give me *darshan*. Then I quiet down and sit for *dhyana* as the sun goes down and the moon begins to show. I wait until darkness comes, illuminated only by the moon and the stars, before reluctantly walking back up the hill to the ashram and my room. At 8:30 Bhatubai brings warm sweet milk for supper.

I feel holy vibrations all around and believe myself to be the grateful and fortunate recipient of many levels and layers of spiritual assistance, unspoken perhaps, but very real nonetheless. I am so very touched by the loving kindness of the trustees of the ashram here. They have decided that Bapuji must have approached Rang Avdhoot (the founding saint of Nareshwar Ashram) in *Swarg Loka* and said, "Listen here, my disciple, Umabahen, is coming to your ashram. Take good care of her!" Indeed they are doing their very best. With immense kindness they feed me without chilies. It is simple food yet totally delicious, as I come ravenous for my one meal of the day.

Three weeks have passed and I have just completed a *lakh* and a quarter of mantra repetitions. Of that number, I pray that there were at least a few which were recited with complete concentration and pure devotion. If there was even one so recited, and if that one gave even the smallest delight to my Beloved Lord, I am most happy. I long to stay here in this, my India, to continue my *sadhana* on the banks of the Holy River Narmada. I yearn to see this River through all Her seasons and all Her changes throughout a year's time. Dearest Master, I confess these attachments. I don't feel finished in India at all. I want to stay and practice *sadhana* until I see God's face – Your face, and know that I am One with That.

Swamini Umamaiya Udasin, a direct disciple of Sri Swami Kripalvananda (Bapuji) since 1979, lived in her Guru's ashram from 1982 until 1989. She then traveled to India to receive her final vows of renunciation, sannyas, in the monastic order established by her Guru. After living in India and following the life of a wondering nun for several years, she returned to the States to care for her parents. After this seva is completed, Swamini Umamaiya plans to return to her life as a wondering sannyasini, or take residence in an ashram in India.

This article first appeared in the ***Om Sri Ram Newsletter***, Spring, 2003.

Finding Peace in Mother Ganga's Lap

Sadhvi Bhagvati

Nothing for sale in America compares to the spiritual bliss that comes for free in India. I sit in silent joy, the cooling Ganga rushing across my toes. A young local ashram child, whom I love as my own, sits in my lap, nuzzling me with the back of her head. My vision is filled with the boundless and ceaseless current of Mother Ganga. The setting sun's light dances off Her waters, reflecting into my eyes and making them tear with joy. Lord Siva sits in the midst of Ganga's waters in all His towering glory. The statue of the Lord, erected for the Kumbha Mela, (Haridwar, 1998), appears to have been there for eternity.

Pujya Swami Chidanand Saraswatiji sings, *Swagatam, sharanagatam, shubha swagatam Gange*: "Hail, O Holy Ganga! We have come to You for refuge." My body is filled with the coolness of the *ghat* and the warmth of a divine child; my eyes burst with the *darshan* of Lord Siva and Mother Ganga; my ears are filled with the song of God – sung during the day by Pujya Sant Rameshbai Oza in his *Katha*, and sung in the evening by Pujya Swamiji on the banks of this holiest of rivers. The mind, the senses and the memories of any other life are gone. There is no more room for them.

"But don't you ever miss America?" People ask me, and I laugh. I came to India in 1996 as a tourist, on a short vacation from my clinical psychology Ph.D. program. I planned to travel, explore, relax, and then return to the white, upper class western life in which I had been raised. In the West we are taught that happiness can be 'acquired' and 'obtained' as though it were a commodity. Having had everything western life had to offer, I was still not deeply happy. Sure, I was happy on the outside, content perhaps, yet never had I even dreamt of the joy that ran straight to the core of my being the first time I stood on Ganga's banks and bathed in the sound of Swamiji's voice. Never had I dreamed of such blissful peace as that given by life in the lap of the Himalayas.

To be in India at all is a blessing. To be here for *Kumbha Mela* is due only to God's grace. It is a time when India's true spirit emerges; a time when the essence, the bloodstream of Indians across the world comes alive and calls them home. They rush, they flock, they flood – as though the call came from so deep within as to be unavoidable. For what do they come? To listen to great saints speak divine truth; to bathe in the holy waters; to offer ghee to the rising flames; to cleanse themselves of sins; to imbibe what their scriptures say is the nectar of immortality. This is the incredible spirit of India. And so it has been since before the dawn of history.

For what will Americans, the 'richest' people in the world, flock in such numbers? For what will they withstand such crowds, heat and inconvenience – a sports event, a rock concert? A McDonald's french-fry giveaway? So, when asked if I miss America, the answer is a resounding "No." Yet it is much more than that. It is "Yes" to India, a country filled with people who will spend their last rupee, and days on a bus, to bathe in the holy water of our Mother. It is "Yes" to a country overflowing with hungry and shoeless children whose eyes and spirits yet shine with the light of God. It is "Yes" to India where everyone understands the ecstasy I am experiencing as I sit with my toes dipped in the holy waters of Mother Ganga, my eyes tearing at the sight of the sun streaming from Lord Siva's open palm, and my soul being carried to Heaven as Swamiji leads the *Arati*, the "Worship with Lights.

Sadhvi Bhagawati, a disciple of Pujya Swami Sri Chidanand Saraswati Muniji, has been residing at the Parmarth Niketan Ashram in Rishikesh since 1996.

H.H. Pujya Swami Chidanand Saraswati Muniji Performing Ganga Arati with H.H. Sri Sri Ravi Shankar

From Hollywood to the Holy Woods

Sadhvi Bhagvati

"Graaandmaaa, buy me a pair of Jordache jeans!" my voice would sing out in a whine as we stepped through the wide glass doors of the department store. My Dad used to joke that I was the only person he knew who called her jeans by name: "my Guess jeans, my Jordache, my Calvin Kleins." I knew when Esprit was in and I wore Esprit matching outfits: starched cotton shirts with pleated shorts joined at the center by the essential thin leather belt. It was too time consuming to figure out what to wear each morning so I would scour my closet the evening before, picking out the perfect clothes for school the next day. At that time every season demanded new clothes: back to school clothes, summer clothes, spring clothes, birthday clothes, party clothes.

Now I live on the holy banks of Mother Ganges, in Rishikesh, India. I sit each evening as the sun's last rays dance off Her waters, a child's soft, dirty arms wrapped around my neck, with dozens of others vying for my hand or a place on my lap. We are gathered together with hundreds of others to offer our prayers, our gratitude and our love to God in a fire and light ceremony called *Aarti*. The stress, the tension and the pains of the day melt into the heat of the flames and are carried swiftly away by the purifying current of Mother Ganga. These children – children who live well below the Western standard of poverty – have an unmistakable glow of joy in their eyes. They sit and sing with their heads on my lap, their voices loud and out of tune. In their young innocence and piety they are oblivious to any sense of self-consciousness. The evening wind blows gently across our faces, carrying misty drops of Ganga's waters onto our cheeks which are already wet with tears of divine surrender. She flows quickly, dark as the night, yet as light as the day. I am surrounded by people singing the glories of God, singing the glories of life.

I wake each day as the sun peaks over the Himalayas, bringing light, life and a new day to us all. I sleep each night in the shelter of Mother Ganga, as She continues Her ceaseless journey to the ocean. I spend the day working on a computer as spiritual songs play in the background throughout the ashram in which I live. It is an ashram not dedicated to one guru or one sect. Its name is "Parmarth Niketan," meaning "an abode dedicated to the welfare of all." My days are filled with *seva.* I do work for schools, hospitals, and ecological programs. Now I never wear jeans at all. I gave my nicest clothes away to others, knowing how happy it will make them. Today, all the possessions I own (mainly books, journals, and a filing cabinet) fit on the floor of a closet in my parent's home.

They came to visit me in Rishikesh last Christmas. Christmas had always been a time for extensive wish-lists, arranged and rearranged in meticulous order of preference. The anticipatory excitement of waiting for Christmas morning was matched only by the thrill of tearing open the wrapping paper to reveal what treasure lay beneath. When my parents came this year it was the first time I had seen them in four months, and it would be another four months before I would see them again. On their last day here they were generously preparing envelopes filled with the equivalent of more than a month's salary for each of the boys who had cared for them during their visit; boys I call, "*Bhaiya*," [brother]: the cook, the driver, the cleaner. After the envelopes had been stuffed, my Mom looked at me with open wallet and said, "Okay, now you. What for you?" "Nothing," I said without a moment's hesitation. "Oh come on," she said, as though my life of simplicity were simply a show for others. "We're your parents." "Well," I replied, "If you really want to give something, you can make a donation to our children's schools."

What happened? How did I go from calling my jeans by name, from being unable to begin the day without a double latté, from a life in Hollywood and Beverly Hills, to the life of a nun on the banks of River Ganga? How to go from being unable to work for more than two hours at a time without a break, from spending more time complaining about my work than actually doing it, to working fifteen hours a day, seven days a week for not a cent, but with a constant glow of joy? How to go from being an avid movie fan, to being someone who would rather work on the computer or meditate? How to go from being someone for whom a 'perfect evening' meant a nice, expensive dinner out and a movie, to someone who would rather drink hot milk at home?

How did this happen? The answer can only be God's blessing. My ego would love to say, "Oh I did it. I decided to make myself a better person. I became spiritual and worked to free myself from the constraints of the Western world." Yet that is only my ego's fantasy; it is not true. What is true is that God picked me up in His arms and carried me forth to the life I am supposed to live.

People frequently ask me, "Wasn't the transition difficult? You must have had to really adapt. Don't you ever miss the western life, the life of comfort?" I say to them, "Imagine that you have size eight feet. However, your entire life people have told you that, in fact, you have size five feet. They were

Shiva Mahadev
Parmarth Niketan, Rishikesh

not being malicious or consciously deceptive. They really believed that your feet were size five. So for your whole life you have worn size five shoes on your size eight feet. Sure, they were uncomfortable and tight, and you developed chronic blisters and corns, but you just thought this was what shoes were supposed to feel like. Whenever you mentioned it to anyone, they assured you that, yes, shoes always feel tight and give you blisters. That is just how shoes are. So you stopped questioning. Then, one day, someone accidentally slippped your foot into a size eight shoe. "Ahhh," you say. "So, that is what shoes feel like!" Still people ask, "But, how did you adapt to wearing this size eight shoe? Don't you miss the way your size five shoe felt?"

Coming home to India has felt like slipping a size eight foot into a size eight shoe – just right. I wake each morning and, just as little children rush into their parent's bed, cuddle under the covers, and lie in their mom's arms before starting their day, I rush down to Ma Ganga, like a very young child. "Good morning, Mom," I say into the wind, as it whips off the Himalayas onto Her ceaselessly flowing waters. I bow to Her and drink a handful of Her divine nectar. I stand in Her waters rushing over my bare feet, an IV of life and divinity in my all-too-human morning sluggishness. I fold my hands in prayer as the sun, rising over the Himalayas, begins to reflect off Her boundless waters:

Thank you Ma.
Thank you for waking me again today,
For letting my eyes open
In the land of your infinite grace.
Thank you for making my legs able
To carry me to Your banks, and then to my office.
Thank you for bringing me forth to this life of service,

This life of light, this life of love,
This life of God.
Let my work today be in service of You.
May You be the hand that guides mine.
And most importantly,
Please, please, let me be worthy of living
on Your banks.

I then walk back up the steps of the ashram into the blinding light of the rising sun, and to my office. It is 6:30 A.M.

The day is filled with work – work on a computer, sitting in an office: proposals for new projects; reports on the projects that already exist; ideas for how to improve the work we are doing; letters to those who generously fund our schools, hospitals, ambulance, and ecology programs; correspondence for the saint in whose service I live my life; and editing beautiful books on the Gita, or on the teachings of the Mother – books written by brilliant Indian thinkers, but checkered with spelling and grammatical errors.

"Don't you ever take a day off?" people ask, and I laugh again. What would I possibly do with a 'day off?' Sit in bed and paint my toenails? And why would I want one? My life is my work. I am more at peace, more joyful, more filled with divine bliss as I work to bring education to the illiterate, training programs to the unemployable, medicine to the sick, sweaters to the cold, and smiles to the teary-eyed, than I could possibly be anywhere else. This work and this life have been the greatest gift from God that I could possibly imagine.

Why am I sharing this with you? Why would people who don't even know me be interested in the joy I have found in life? Because this is not what we have been taught. We are taught that joy in life comes from having money, a good education, the latest material possessions, relaxing vacations, the right partner, and a white picket fence around our home. If we have all of those things and are not happy, they simply say, "Acquire more. Make more money, get another degree, buy this or that, take another sun-soaked trip to Mexico, start a new relationship, and build a higher fence." Who ever says, "You have the wrong things! You are looking in the wrong places!" No one ever tells us that money, education, possessions, and vacations are wonderful, that they may bring comfort, but that they are not the key to happiness. No one tells us that to be in service is one of the greatest joys in the world.

Of course, there are clichés like, "It is better to give than to receive," yet these words are more likely found in a book in the self-help section of a bookstore than on our lips or in our hearts. Today, as I see an advertisement for a skin cream which will "restore your youthful beauty" for only $30, I think of twenty children, shivering in the Himalayas, who can have sweaters for that same amount of money. Which, I wonder, will truly bring youth to my being: the skin cream or the knowledge that twenty children are no longer suffering?

I have found that all the things I used to believe were essential – as much sleep as my body could take, meals whenever I wanted them; an air-conditioned car – don't begin to bring the health to my being that being in service does.

On a recent trip back to America I had just arrived in Los Angeles after forty hours of travel, preceded by days of unusually long hours in preparation for my upcoming two-week absence. At 9:45 PM, I received a message that I must write and send a fax to Bombay to people who want to send six truck loads full of clothing, utensils and food to earthquake victims in the Himalayas. They had contacted our ashram requesting specific information immediately in order to dispatch their trucks. I had not slept in over forty-eight hours (other than a few hours caught on the airplane), and was just about to brush my teeth and head for bed. Yet the knowledge that these people were going to bring shelter to those who were stranded, that they were going to clothe those who were without, that they were going to give food to a region which for weeks had been without water or electricity was enough of a catalyst to send me straight to the computer. As I stood over the fax machine, trying to get through to Bombay, my mother came over for the third time, insisting that I go to sleep: "You haven't slept in days. You have to get up early in the morning and it's already 10:30. Please go to sleep." What? Trade six truckloads of disaster supplies for twenty minutes of sleep? In whose world!

This was the rationale I used to believe: that my needs came first. Only once they were met could I then help others. It's like on airplanes when they describe what to do in case the oxygen masks drop, "First, secure your own mask. Then, help others." I have discovered something different in life. I have discovered the incredible health – not only mental and spiritual, but physical – that comes from being selflessly in service. Any friend of mine will vouch for how somatically focused I used to be – always running to take care of this ache, that pain, this 'signal' from my body. I would panic at the prospect of getting less than the 'necessary' eight hours a night, because then I would undoubtedly get sick and my world would come to an end.

Yes, it is true that there are times when it is important and healthy to nurture oneself; when one must first take care of one's own needs, be they physical, emotional or psychological. There are times in which such work can make one more able to be serve selflessly later on. However, I feel that our culture today is focused backwards. We are taught that the majority of our focus should be on ourselves and once our needs are met, we should give a token amount of time and energy to charitable endeavors. Then we wonder why we don't feel a divine connection; why we don't wake up each day filled with ecstatic joy at the thought of jumping from bed and beginning a new day. Could it be that we have our priorities backwards? Yes, we must take care of ourselves, but our own satisfaction does not have to be our primary goal. Could it be that changing the lives of others is exactly what we need to help us change our own? Could it be that a beautiful divine connection can also be found in simple surrender to His will, not only in ardent, arduous, spiritual 'practice'?

For me, it has all been about surrender – surrendering to truth, surrendering to joy, surrendering to God's will. What are my plans? Only God knows. I have no plans, per se. If I were 'in charge,' I would stay in India forever, building schools, orphanages, and hospitals, and ceasing work each day only for *Aarti* on the banks of Ganga. Yet one thing I have learned is that we are not in charge. Who can know what will befall them? A sudden accident, sudden illness, sudden lottery win, sudden ecstatic epiphany?

I

I

I have found that rather than pretend to have any semblance of control over my life it is better to simply turn it over to Him. "May I live as your tool," I pray. "May Your will be my will." Then the messages come clearly. His voice is loud and unmistakable, if only I am quiet and still enough to hear. Sure, there are times when I will say to Him, "But why this? That's not how I would have done it." Yet, the answer usually comes quickly. A few hours, days or weeks later I will understand why He pushed me to move in a certain new direction.

My life is in God's hands. If He ever asks I will certainly tell Him that all I want is to be able to stay on the banks of Ma Ganga forever. Yet He has not yet asked. Still, by His divine grace He has kept me here, and every day I am more and more grateful.

With Maharaj-ji, Neem Karoli Baba

Gita Gendloff

When I look back at my years in India it now seems like a dream. Leaving for my second trip, in 1973, I had a strong yearning for oneness with God, determined to spend time with realized beings and daringly hoping to meet my Guru. My plan was to take a meditation course in Bodh Gaya and then proceed to Bangalore and spend time with Sai Baba, whom I had had *darshan* of two years previously during my first trip to India. Since that time he had been haunting my dreams and I felt a strong connection with him.

My friend, Mira, met me in New Delhi when I arrived. We were planning to travel together. She had just come from Brindavan where she had had the *darshan* of Neem Karoli Baba. She said she was coming to meet me and felt we should stop off in Brindavan on our way. We had a ride with a German man in a VW bus, and there were other passengers who were also going to Bodh Gaya.

We arrived in Brindavan in the evening. At the time there were approximately twenty five Westerners, mostly Americans, staying in town so that they could to be with Neem Karoli Baba (Maharaj-ji) as much as possible. He wasn't seeing any of them at the time, and hadn't for several days. He sent word that we were to be given rooms in the *dharmsala* next to his ashram. A couple of days later I had my first *darshan* with Maharaj-ji. From the first time I was with him it was a relationship like none I had yet experienced in my life. The love I felt for him was a combination of lover, father, best friend, and other feelings which were new to me.

With no thoughts or dreams of Sai Baba coming after a couple of weeks, I prayed to him and asked why I didn't feel the need to come to him. That night Baba (Satya Sai Baba) came to me in a dream. He kissed me on the forehead and said that he had brought me to this place. This was where I belonged now and he was letting go of me.

I stayed with Maharaj-ji for the last six months of his life. On the average, I was able to sit at his feet four to five hours a day. No thoughts or desires came to me to be anywhere other than where I was, or to do anything else during that time. In the night I would sometimes get up and look at his window just in case I could get a glimpse of him. The yearning was so intense.

Many so-called 'miracles' happened in his presence. They are, in themselves, nothing compared to the general feeling of complete, unconditional love one felt from him, but I guess they were something for the memory to hold onto. He was great at reading minds and pretending not to know that he was doing so. There was no ego involvement there at all. I will relate a couple of incidents as I recall them.

While I was at Maharaj-ji's Himalayan ashram at Kainchi, where we went in the spring and summer, I got a telegram from my parents that my grandfather had passed away. I was thinking strongly about my grandfather and the whole situation. After some time, Maharaj-ji sent me, and also a young Indian man named Ravi, away from his presence. This was unusual, as I did not speak Hindi at the time, and he usually always let me sit with him during these hours. I told Ravi that I didn't understand why we were being sent away. He also was troubled and had no idea why this had happened. I asked him what Maharaj-ji was talking about. He said that Maharaj-ji just kept saying over and over that when someone dies it is just the body that dies and we should not be concerned or worried over this. I told Ravi about my grandfather and that I felt we could go back now. When we returned we were welcomed. Maharaj-ji asked me if I was OK. I told him about my grandfather and again he repeated

how it is just the body that passes, and the importance of knowing that.

Another time I awoke in the morning with a horrible flu. I was so sick that I was unable to leave my bed. By late afternoon I was still feeling the same way and didn't know when it was going to pass or how long it might last. Suddenly there was a knock at my door. Maharaj-ji was there! I made it to the door and fell at his feet. As I lay there touching his feet I felt the flu being lifted and taken from me. He asked me if I was OK, and I was. The flu was gone!

There were numerous incidents like this in his presence; many things that he said that were to make sense only years later. As his teaching was very unconventional and just given in the course of being in his presence, not in any formal manner, I was left with examples more than words about how to live in this world. A couple of these impromptu teachings were left as great examples for living a life in the world, as I live now. "Give and you shall always have," he would say; "Don't give and you will never have enough." Or,

Gita and Ravi Khanna with Maharaji
Summer, 1973

"Whatever you give, double will come back to you." There were teachings on marriage, friendship and feeding people. These teachings continue to come even today in many diverse ways. It is hard to even imagine, let alone express. Those years in India are among my greatest blessings. They helped shape my life and my values. Not a day goes by that thoughts of Maharaj-ji and India do not come back to me. The grace of the Guru can never be underestimated!

Gita Gendloff resides in Leucadia, Califorina, where she maintains a real estate practice.

Mahabharat Yatra: Reflections on the North India Tour with Amma, 2006

Ranganatha White

My humble prostrations at the lotus feet of my most beloved Satguru, Mother and Friend, Sri Mata Amritanandamayi Devi, affectionately known as Amma.

For the last twenty years Amma has been traveling the globe soothing minds, healing hearts, and physically embracing all who come to Her regardless of race, religion, caste or creed. She is love incarnate, reminding us all that we are being embraced by the Divine at all times. During the winter of 2006, Amma embarked on Her seventeenth North India Tour which starts at Her main ashram, Amritapuri, in Kerala, South India, and stretches toward the north and then to the east, ending in Kolkata. Accompanying Amma were more than 150 international devotees, including myself, approximately 200 Indian *brahmacharis* and *brahmacharinis*, a handful of senior monastic swami's, a few Indian householders who reside at the ashram – and our tireless bus drivers. It was the longest tour to date: eight very full weeks. On seven buses we traveled over 4,600 miles through seventeen cities to witness and imbibe the profound love given freely to hundreds of thousands by one of the most phenomenal saints our blessed Earth shall ever celebrate. Words alone could never convey the transforming potency of such a journey. I offer this humble attempt with love.

It is true that India can be a bit overwhelming, especially on a fifteen to twenty hour bus ride leading to a public program of anywhere from thirty thousand to one-hundred thousand people, where one might be asked to help out with crowd control! Everyone is there for the same intrinsic desire: to be awakened to one's true nature. Though this was my third (and a half) North India Tour with Amma, I can truly say I will never be without a feeling of complete awe at the magnitude of this five foot tall woman who has the peculiar habit of hugging thousands of people for up to twenty hours at a stretch! Aside from listening to the countless pains of individual lives during *darshan*, Amma also assesses many other topics such as the details of Her countless charitable activities, Ashram matters, or simply the well being of Her children who are traveling with Her – all the while remaining 108% present with those individuals who are receiving *darshan*. Truly a supreme multi-tasker!

If it is a one-evening program, as opposed to a few days of programs at one of the branch ashrams, we leave fairly soon after it is over for the next stop. One might think that after an all night hugging fest of thirty to fifty thousand people with no rest or food, Amma may want a little shut-eye. Nope. This is where the nectar comes in. Though we may all beg Her to take some rest, She will insist on meeting up with us somewhere on the road for a lunch stop. She may even let us know that She missed us and didn't see enough of Her children the night before. The fact that spending time with us was more important than rest to Her made my eyes fill with tears on more than one occasion, reflecting upon such loving sacrifice.

We may sit under a tree near a cotton field, or maybe near a river somewhere in Rajasthan. Perhaps it is in a gas station parking lot, as we did a couple times on this tour. No matter where we sat with our beloved Guru we would be instantly transported to a profound place where fear and hatred could not exist. After sharing words of wisdom, or passing a microphone around at Her request for jokes (spiritual, of course), or singing a few *bhajans*, lunch is served. Amma, Herself, passes all three hundred individual plates out to the devotees while the food is being dished out and handed to Her. This is *prasad* at its finest! Before eating, the recitation of the 15th chapter of the Bhagavad Gita is melodically chanted by the ashramites. This is the chapter wherein Lord Krishna describes the nature of the Supreme Spirit. After leaving the newly sanctified area we head out for more time on the road. Times like these easily wash away any discomfort associated with the long bus rides. Will we be stopping with Amma again for evening chai and *bhajan* under the stars? We never know for sure, but such thoughts keep our minds focused on the divine play of which we are a part, and the immeasurable blessing of being with Her.

The day after the program in Talessary, still in Her home state of Kerala, Amma wanted to sit with all Her 'tour children' on the top floor of the branch ashram. It was a sweet time of joyful laughter and deep wisdom lavished by all. Amma was just about to join the ashram musicians in a makeshift recording studio. There She would record soul-stirring *bhajans* sung in the local language of the state that we would be traveling to next. Time stood still as She silently gazed around the room with a most benign and enchanting smile. A Western devotee ventured to ask Her: "Why is Amma smiling"? Her reply penetrated all of our hearts: "Amma feels as though She is standing in a beautiful meadow filled with fully blossomed flowers." Not a word was spoken as three hundred pairs of innocent eyes were filled with the purest love and gratitude. To be seen only for who we truly are rather than for our limited little selves was a reminder of our Guru's love for us. The *Satguru* sees what God sees, our true Self, which is always abiding in the pure peace and bliss of Itself. Such is the love of our Divine Mother. Dear friend, may I humbly remind you that you too are a flower in that beautiful meadow?

Om Lokah Samastah Sukhino Bhavantu
"May all beings in all the worlds be happy."

Ranganatha White resides in Santa Barbara, Caifornia.

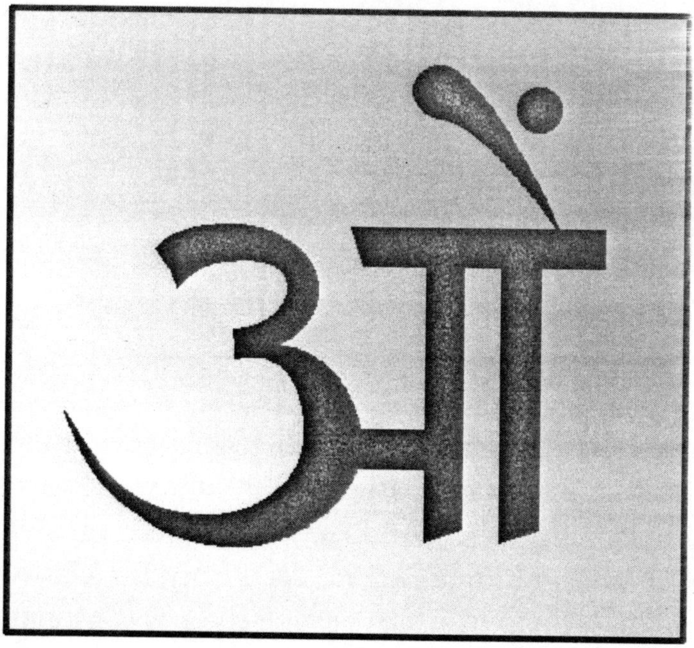

Tungnath

Colin Kenney

In the fall of 2004 I had the amazing good fortune of traveling to India with a dozen of my good friends. We traveled all around Northern India, visiting Delhi, the majestic Taj Mahal in Agra, Shiva's holy city of Kashi (Varanasi or Banaras), Haridwar, the "Gateway to the Himalayas," Rishikesh, and many other beautiful, holy, uplifting sites. This is the story of how perseverance, dedication and devotion rewarded me with one of the great adventures of my life.

We had been in India for about two weeks, traveling through the beautiful hill country of the Himalayas. We had been to many sacred and holy places, temples and ashrams, and had visited various saints and *sadhus*. We spent several days at the Yogoda Satsanga Society Ashram at Dwarahat, and visited the most holy cave where Babaji Maharaj, my great-great-grand Guru, initiated Lahiri Mahasaya into Kriya Yoga. From there we headed north to the high Himalayan shrine dedicated to Lord Narayana at Badrinath. Badrinath is a magical place which is saturated with blissful love and the devotion of millions of devotees who have made pilgrimages to there throughout the centuries. One can't help but be uplifted just by breathing that holy air which has been breathed by saints and yogis for millennia. After the rigors of navigating the narrow mountain roads on a bus that seemed just a little too wide for them, we received a much needed recharge at Badrinath!

Reluctant to leave, yet eager to continue our journey, we made ready for our next destination: Kedarnath. As we were leaving Badri, however, it was beginning to rain. We knew that didn't bode well for the fourteen kilometer hike required to reach Kedarnath, where the altitude is considerably higher. We then heard reports that it was already beginning to snow at Kedarnath. It was suggested that we visit the second most holy Shiva shrine in the area at Tungnath instead. Tungnath is intimately connected to Kedarnath as one of the five Kedar shrines known as "Panch Kedar." Hearing that we were already not far from the temple at Tungnath, four of us decided to leave the group and take a day trip to that shrine. It was arranged that we would hire a jeep to take us to the trail leading to Tungnath, while the rest of the group would meet us in Rudraprayag where accommodations had been arranged.

We took our jeep to the small village of Chopta at elevation 9500 feet, which is the starting point for the pilgrim trail to the temple. By the time we arrived at Chopta, it was pouring rain. Doubts were starting to creep into our minds, yet at the same time, we were determined to make it up the mountain. We waited for a break in the rain. Time went by and if anything, the rain just got heavier. Sitting in the jeep and listening to the rain falling, we began singing a Shiva *bhajan* to focus our thoughts on the Lord, and to remind ourselves of the purpose of our journey. As soon as we started singing, the rain lessened. By the time we finished the song not a drop of rain was falling. It seemed like the sun was actually beginning to peep through the clouds. Seizing the moment, we bundled ourselves up against the cold and headed for the trail. Our driver said that he would wait for us in the village while we made the trek up the mountainside to the temple of Tungnath.

We began our hike on the ancient path made up of thousands of flat stones placed up on their sides and packed together with mud, grass, and moss. The path wends up and up through the most beautiful dense old-growth forest, and through picturesque alpine meadows (picture the opening to *The Sound of Music*) with astonishing views of the Himalayan peaks. The area around Tungnath is the most densely forested part of the Garhwal region of the Himalayas. It is absolutely breathtaking!

The hike to Tungnath is breathtaking as well – literally! The trail from the village up to the temple is about four kilometers (2.5 miles), and it is quite steep. We were coming from Southern California, after all, and hiking at that altitude on a steep slope of slippery rocks was tougher than we had thought it might be. Nevertheless, we kept trudging along, pausing occasionally to catch our breath, only to have it taken away again by the beauty of our surroundings.

After walking for an hour and a half or so, we could see fog gathering on the hill above us. The clouds were getting thicker and the air was getting colder. As we came to the top of a ridge, the first few flakes of snow began to fall. We kept on but the snow got thicker and heavier. It was then that we came upon two young men on their way back down from the temple. Exhausted yet eager, we asked them how much farther it was to the temple. Neither spoke English, so we pointed up the hill and said, "Tungnath! How much further?" Eventually one of them did seem to understand what we were asking. He pointed up the hill and all he said was, "Half, half." Our hearts sank. Only halfway! We didn't think we could make it to the top if this was only halfway but decided to press on a little longer, just to see how far we could get. The snow was quite heavy now, and we were all wet and very cold.

We then came upon a small hut which was really nothing but four poles with plastic tarps for walls and a roof. We asked the occupant if we could come in and warm up by his fire. We were delighted to discover that the hut was actually a little chai shop. We were able to warm ourselves with hot tea also – a welcome relief! The shop owner, of course, spoke no English at all, but somehow we all had a good laugh together. By this time the snow and fog were so thick that all we could see outside the shack was a solid wall of white. I was completely soaked as I had 'cleverly' worn sweat pants, socks and sandals that day! As I was drying my socks on the clay stove I looked up at the wall and saw a photo of the temple that we were trying to reach. Pointing to the picture, I said "Tungnath!" The shopkeeper nodded and repeated, "Tungnath!" We asked how much further it was. Not understanding our words, he just pointed up the hill in the direction of the temple. Again we asked how far, but it was in vain. Slowly it dawned on us that he was not pointing a long way off at all. He was actually pointing at the temple itself – we had arrived! The relief we felt might be described as something like 'glorious!' The young man who had told us, "Half, half," did not mean that we were only halfway there; he meant that we were only half a kilometer away. We were that close yet couldn't even see the huge temple through the icy fog! Hurriedly we paid for our chai, thanked the shopkeeper immensely, and made our way up the last few hundred feet to the temple.

The temple at Tungnath is beyond description. I don't really mean the way it looks, for its appearance is similar to many other temples in India. It is the feeling that is there that cannot be put into words. I could actually feel the peaceful joy of the saints who have been visiting this remote shrine for thousands of years. I imagined I could feel the presence of the Pandava brothers who built this temple with their own hands. And best of all, I could feel the living presence of the Lord permeating the very stones from which it is built.

The elevation of Tungnath is about 12,000 feet, making it one of the highest temples in the Himalayas, and the highest Shiva temple in all of India. We could not enter the temple with our shoes on so we had to leave them in a room across the courtyard and walk barefoot to the entrance through the snow. Entering the temple, we stepped into another world and another time. The vibration in the inner sanctum felt as though it had remained unchanged for eternity. It could have been a thousand years ago... or a thousand years from now. The feeling would have been the same. The small room which houses the ancient *lingam* seemed to be a pocket which was somehow removed from the flow of time. The local *pandit* chanted the appropriate mantras, blessed us and gave us *prasad.* Then we began our slippery hike back down the hill. We again visited our newly found friend in the chai hut to warm our feet and hands before braving the steep, snowy trail back down the mountain. Saying goodbye, we took our time going back down.

We all slipped once or twice but our spirits were soaring. When we finally reached our waiting taxi we piled in shivering. We were cold, we were soaked... and we were very, very happy.

Hara Hara Mahadev!

Varanasi, October, 2004

Colin Kenney and his wife, Tiffany, reside in Fort Collins, Colorado. Along with friends, they founded the kirtan band, BOLO!

The Many Blessings of Lord Narayana

Colin Kenney

There is a very potent *mantra* with which you may be familiar. It is the *Mahamantra* of Lord Vishnu in the form of Badrinarayana. This mantra, *Om Namo Bhagavate Vasudevaya*, is emblazoned on a golden plaque over the *murti* of Lord Badrinarayana in His temple at Badrinath high in the Himalayas of Northern India. These few words carry within them an amazing amount of spiritual energy. If they are chanted diligently and with intense devotion, they can give great spiritual blessings to the ardent devotee. Badrinarayan is a very important deity in the Hindu pantheon, and His temple at Badrinath is one of the four main pilgrimage sites in the Himalayas, which are known as the *Char Dhams*. Devout Hindus try to visit them at least once during their lifetime. Over the centuries, Badrinath, which is inaccessible for half of the year due to heavy snows, has been host to countless *sadhus* and saints, *mahants* and *mahatmas*. Paramahansa Yogananda said in his *Autobiography of a Yogi* that, "The northern Himalayan crags near Badrinarayan are still blessed by the living presence of Babaji," the great immortal founder of the Kriya Yoga lineage that Paramahansaji brought to the West in 1920.

It is said that in the spiritually elevated Golden Age, the Satya Yuga, Lord Badrinarayana, Himself, was visible to all who visited this holy *tirtha*. As human consciousness descended and passed into the Treta Yuga, only *sanyassis*, and the most steadfast devotees, had the vision of the Lord in the temple. As the collective consciousness descended further and entered the *Dwapara Yuga*, only the most advanced yogis were able to have the Divine *darshan*. And when the Kali

Yuga took hold of the world, and humanity was plunged into spiritual darkness, the vision of Lord Badrinarayana was hidden to all. It then became necessary to install a *murti* in the temple. This *murti* was installed by Adi Shankaracharya, the great saint and reformer of Hinduism, and founder of the monastic order of which most modern-day swamis are a part.

We were fortunate to be able to visit this most holy site in the fall of 2004 on our pilgrimage tour of North India. It was one of the most inspiring experiences of my life. The energy built up by the countless devotees making that long and difficult pilgrimage, often on foot, was easily perceptible. We spent our time chanting and meditating upon Lord Narayana and drinking the blissful nectar of God's propinquity which is felt so strongly here.

When we left Badrinath, Lord Narayana's presence was still strong in our hearts and minds. We found it difficult to chant to anyone but Him. We were bussing down the narrow Himalayan 'highway' – which is oftentimes only one lane for both directions – on our way to Devaprayag where the two main tributaries of the Ganga, the Bhagirati and the Alakananda rivers converge. It was not long after the end of a late monsoon season. The ground was saturated by the heavy rains, the hillsides and roads were unstable and landslides were commonplace. From time to time we would have to wait while road crews cleared the rocks and mud that had fallen, blocking the way.

On one particular occasion, the landslide was so bad that traffic was backed up for well over a mile. While we were waiting we heard crews using dynamite to clear the huge rocks that were blocking the roadway. Inching forward, we hoped to be able to continue on our way. Soon, however, we saw that one of the men working on the road was making his way from vehicle to vehicle. After speaking with him our driver turned off his engine and we knew that we were in for a wait.

As we all got off the bus to stretch, we were quickly joined by a large group of school children from two other buses which were parked just in front of ours. They were eager to meet us and wanted to know all about where we were from and what we were doing on the Rishikesh-Badrinath highway. We soon discovered that they were also coming back from a pilgrimage to Badrinath, which they had visited as part of a school outing. They were all from the area around the beautiful mountain town of Nainital, and reflected the innate sweetness, purity and guilelessness so typical of Indian children – especially those who are from the countryside.

We spent quite a bit of time with these wonderful kids and their teachers. They even demonstrated a type of team sport that they play together. We still had no word as to how long we would have to wait for the road to reopen. Well, in India, whenever there was some free time we would usually spend it chanting, so we thought of doing kirtan with all of the children. Directly in front of our bus there just happened to be an empty truck. If you have been to India you know exactly what I'm talking about. They are what they call 'Goods Carriers' – brightly painted and decorated with OM symbols and pictures of deities. Well, one of these happened to be right in front of us and it was empty! We found the driver and asked him if we could climb in the back with our kirtan instruments – harmonium, *dholak*, and so on – and do some chanting. He looked at us like we were a little crazy, but agreed. So we dropped the tailgate and climbed in!

Having just left Badrinath, naturally we had to sing to Lord Narayana. The *bhajan* began slowly, just like a lullaby:

Narayana Hari Narayana Hari Narayana Hari Narayana
Narayana Narayana
Sri Vasudeva Murare Sri Vasudeva Murare

Then we started to rock! Hilary was playing the *dholak* with everything she had.

Narayana Narayana Jaya Jaya Govinda Hare!
Narayana, Narayana Jaya Jaya Gopala Hare!

As we reach a crescendo and continued to speed up, I was swept away by the chant. Lord Narayan made His presence known to all of us. The kids were shouting, jumping and laughing, while the adults were fervently chanting. It was an amazing scene – one that would have been simply unimaginable in the West. There we were, stranded by a landslide, not knowing when we might be able to continue our journey. Yet rather than brooding over our situation, we were joyfully singing God's Name with unbridled enthusiasm!

Jaya Bharat! Hail Mother India!

When we finished the chant, all the kids screamed and clapped, apparently in awe of the Americans who sang kirtan. Afterwards, we were approached by two elderly ladies who were on their way up the mountain to Badrinath. It was the first time, and probably the only time in their lives, that they would be making this long-desired pilgrimage. They felt that God had blessed them by coming in the form of this group of Westerners who chanted His divine Name with so much devotion. He did indeed bless their pilgrimage, even as He blessed ours and the children's. All these souls who had never met before and may never meet again, brought together by a natural 'accident,' with nothing in common except love for God. It was truly beautiful. I have been blessed on many occasions to play music with many of the top kirtan artists in America, yet with all my experience chanting the Divine Names, there are none that can compare with chanting to Lord Narayana while stranded on a mountainside in Northern India. The sweet sincerity of the children and the pure devotion of the adults made this an experience I will never forget!

Om Namo Narayanaya!

In India with Ammachi

Komala Saunders

There is a spirit in India that is palpable. You can tune into it and ride that wave of Spirit. If you surrender your mind and your heart, many beautiful and profound divine experiences can be had. India can take you places, both externally and internally, where you may never have been before – beyond the mind to the soul. India is where the name '*Satchidananda*' comes from, and India can show you that it is entirely possible to tune into that uncaused bliss-consciousness. It seems easier, somehow, to experience that in India. I think it is because of all the masters who have lived in that land, plus all the *yajnas* and spiritual ceremonies that have been practiced there throughout the ages. It is also because the people, as a whole, are simple, guileless and very devoted to God, as they have always been.

Starting around 4 AM you begin to hear the temple bells for *mangala arati*, and chants being sung over the loudspeakers to the various forms of God. Incense is being offered and conches blown. It is all-pervasive. That has been going on all over this land for thousands of years. There are no sound control laws in India! You will hear Hindu chants, Muslim prayers and Christian hymns all intermingling in the darkness before the sun even rises over the countryside. That is my experience of India.

The more I become aware of what spirituality really is the more I see how the mind blocks our perception of Spirit. Yoga is 'yoking' the mind to Spirit; calming the mind down, and awakening the heart. So many amazing masters have lived in India and I think they have consciously blessed and sanctified that land so that it is easier to perceive the Divine presence there. You hear so many stories of *avadhuts* who are not bound by society or any convention; saints who may just show up to bless or heal and then run away with a pack of dogs. Sometimes they may look or act crazy, but they are really liberated beings. You just never know. It is so mysterious.

One thing I often notice when I return to America is what it is that I have left behind. I feel as though I have left an environment that is swimming in a sea of consciousness. Of course, it does make a difference when you to go there on pilgrimage to visit holy places. So much of what we perceive has to do with our own sincerity and receptivity.

I remember once when I was staying in Varanasi on the Ganga at the Sita Guest House, which is near Hanuman Ghat. There was a small ashram close by and you could hear them chanting every morning. These *sadhus* would come out all dressed in their *gurua* robes with their staffs and *damarus*. They were covered with ash – the typical image of Hindu holy men – and off they went just parading down the street! I would think, "This is amazing. How wonderful!" Everyday is like a festival day in India. It really is. There is such a sense of freedom. You can worship anywhere, anytime and pretty much in any way. The people are so innocent and simple because they have such sincere devotion. I really hadn't experienced anything like that before and I loved it. I loved the freedom and the acceptance. Even though I was a Westerner, I could still chant *bhajans* while walking down the street, use my *mala,* or sincerely cry to God in a temple and people would understand.

It was in 1998 that I made the decision to go to India for the first time. I had been deeply attracted to Ammachi and had had *darshan* with her on several occasions in the States.

When I heard that she was doing a North India tour that year, I decided to join the devotees who were traveling with her. I went alone, although I did have friends that I planned to meet after I arrived. I was filled with a mixture of emotions, however, as I landed in Bombay in the middle of the night with no one there to meet me. On the one hand there was the fear of being in a very foreign place alone in the middle of the night. Yet, as I was sitting in the airport, waves of spiritual energy seemed to be pouring over me. I remember feeling quite overwhelmed by it. Not knowing what to do next, I sat in the airport alone all that first night.

The next day I connected with some of my friends, and together we went to Amma's program. At that moment, Mother just sent out so much loving energy to me. She connected deeply with me and I with her. I was sitting in a chair and feeling so, so protected. Even though there were many people present, I knew that Amma knew that I was there. I had come all the way from America to be with her in India for the first time and I just *knew* that I was in her grace. I felt it. It was as if she had merged into my being. I remember feeling, "Everything is OK."

On that tour Mother was still doing *Devi Bhava*, which she doesn't do any longer since so many people come and the *darshans* are so long. This was a very special tour and I felt so grateful to be able to be a part of it. The schedule was extremely tight. We would have one morning program that started around 10, and Mother would give *darshan* until perhaps 5 in the evening. She would then come back out again at 7:30 and would give *darshan* until around four in the morning. In *darshan*, Mother gives a hug to everyone, which is one of the many ways she blesses those who come to her.

As Westerners who were part of the tour group, we were allowed to stay on stage with her. We would sit there with Mother all night long. It was a big deal, having a seat. Everyone would just sit and 'glue' themselves to Mother. There was always a tension between us as Westerners and the Indian *brahmacharis* who thought they should be closer to Mother. The Indian devotees would literally fight for seats, so when you got one you stayed there! That's how I spent my nights on the tour – just absorbed in Mother – merged in her. You know when you are with her that she is totally aware of you and everything you are doing. At the same time you feel this comforting love and light emanating from her. The mind quiets down and you go into a deeper part of yourself. Sometimes the unpurified aspects of my mind would arise. It was very scary for me then because I was aware that Amma knew my thoughts.

Those of us on the tour would never be able to get *darshan* in the sense of getting a hug, but we had various positions of service such as rolling *prasad*, or giving it to Amma to hand out. We would bundle candies and *vibhuti* and pass them forward. It was Mother's way of giving us an opportunity to serve her and to be close to her – and to have something to do all night!

When the program would start, Mother would give a *satsang* in Malayalam, her native language, which would then be translated into the language of the locality where we were visiting. Those of us on the tour were never able to attend the *satsangs*. Then the *bhajans* would start. For me, the *bhajan* programs were always just 'out of this world.' They were the highlight for me, without a doubt. Amma would lead the chanting, and she transmitted so much feeling and devotion for God – so much love and passion – just burning. We would sing with her and I often felt that a lot of emotional baggage would be cleared up at those times. I felt that I was being purified, that my heart was being opened and given the space to know what real devotion is. It was her gift. I felt like she would make a *sankalpa* for us to experience true devotion and love for God. That is one of Mother's greatest gifts.

Mother sometimes commented on how the Westerners are very mental. She never really answered many of my questions. That would just have kept me in that mental realm. I wouldn't have been able to drop into the heart and see the reflection of my Self. The mind often locks out the real feeling of the Self. Mother is the fullness of love, and that is what our hearts are seeking.

She would encourage us to stay up all night. There was a lot of *tapas* on the tour. There were some elderly people with us and a bus would leave after the *bhajan* program for those who wanted to go. If you didn't take that bus you would have no recourse but to remain until the conclusion of the program. Mother always encouraged us to remain. She really wanted us to go beyond what we considered to be our limitations. She wanted us to push forward and to feel the power of God behind our lives, that great power that sustains us. That is what this tour is really all about: surrendering to that power which is Amma and riding the wave of Mother's grace.

We were staying up very late – sometimes all night – then trying to sleep a little while bouncing along rough roads in old buses with the windows open and the dust blowing in. Sometimes we might get a cold or become sick. The response was always, "It is Mother's will for you. It's just purification," or, "Mother is relieving you of some of your *prarabdha*."

Mother herself sometimes confirmed that this was, in fact, the case. We would finish one program at 5 in the morning, pack up and leave around 6:30, drive a few hours and start a program again. This would be followed by another program in the evening, and Mother required us to be at all of these programs. So you can imagine – coming to India for the first time and then having a routine like that was just incredible. I could hardly keep it together!

We went from Bombay up to Delhi where Amma inaugurated a new temple with a *Brahmasthanam* celebration. This was an amazing experience. What she was actually doing was empowering the whole temple with the energy and the love of God's presence, as well as infusing life into the *murti*. Drummers were beating their drums; temple trumpets were blaring. The temple was packed with people. The energy that was created was just amazing. They had built a platform for Amma to sit on and she had her hair tied up in a knot on top of her head, which she only did for occasions such as this. She would sit in meditation and then pour water and other sacred offerings over the Deity. I had never felt an energy like that. It felt like she was calling in the whole Universe! I deeply felt the presence of God at that time. Amma would say that we were beginning to feel more of her real nature. We couldn't take it all in. It was just too much.

One of the beauties of India is that they know how to use different methods such as drums and what one might call 'ecstatic ambient noise' in such a way that, although it may not be particularly pleasing to the ear, carries a tremendous divine vibration. That music calls in the Spirit and shuts down the mind. Then God can come in.

Brahmasthanam Dedication
New Delhi, 1998

I didn't socialize much during that first trip to India. I was by myself most of the time and just clung to Mother. I kept her in my heart and the grace I felt from her was incredible. Her *bhajans* were so ecstatic! When she would break into, "Ma, Ma, Ma, Ma, Ma, Ma, Ma, Ma, Maaaa!" I felt that she was doing that for all of us so we could feel her love and her devotion. Then we would fall into spontaneous meditation. She would extend herself to everyone so that we could understand, so that we could have that experience of God – that Love within ourselves. When she chanted, the *shakti* was very strong. I realized I already had that perfection within me. The soul is eternal, and in the realm of eternity that divine consciousness is already mine – because she is here; because the guru is here. She gave me that experience, that understanding. In the realm of time – no matter how long it takes – that is nothing compared to eternity. I just wept, realizing what blessings we were receiving! What a gift the guru is. It's huge – bigger than anything else. The tour with Amma ended in Calcutta and I was feeling very full.

Some of the devotees wanted to go up to Dakshineshwar to the famous Kali Temple because Mother speaks very highly of Sri Ramakrishna and Sarada Devi. But for some reason I decided not to go. I kind of felt I missed the boat on that one since the people who came back were saying what a beautiful experience it was. I then decided to go on my own. I was really in an uplifted state at the time. When I got to Dakshineshwar it was like I was in another world. It all seemed so familiar to me. I especially felt a deep connection with Sri Sarada Devi. Visiting the shrine which was dedicated to her was absolutely thrilling.

Kali Temple, Dakshineswar

I then went to the Krishna Mandir inside the Kali Temple complex where I had an interesting experience. Looking at the image of Lord Krishna I just got this 'hit' from the *murti*. That's the only way I can describe it. I just kept on repeating, "Ma, Ma, Maaa…" The next thing I remember was that I was lying on the ground. Something happened. It was as though I were floating in light. As I started to regain awareness I noticed that there was somebody next to me; really close next to me. In fact, he was almost touching me. I felt the light coming up my body and as I opened my eyes there was a little boy right next to me. He was just there, and I felt a very close relationship with him. Yet as soon as I began to open my eyes, he got up and ran off. Then I started to feel that everything was *karma*. I started to understand that there were ancient and deep connections to everything and everyone around me. Who was that boy? Did I know him? Did he know me?

From there I went to see Bhavatarini Kali! I hadn't been to very many temples in India, yet as far as my temple experience had been, this place was the best.

I then decided to serve at Mother Theresa's Mother House for awhile, taking care of the handicapped children. Many of them were born deformed and needed to be exercised. One little boy in particular drew my attention and sympathy. His name was Pintu. He was severely deformed and very sensitive. My heart just went out to him. I would stroke his head, hold him and do whatever I could for him. He touched me deeply.

While staying in Calcutta I heard from another Westerner that there was something very special happening up in the Himalayan foothills not far from Darjeeling at the Tibetan

Buddhist monastery in Siligiri. I had long felt a connection to Buddhism, so I decided to go. Kalu Rimpoche was very well known and highly respected in both the East and the West. He passed away and was reincarnated into a Tibetan family that worked at the monastery. When the young Kalu Rimpoche was about 10 years old, his father passed away. The ceremony the lamas were performing included 49 days of *pujas* to guide his father's soul through the bardo.

I found the monastery and they actually gave me a room there. I heard the blasts from the ceremonial trumpets and the huge gongs, so I walked up and looked into the hall where the *puja* was taking place. The energy in there was so strong. It felt like the lamas and *rimpoches* were on another plane of existence. There was a huge number of them all lined up. My jaw just dropped!

One of the main *rimpoches* was an incarnation of Mahakala, the protector of the whole Tibetan Buddhist lineage. Another, Bokar Rimpoche, was the embodiment of Green Tara, the Goddess of Compassion. He was very, very sweet – almost feminine in nature. These were amazing beings. They let me come in and sit with the little boy monks who were required to be there.

These *pujas* just went on and on, eight hours a day for two more weeks. Even though I couldn't see the other planes that they were working on, I could sense the power of all the Buddhas and the great beings in the spirit realm. I remember going back to my room and seeing – just for a moment – that I was there as part of a chain of interrelated events – sort of like playing back a tape. It felt like a part of me was going back and back in time. There are so many dimensions. Once again I realized that there was no mistake as to why I was there.

I had some very special times with a group of the Tibetan nuns. They were so precious! They were always happy to see me and would serve me their yak butter tea. They were just beaming. Even though I was allowed to attend the *puja*, they were not – because they were nuns. There were about twenty-five of them and they had their own little room where they would gather. They would all have their prayer wheels going. Their bodies were old and big. They reminded me of little walruses! They were wearing rags for clothes and they stunk. Their faces were like raisins, but their eyes were just beaming. I was so amazed to see them and they were amazed to see me. They were extremely devoted to their spiritual practices.

Once you are in India for awhile you begin the have the feeling that anything could happen. An interesting thing did, in fact, occur one day while I was out walking in the woods. I had just passed by the temple where the *rimpoches* were chanting. I looked inside and felt that something really big was taking place in there. So I walked away out into the forest, and came into a small clearing surrounded by trees. I looked up and there was this 'light-being' kind of floating in the air. It was coming towards me and I had the understanding that it was one of the protectors of that area. It had somewhat of a form, but it was a moving, shifting form. I wasn't afraid at all. It was transparent, yet visible, and seemed very gentle. I got the feeling like it was asking, "Who are you? What are you doing here? What is your intention?" I remember saying mentally to it, "I have only good intentions. I am here to learn," and I just opened my heart. It seemed like a normal thing, just as natural as seeing a deer walking through the forest. India has a way of making things which we may often think of as strange or unusual just a natural part of daily life. In India there's not so much of a distinction between the physical world and awareness of the other dimensions.

Komala says, "Yogananda is my Father and Amma is my Mother." She resides in Encinitas, California, often making pilgrimages to the holy land of India. Komala is an excellent bhajan singer, singing at the local Ammachi Satsang and elsewhere in the Encinitas area.

Radha's Love

Komala Saunders

At one point while I was traveling in India I was carrying this huge heavy back pack full of all sorts of herbal remedies and this and that, as well as a couple of hand bags. I had already been on a couple of buses this day, and I hadn't eaten a thing. The back pack was getting pretty heavy. I was just trudging along and here I see this *sannyasi* going by. He was carrying only one orange bag – and there wasn't much in it. He had a definite spiritual presence about him, and he was walking towards me. Just then I strongly heard these words in my mind: "What a heavy load you carry!" As I heard that it felt like my pack just got ten pounds heavier! As he passed by our eyes met for just a moment – and I knew… I knew the message was meant for me. Right then I just sat down by the road, unzipped that pack and started giving everything away. I felt so free. What on earth do we need all these things for? It was another opening for me. That is one of the greatest gifts of India: the ability to learn to live simply; to be happy with few possessions. It's one thing to read about or hear people say that happiness and unhappiness are all in the mind, but to actually see people who live such extremely simple lives and yet are so full of life and joy is amazing. It awakens some deep memory that complete fulfillment is our real nature. These people may struggle sometimes, it is true, yet overall they are happy.

So Mother (Ammachi) would give her *satsangs* in Malayalam, and by the time I returned to India on my next visit it was very nice. She had one of the swamis who spoke English meet with us Westerners during the afternoon break to translate the *satsang* so that we could understand. The subjects varied. Oftentimes they were directed more toward the Indian people, while at other times they were more broad-spectrum. Yet at the end of every single one of her talks that I can recall she would always talk about Lord Krishna and the *gopis*. Amma would talk about how Radha would steal away in the middle of the night, running into the woods to be with Krishna. She would tell stories about how the *gopis* would bring gifts for Krishna. Some of them would write love notes or poems of their longing for Him. Some would bring fruits, flower and sweets. They were always wondering why Radha never did any of those things, and why Krishna still seemed to prefer her. So one day they asked Him outright: "Krishna, why do you say that Radha is your special one. She never gives You anything!" The Lord replied, "Every thought Radha thinks is of Me and only Me. Everything she does she offers to Me. I don't need anything else."

Every time I heard those stories my heart would just melt. Previously I had felt very close to Ma Kali, the "Dark Mother." I always thought She would take away my darkness. Now something else was happening. My heart was opening to that love and longing expressed by Radha. Amma would sing such beautiful songs of longing for Krishna. A deep desire was growing inside me to understand this love of Radha for Krishna. For so long I had been centered on, "Take away my darkness; take away my darkness!" Now it had become, "Oh, let me love You; let me love You!" It felt like an initiation into new territory for me and my relationship with God – a God of love, joy and laughter. It also gave me a clearer understanding of the Christian approach in which I had been raised: how one might take Jesus as the supreme goal of our love.

So out my own curiosity to know what the deepest love one could experience was, my love for Krishna began to grow through Mother's grace. She was showing me the true essence of the soul, which *is* love. That is what our souls are naturally longing for. We were at Amma's Delhi ashram during Devi Bhava and I didn't want to waste this precious opportunity of being with a master in this holy land. I kept praying and praying to know the love of Radha and the *gopis* for Krishna. I just wanted to experience a taste of That! I was becoming infatuated with Radha and wanted to know what this quality of deep soul-longing for God really meant.

Devi Bhava ended and Amma was standing up showering everyone with flower petals, as she does. I just started crying and crying and praying, "Show me Radha! I want to know what Radha is like. Mother, please show me. Please show me!"

All of a sudden Mother's eyes began to twinkle with a beautiful light. She looked over at me out of the corner of her eyes, and it was like she was shining a spotlight on me. It was a playful 'Krishna' kind of look. I remember feeling so much exhilaration and joy. I got a glimpse of Radha. Since that experience I always think of Radha as Divine light. She isn't a *Shakti* of this material world; She is a *Shakti* of the spiritual world. She is like a million sparkling stars – and She is so blissful – Radha! ...and She can be experienced in our souls.

O India!

Swami Atmarupananda

To me the social India, the political India, the economic India, is more or less superimposed over spiritual India. Spiritual India is the heart of India. That's the real India and everything else takes place over the top of it, we might say. No matter how chaotic the political and social scene appears to be at times, there is the Reality underneath it all.

My first introduction to Indian spiritually came when I was young, through reading Somerset Maugham's book, *The Razors Edge*, wherein the protagonist, Larry, meets a swami of the Ramakrishna Order. He goes with him to India where he studies Vedanta and finds the truth he was looking for. The book ends with him returning to New York after two years of study in India. I was so inspired by that book! Inwardly I thought that I would love to live my life like that. I was a high school student at the time and couldn't actually go to India, so I did the next best thing and that was to read as much as I could on Vedanta philosophy. In that way found what I was looking for. That began a fascination that has lasted through the present. From the time I first read that book, India became to me a mystical land of promise, a land of fascination; a place where people lived philosophy and not just talked about it.

About a year later I found my way to the Vedanta Center in Chicago. I stayed there for a little over a year and was then sent to India to receive initiation. I had tremendous anticipation about finally going to India, and there I was on a plane actually going there. As we know, sometime the more we build something up in our minds the greater the disappointment can be, yet when I got off the plane I felt something that many people, I'm sure, feel to one degree or another. There was a magic in the air that was tangible yet at the same time indescribable. I was too shy to do it at the time but I felt like getting down and kissing the earth! I had already traveled to Europe and the Soviet Union, so this wasn't my first trip abroad, but there was something very different here.

I was only able to stay in India for 28 days on that first trip, yet everywhere I went I felt that there was a divine Presence which transcended the superficial realities of daily life. I became aware that even though many people in India don't have much by material standards, there is a certain "carefree" sense that impressed me deeply. Swami Vivekananda used to say that in the West everything is laughter and so-called happiness on the outside, but there is much misery on the inside. In India there may be difficulties on the outside while on the inside there is a lightheartedness.

After returning to the States, I continued to live at our ashram in Ganges, Michigan, for four more years, returning to India in 1975. This time I was to remain for seven years. Swami Ashokananda, a very great swami who had been in charge of our ashram in San Francisco for decades said, speaking to a Western audience: "When you go to India the first thing you will see is poverty and squalor. It will be a great contrast with the opulence of the West." He then continued, "Yet if you stay long enough, you will find something happening. The hard covering around the heart, that is so prevalent in the West, begins to soften." I realized *that* within myself. When I did return to America after those seven years, I knew that of all the things that happened to me in India – and there were many wonderful things – the most lasting and most important was that softening of the heart, that opening of the heart. There is a place for individuality, but that exaggerated sense of self-importance begins to dissolve in India, and for that I am eternally grateful.

When I first began reading books on Vedanta, the thoughts expressed seemed to be my own. I felt that these were my thoughts, my beliefs, although I hadn't fully awakened to them yet. While in high school I was an exchange student in Stockholm. I could only find one book on Vedanta there but there were several on Buddhism and Taoism, so I studied those as well. For a while my thoughts turned toward China. I felt such a deep attraction to China that I took two semesters of Chinese and loved it. Later, upon returning to the States, I hitch hiked out to Berkeley where I found a great many books on Vedanta at the Shambala Bookstore. Reading those books, I regained my focus on Indian spirituality and knew that was what I really wanted. So I decided to leave college and join the Vedanta Ashram. For the next five years, though, I still retained a love and fascination for China. During the first two years of my seven year stay in India, even though I loved India and the culture there, I nevertheless kept my Chinese books with me, hoping that one day I would find time to study them. After my two year training period as a monk was over I was going by taxi from our ashram at Belur Math to the Advaita Ashram in Calcutta. I had all my books, including my Chinese books, with me as I was being posted to the Advaita Ashram. Suddenly – and I remember it so clearly – something 'snapped' inside, on a deep, deep level. I realized I had no more connection with China. The *karma* associated with that attraction had gone. If I had had a watch with me I could have told the exact moment that occurred. It was that precise. From that moment on I knew my spiritual home was here in India.

A wonderful part of living in India is meeting with many great holy men and women; that and going to holy places, of course. Meeting holy people is more important than going to holy places, but both are important. Since I am a monk in the Ramakrishna Order, naturally most of my associations were also with members of our order. My Guru was one of the former presidents, Swami Vireshwarananda, a disciple of Holy Mother, Sri Sarada Devi. He was one of the holiest people that I have ever had the blessing to meet.

The president of the Order has his seat at Belur Math, across the Hugli River from Dakshineswar, a suburb of Calcutta. I lived at Belur Math during the first two years I was in India. When I was subsequently posted in the Himalayas for five years, I would return to Belur Math from time to time for short periods. During those times at Belur Math I would see Swamiji almost daily, except when he was traveling. He was one of those great souls who, when I saw him, it was a strange experience. The holiness of the man was actually visible. It's not something which you can describe, yet when you looked at him it was as though you weren't seeing a physical body. Yes, I was aware of all the details of his physical body. That is true. He was in his late eighties and early nineties when I knew him, and he was very short. He must have weighed less than a hundred pounds. Yet when you would see him there was such a feeling of power about him. With him it was a gentle power. He could, of course, be fierce if he needed to be. I once saw him scold a *brahmachari*, who, from my own experience, very much needed the scolding! Yet normally there was a softness - a gentleness about him. Looking at him, both in his eyes and his entire body, it seemed as though you were looking at a bundle of energy rather than a solid body. I can't describe it, yet it was visual – something you could actually see.

There was another highly advanced *sannyasi*, Swami Nirvanananda, who at that time was vice president of the Order. He had been blessed by one of Sri Ramakrishna's great disciples, Swami Brahmananda, that he would have the knowledge of Brahman in this very life. He was also very elderly. I would go almost daily to make *pranam,* pay my respects and receive his blessing. He also, when I would look at him, would seem to not be of this world. You just knew that you were looking at embodied spirituality. When I returned to Belur Math from our ashram in the Himalayas where I had been living to return to America and to take leave of the *swamis*, I asked for his blessing that I would continue to be a good *sadhu* and continue my spiritual life in America. He did bless me, but I was thinking that if only he would have worded his blessing in a slightly different way how much satisfaction it would have given my heart. As I thought that he stopped, looked deeply at me and said, "No. I bless you…", and then he repeated just the words that I had thought. Even though he was advanced in age and his memory was often severely affected, he knew who he was and he knew Truth. When someone came to him with a spiritual question, he responded precisely and incisively.

Another great swami was Saradeshananda, also known as Gopesh Maharaj. In our Order swamis are often called by their pre-monastic name with 'Maharaj' added to it. Swami Saradeshananda was a direct disciple of Holy Mother, Sarada Devi. He was highly regarded as one of the very saintly members of the Order when I was living there. He usually resided at our ashram in Brindavan but during our monastic training he came and stayed at Belur Math for two months. I would go as often as I could just to watch him. He would be walking in the courtyard in front of his quarters in the late afternoon. There was so much beauty in everything he did. His spirituality, again, was self evident. He had a quality that I have never seen in anyone else. His eyes were like those of a little child – an infant. You could look at him right in the eyes for minutes at a time with absolutely no sense of embarrassment or self-consciousness. It felt like you were looking into a vast ocean.

I remember once when he came into the dining hall where we were all seated on the floor in rows. The dining hall at Belur Math is very large and there may have been 150 monks there at the time. Gopesh Maharaj came in and started walking up and down the rows, looking at each person and smiling as he went by. It was one of the most beautiful sights I have ever seen in my life. He had the most blissful smile, like that of a happy child, with a look of wonder in his eyes. He wasn't trying to teach anything. You just had the feeling that he was getting so much joy out of just seeing so many brother monks seated there together.

Another very great holy man that I met was Swami Gaurishwarananda, also known as Rammoy Maharaj. He met Holy Mother while he was still in his teens and had been very close to her. He was a simple village boy and Holy Mother would allow him freedom to do things that she would not allow anyone else to do. He was with her almost on a daily basis at Jayambati. Of course, when I met him he was a very old man, yet he was the simplest person I have ever met in my life. One's first impression might well have been, "This person is so simple, what could be so special about him?" Yet when you looked a little longer you would realize, "No, he is so simple, that is exactly what is special about him." No person could achieve that degree of simplicity without it being a transcendental simplicity.

These great souls whom I had the good fortune to have been acquainted with, plus many, many others, are the true wealth of India. Today India must look to her material development in order to maintain a position in the modern world. Yet my conviction is that India will come back full force to her spiritual roots. That can never die. It has been there for thousands of years and is an expression of eternal Truth. So in India you will find these men and women of God. When you meet them you cannot but feel that they have something you want, something that is worth whatever effort it takes to go in that direction. That is the blessing of holy people.

Then there are the holy places where there is a tangible atmosphere of holiness. Every place has its own mental atmosphere. The tradition of spiritual aspiration in India has been going on for thousands of years by millions of people. Wherever you go in India you will feel something of that vibration, and there are countless special places where the spiritual consciousness has become more solidified, more accessible. It is easier in those locations to feel the Divine presence. The mind becomes spontaneously uplifted.

One of my favorite such places was Banaras (Varanasi). I have been there many times. I would go to bathe in the Ganga at 3:00 AM and then go to the Vishwanath Temple. It is not a large temple, and you are walking on water, flowers and offerings. You are literally wading through all kinds of stuff. You can't just spread out an *asan* and sit to meditate. So I would find these little places along the wall inside the temple where there was a ledge and I would use that as my seat. It was just enough to keep me from sliding down the wall. I would meditate in that way for an hour and a half or two hours.

Where I lived in a remote part of the Himalayas at Mayavati there was also a wonderful spiritual atmosphere. It was one of the few ashrams founded during Swami Vivekananda's lifetime. He had stayed there and had a special love for Mayavati. Mayavati is about 50 miles east of Almora, 15 miles from the Nepal border, and 75 miles south of Tibet, in the province of Uttaranchal. I had been in many quiet places yet there was a deep silence at Mayavati that I had not experienced elsewhere. There was such a quality to the silence that I often felt that when one did hear a sound, such as that of a bird singing, the sound itself was made of silence. Silence seemed to be the material and sounds were made out of that silence. Silence was simply the nature of things and would take form in sound. The five years that I spent there was a wonderful time.

During those years in the Himalayas I made a pilgrimage to the famous ice *lingam* at Amarnath. At that time there was great amity between the Moslem majority and the Hindu residents. I recall one time when I visited the largest mosque in Srinagar. There were many men in prayer. I was dressed, as usual, in the *gerua* robe of a Hindu *sannyasi*. They called me inside just to inquire who I was. Everyone was very cordial, respectful and genuinely friendly. In fact, a brother swami, who was Indian-born, was returning from a pilgrimage to Amarnath around that same time. He flagged down a bus along the side of the road in the countryside. The bus stopped yet the other passengers complained to the driver saying, "Go ahead! Go ahead! The bus is full. There is no room for anyone else." The driver, who was Muslim replied, "Nahin! Nahin! Swamiji hamara guru hae." That is to say, "No, Swamiji is our guru. We must take him!" He said it with great respect and true humility. At that time the Hindu - Moslem harmony was still remarkable in Kashmir.

By the time I reached Amarnath it was at the end of the pilgrimage season and the ice *lingam* was greatly diminished. Still it was a wonderful and blessed experience. The beauty of the Himalayas at that high altitude is unparalleled. You must cross over the Mahagunas Pass at 14,000 feet; the cave itself is at 13,500. You are walking over glaciers and ice bridges. It is really indescribable.

It was while I was living at the Mayavati ashram that I took *sannyas.* I returned to Belur Math for a brief time while receiving *sannyas diksha* and then went on pilgrimage in North India begging for my food, or what is called *madhukari biksha.* That was a wonderful experience in itself. Although in our order we are only required to beg for our food for the first three days after receiving *sannyas*, I enjoyed it so much that for the next two months, while I was on pilgrimage, I would beg for alms from house to house whenever it was possible to do so. It gave such a sense of freedom, being willing to accept whatever was given and to be satisfied. That *yatra* was a great help in solidifying the belief that I was now a new person, reborn in a dedicated spiritual life.

The fact that I was a Westerner seemed to come to my aid while begging, rather than the reverse, as one might imagine. I probably had better luck than did many of the Indian initiates. People were very curious and interested in what I was doing. Nevertheless, as I was practicing the discipline of renunciation to really establish those *samskaras* in my mind, I would not talk with them. People would ask all sorts of questions, and I would only reply, "I'm just a simple *sadhu*." People were generally quite friendly. Once, though, when I was in Rishikesh, I was heckled by some teenagers. It was my discipline at that time not to look to the right or the left but just to gaze ahead, so I ignored them and kept walking. They kept taunting me, trying to get my attention by joking and singing. I never paid the slightest attention to them. Finally I heard one of them say to the other in Hindi, ""Oh, leave him alone. He's crazy. He's crazy."

Later, on a subsequent trip in 1991, I was fortunate to visit the famous holy shrines in the high Himalayas of Kedarnath, Badrinarayan and Gangotri. I loved Badrinath, but since I've always felt a close affinity with Shiva I preferred being in one of Shiva's places at Kedarnath. I've always loved being away from cities. In fact, except for the years I spent at the Vedanta Center in San Diego, almost my entire life had been spent away from cities. So I was especially attracted to Kedarnath for that reason. You can take a bus directly to Badrinath and drive right up to the temple, but to get to Kedarnath one must hike a long way. It is a small isolated village, very remote – and the abode of Shiva – so naturally I was drawn there. I also like Shiva temples because you can go right into the temple, to the Shiva Lingam, and offer your own worship, whereas at Badrinarayan, for example, a priest must make the offerings for you.

After my *yatra* to Kedarnath and Badrinarayan, I went on to Gangotri. I enjoyed it there the most. At Gangotri I had a *kutir* all to myself. It was right next to the Ganga and next to a waterfall that made so much noise that it was like another type of silence. There was so much noise from the waterfall that you couldn't hear anything else! I could see across the Ganga, which is quite narrow at that point, to the bus stop and market place, but I couldn't hear any sound at all. It was the strangest silence because it drowned out everything else. If you've ever seen that wonderful video about the life of Swami Abhishiktananda (*Abhishiktananda: An Interior Voyage*), that raging waterfall is shown several times. That is the location of the *kutir* in which I was staying, and what a wonderful time that was! I spent hours and hours each day in meditation.

I also hiked up to Gomukh, where the Ganga actually emanates from an ice cave in the face of the glacier. 'Gomukh' literally means "the face of the cow." I took a bath there twice in the icy water – full immersion – and it was extremely painful! I climbed up over the glacier to a high plateau call Tapovan, which is much higher than Gangotri. There I found some caves and an Indian *sadhu* that was living there whose name was Simla Baba. He let me stay is his cave that night. He had a German woman disciple who had her own cave nearby and had been with him for two years. He would live there from May through November.

I also met a wonderful *mataji* living in a cave there at Tapovan. She would remain throughout the entire year! In fact she was the only one that I met who remained there when everything was covered in snow. During the winter she was snowbound and could not leave her cave. She kept some potatoes, and enough water and firewood to pass the six months of winter. It was amazing to see this simple woman, a *sannyasini*, living such an incredibly rigorous life. Previously she had resided at Gangotri and would stay there year round as well, even though almost everyone else would leave during the snowy winter months. Tapovan, however, is at a much higher elevation and the weather even more severe.

During the five years I lived at our ashram in Mayavati, which is called the Adwaita Ashram, I was focusing on *sadhana* and was also the editor of our ashram magazine, *Prabhudda Bharata.* We had some visitors at the ashram, mostly in the spring and fall. In the summer the rains were very heavy and the roads would often wash out. In winter not many came because of the snow. We do have a very nice guesthouse for visitors, and guests, both men and women, are welcome. The facilities are very nice by ashram standards. It is a beautiful, peaceful place well worth visiting. I highly recommend it!

Adwaita Ashram, Mayavati

Swami Atmarupananda has been a monk in the Vedanta Society since 1969. He traveled to India for one month in February, 1971, to receive spiritual initiation and returned in 1975 to remain for seven years. Swamiji received sannyas diksha in February, 1979. He has made several subsequent visits to India and currently resides at the Vedanta Society Monastery in Trabucco Canyon, California.

Meeting a Saint on Mount Abu

Myriam Machado-Baker

My husband, Larry, and I arrived in India through the city of New Delhi where we stayed for a couple a days awaiting the arrival of the *Darshan Tours* pilgrims. We were joining them for the second portion of their pilgrimage to some of the holy centers along the Ganges. They had just come from the mountain portion of the tour where they had visited many sacred sites in the beautiful Himalayas. Larry and I were fresh, awake, and ready to experience all and everything in India. The group arrived in the late afternoon, looking as though they were already settled into the slow and earthy rhythms of India. We couldn't help but notice their beatific smiles: the proof of living and experiencing so many divine moments in the mountains. I thought, "Why didn't we come earlier?" The next morning we introduced ourselves at breakfast and headed to the airport – destination, Varanasi.

Varanasi (Banaras) was my first real experience of India, and it was unique. The people in the airport, the children dancing in their costumes to get some money, lots of guides, vans, mini buses and big buses; everybody was waiting for the tourists – and here we were!

The road from the airport to the hotel was bumpy as we drove in our minivan through the poor areas of the city and past many small shops. There were cows, children running and playing, women in bright saris; men just 'hanging'... colorful fabrics everywhere; everything seeming to coexist in a peaceful dance.

We checked into a very comfortable hotel and rested until the sun set. We then went down to the main bathing *ghat*,

Dasashwamedh Ghat, to see the *Ganga Aarti* ceremony from a boat. We took bicycle rickshaws and moved slowly through the crowded and narrow roads. Everything was so overwhelming! All our senses were being bombarded by the most extreme sensations: loud sounds such as chanting to various forms of God; so many colors and smells. I couldn't think. I was just being present. It was amazing!

We got out of the rickshaws and walked toward the holy river. I will never forget my first sight of the Ganga. The water seemed so still. There was no movement. Even my breath became still. The colors of the sunset were falling over the river and the warmth in the air was embracing my heart. The emotions of remembering all my years of reading the *Autobiography of a Yogi* with my Guruji's description of the Gange, and there I was, looking at the river that has inspired the lives of so many great divine masters! I couldn't talk; I could hardly breathe. Time stopped for I don't know how long. I remember walking under a balcony, just following my husband. There were covered people lying in dark corners; some fetid smells combined with incense and burning candles… and lots of people... lots and lots of people!

We got into a small boat and someone gave me flowers, incense and a candle in a little arrangement. I sat on the boat and just burst into tears. My heart couldn't take so much emotion – so much gratitude and so much love.

We stayed in India for a little over two months, visiting many special places such as the *YSS* (Yogoda Satsanga Society) ashrams and centers, palaces, forts, temples, simple devotees homes, and caves... caves where renunciants have lived for many years in search of their own Self-realization.

One very special experience occurred while we were visiting Mount Abu, which is revered as a holy town in the southwestern mountains of Rajasthan. It is a very beautiful location with many hidden caves that are inhabited by holy men living in seclusion.

We were discussing our proposed itinerary with a local guide when I mentioned that I was a yoga teacher and that my husband taught *Vipassana* meditation. He seemed surprised and told us that he would change our 'tourist' itinerary and take us to see a holy man. So off we went. Walking up a trail, we climbed a small hill facing the lake that is surrounded by the town. We soon arrived at a cave that had been made into a small room with a door. Our guide knocked and a *swami* welcomed us with a bright and friendly smile.

We were invited to come in and he promptly prepared chai. We sat with him and started to talk with the guide as our translator. Our guide told him that we were meditators. The saint said that he knew. He said he could feel that we were talking the same language even if we couldn't literally 'talk the same language'. Every word he said seemed full of joy and truth. We felt so good and happy. Our consciousness was moving into a higher level of awareness. We really felt blessed, sensing that we were in the presence of a genuine holy man.

A spontaneous *satsang* developed and he told us that he had been living there for about 30 years. He said he was taking care of some cows and receiving donations from the local people. He was just a simple renunciant and we could feel that he was completely happy in his simplicity. How could we know that? Because we were happy just being there

Varanasi Ghats

Ganga Arati, Varanasi
October, 2006

Are there not many places on this earth?
Yet which of them would equal in the balance
one speck of Kashi's dust?
Are there not many rivers running to the sea?
Yet which of them is like the River of Heaven
in Kashi?
Are there not many fields of liberation on earth?
Yet not one equals the smallest part of the city
never forsaken by Shiva.
The Ganga, Shiva and Kashi:
Where this Trinity is watchful,
no wonder here is found the grace
that leads one to perfect bliss.

Kashi Khanda 35. 7-10

with him. He had the power to uplift our consciousness just by being in his presence. He was talking from his own experience, not from books or from what other people might have said. He told us that he was a *bhakti yogi*. He said that he does study the Vedas but that his most important spiritual practice is to feel the presence of God everywhere and in everything. He said that he could feel only love and joy – and more love and more joy – for everything and everyone. He smiled and looked directly into our eyes.

I asked him about the secret of this earthly drama. Why, if we are already in the Divine Presence – in the bosom of Divine Mother – in the bliss of Spirit – do we get lost and need to find our way back Home again? He responded, through the translator, that we have never left the bosom of the Mother Divine. We have never left our eternal Home. He then told me that I was just dreaming in a very light sleep and that soon I would wake up. He said, interspersed with the purest and most sincere smiles, that in order to awaken earlier and faster from this dream, I could practice seeing the light of the Divine vibrating everywhere. He pointed to the trees outside and said, "That is what I see because I practice day by day, year by year. I practice seeing the presence of God everywhere and now I *can* see It. It is simple like that."

We stayed there talking, smiling – just loving each other. We were drinking chai together like close friends – like family, and as devotees. We sat talking with a man who couldn't speak English and who we had never met before and probably will never see again. Yet for me it was a moment of awakening: a glimpse of the fulfillment of my life's dream.

Your humble devotee in the practice of Your Holy Presence.

**Jai Jagannath! Jai Bhagavan! Jai Kali!
Jai Durga! Jai Jaganmata! Jai Gurudev!**

Myriam Machado-Baker and her husband, Larry, reside in Encinitas, California, where she teaches yoga and maintains a Body Talk healing practice.

How I Became a Kirtaniya

Vaiyasaki Das

I was born in England but when I was five years old my family migrated to Canada. I was always into music. My mother sent me for violin and music theory lessons at the age of seven. I also sang in the school choir. By age fourteen I already had formed my first rock band and began playing locally.

My first introduction to India came after college while I was working for IBM in Toronto in 1968. I met an Indian gentleman at work who would tell me mystical stories about India. He was fun and jovial and invited me to his home. He cooked delicious Indian food.

Then I met someone who left an even deeper impact. He was from Bengal and his name was Mr. Sengupta. By that time I was already reading the Bhagavad Gita – a small pocket edition. He invited me for dinner at his home on a Friday night, so I invited a friend and we went. After being introduced to his wife, we chatted in the living room while she returned to the kitchen to finish cooking. In the middle of our conversation his wife suddenly returned with a tray of food which she placed on the mantle and made an offering. I didn't know what she was doing at the time. That was the first time I had tasted *prasad.*

By the time we finished dinner our hosts could see that I was very interested in their traditions. They told us about *Vaishnavas* and that word stuck with me. They said that there was a temple in the Indian community and that they met there on Sundays. Would we like to come? "Of course!" When we arrived the next Sunday the program was already in full swing and a group of musicians were chanting and playing harmonium, tabla and other kirtan instruments. I loved music so I was concentrating on how they were playing and what they were singing. I could make out the words Hare, Krishna and Rama. They were chanting the *Mahamantra*: **Hare Krishna Hare Krishna Krishna Krishna Hare Hare / Hare Rama Hare Rama Rama Rama Hare Hare.** It was the first time I had ever heard *kirtan* – and from Bengalis! All of a sudden I became filled with emotion and tears came from my eyes. It moved me so much. I didn't know why this music was having such an effect on me but that was the trigger that turned my life in another direction.

I was doing a lot of reading at that time, trying to understand the basic questions about life. Paramahansa Yogananda's *Autobiography of a Yogi*, was one of the first books I read and really liked. At the same time I began reading books by Swami Vivekananda and other books on yoga philosophy. I began seeing the Hare Krishna devotees on the streets. Soon I left IBM and returned to college in Vancouver. I was becoming more and more disenchanted with academic studies. In December, 1968, when I was supposed to be studying for my exams, I went to a Moody Blues concert. I was sitting on the floor in the midst of more than 3000 people, and a powerful realization came to me. I had been studying evolution, and it struck me that evolution was really about the evolution of consciousness. It was an evolution from the lowest to the highest consciousness, the highest being God. The second realization that came to me at that time was that there was a secret, one might say. If you knew that 'secret' you could 'pop out' of this process of evolution and go straight back to the Supreme. I was overwhelmed by these revelations.

I wanted to make music my career so I decided to return to London where I was born. The music scene was really happening there at the time. One day as I was walking down Oxford Street I heard a familiar sound – *ching, ching, ching / ching, ching, ching* – it was that sound again, the sound of *kartals* and drums.

I saw the Hare Krishna devotees, and I remember thinking, "They're here too!"

It was 1972. I auditioned for a spiritually oriented rock band called *Quintessence*. The lead singer's name was Shiva and everybody in the group had a spiritual name. The girl friend of Shiva was a devotee of Bhaktivedanta Swami from whom I also took initiation later on. I had already been a vegetarian for four years, having been attracted to a cruelty free diet while I was still in college, so I was receptive to the process of *Bhakti Yoga*. She introduced me to the Hare Krishna mantra, the philosophy, and also *prasadam*. I gradually realized that this was the path I had been looking for.

The first time I went to the temple in London I wasn't particularly attracted to the *kirtan* because I loved the way the Bengalis had done it back in Toronto. These Westerners weren't really very musical. I wasn't attracted to the *prasadam* either, because I was on a diet of dates and goat milk at the time. What really attracted me to follow the Hare Krishna path was the way they honored each other. They would offer obeisance to one another. I knew that the foundation of spiritual life was humility, so this impressed me the most.

After being initiated by His Holiness Bhaktivedanta Swami Prabhupada, the founder of the International Society for Krishna Consciousness (ISKCON) in San Francisco in 1975, he requested that those who held British Commonwealth passports (which I had) to come to India because they didn't need visas at that time. Americans required a visa and were not allowed to stay very long in India. I heard my Guru calling, so I decided to go. Before going to our own ashram, I decided to visit Rishikesh where I stayed at the Sivananda Ashram (Divine Life Society). There I became close to Swami Nirmalananda, who was originally from Trivandram in Kerala. He knew my Guru and loved his chanting. He asked if I had any tapes of Srila Prabhupad chanting. I did, so I offered one to him.

In Rishikesh I was staying in a dormitory that had flimsy lockers for personal belongings. I had only been there a few days when everything I had with me disappeared! So there I was, penniless in India! One of the Westerners gave me 20 rupees to get back to Delhi. I stayed at our ashram there for a while and then left for Brindavan. That is how I reconnected with our mission. It wasn't long before I started traveling all over the country as a renounced monk, wearing only a bottom cloth and a top cloth to cover me, and wooden pegged shoes. I would not wear any sewn clothing. That was our tradition.

My message to everyone was, "You are Indians. This is your culture, your traditions. The Vedic teachings are the highest in the world. They are completely focused on God-realization. Please do not chase after western 'progress.' I am from the West. So many young people there are embracing the Vedic ideals and lifestyle. Please don't give that up."

One of my god-brothers and I were doing so well that we were requested to travel throughout Southeast Asia to disseminate Vedic knowledge. We went to Thailand, Singapore, Malaysia, and even to Indonesia (which is a Moslem country); Bali, Hong Kong and the Philippines. We were distributing our spiritual master's books and trying to awaken people to a spiritual lifestyle.

On the way back to India in 1978, we visited Bangladesh. We had heard that Bangladesh was a fantastic place for *kirtan* and traditional Vedic culture. The British had never gotten a foothold there, because there were too many rivers! Much of India had adopted the 'way of the British,' but Bangladesh had retained the ancient traditions. We stayed at the Gaudiya Math in Dhaka. Hindus were a small (15%) minority of the population, but most were Vaishnavas in the line of Chaitanya Mahaprabhu, which is the same path I was on.

We began traveling around the country. In Chandpur, my friend and I parted ways. He went south and I decided to go north. I boarded a launch on which I saw a group of musicians. They had their instruments with them – various types of drums and folk instruments. I introduced myself and spoke a few words in Bengali, asking them if they were a band and where they were going. They said that, yes they were, and that they were going to a festival. Pretty soon the launch arrived at the next stop. They said goodbye and left the boat. I watched as they walked away across a field. Other passengers had gotten on board and the boat was just about to take off. Suddenly, I jumped off the boat and started running after them. That spontaneous act was to change my life forever!

We arrived at the festival site and the organizers, the hosts, were very surprised to see a Westerner. When they found out that I was also a *Gaudiya Vaishnava*, a vegetarian who loved *kirtan*, and following the *sadhana* of their lineage, they were very excited. The festival was in honor of the departed father of the host. He considered my arrival to be an auspicious sign.

The festival took the form of a 72-hour *akhandanama kirtan yajna* – that is, non-stop kirtan for three days! There were six kirtan groups and each group would play for two hours. In Bangladesh you always sing the appropriate *raga* to the correct time of day. At 8 o'clock you sing the 8 o'clock *raga*, etc. – without fail. They first look at the time to see which *raga* should be sung. The musical side of traditional Indian culture is highly developed. The *puranas* explain that the *ragas* and the *raginis*, the male and female melodic forms, are actually living beings. They are the personification of the musical scales that are in tune with the universe at various times of the day and night. Then I found out that they have personalities! They personify different moods and feelings which are archetypal and central to the practice of *Bhakti Yoga*. It is said that if we perform them incorrectly, or at the wrong time, it is actually painful to these *devas*. So the musicians are always faithful in performing the *ragas* at the correct times. In Rajasthan, especially, you will see miniature paintings which depict these *ragas* and *raginis*, with names such as Bhairvai or Kalyani, expressing the deep-seated emotions such as joy, yearning, or separation from the beloved. This is the magical and mystical side of Classical Indian music which is being lost in modern India when musicians concentrate only on the mathematical precision of the *ragas* instead of their divine potencies.

I had never heard *raga* kirtan before. It was a new experience. I was amazed and thrilled. Each group had three lead singers and they would alternate. The audience did not sing in response. They simply listen and enjoy. Each group had different instruments such as esraj, dottara, violin or flute – some had only one or a combination of those instruments, but there were always two drummers who would play in unison. It was so amazing because they would play these incredibly intricate *tals* and then come back together right on the beat every time! There were usually three *kartal* players and everyone was brilliant. Just amazing players! Some groups had children who were apprentices. They would begin by playing *kartals*. If they were inclined to sing, they would be encouraged to do so. Everyone loves kids, of course – and they were great. We would hear these young boys of nine, ten or eleven years old singing the *ragas* so beautifully. Their family tradition was to be a *kirtaniya*, as their fathers and grandfathers had been for generations.

I became friendly with two *kirtan* bands in particular. One was called the *Gauranga Sampradaya*, the other the *Nityananda Sampradaya*. I remained in Bangladesh for three years and followed them around the country. I had a tape recorder and would record them at every performance. In this way I became steeped in their style of *raga kirtan*. I still have many of those wonderful recordings. By listening to them over and over again I learned their styles myself.

I decided not to study the Vedic school of singing under a teacher because I didn't want to sound like a trained singer. After learning the basics of Indian classical vocal music, I taught myself by listening. One of the great singers from the *Baul* tradition in Bengal, Purnadas Baul and I became friends. He told me that if you really like the way someone sings and want to sing like them, just listen to them as much as you can. By hearing them over and over again, you will naturally imbibe their style.

Bangladesh is famous for kirtan and for cooking! 'Food' means *prasad*, because all food in Bangladesh is offered to God. The residents hold many elaborate festivals which help to preserve their traditions as a minority. During the three years that I was living there I was able to register the first official Hindu cultural organization, the Chaitanya Cultural Society (CCS). Of course, Sri Krishna Chaitanya Mahaprabhu, the great saint and reformer of Hinduism in India, was the founder of the popular *sankirtan* movement of the 16th Century. The word, *"chaitanya,"* in Bengali, means "consciousness," so we were able to register the organization as meaning, "a society for preserving the consciousness of our culture." To Gaudiya Vaishnavas, however, it held a double meaning. The CCS is still in existence today.

Being involved in this way, we were able to meet all the top leaders in Bangladesh – and all the top singers. Bangladesh was so poor that whenever we went to India we thought, "Wow, we can get anything here!" It might be compared to someone from India coming to America. The life in Bangladesh is so simple, yet that simplicity is also very charming. We loved the feeling of ancient Bengal. We loved the customs and we loved the traditions.

I became aware of one of these ancient traditions later on while I was living at Jagannath Puri, in Orissa. The famous Jagannath Temple is so traditional that they cook and offer the same fifty-six food preparations to the Deities every day. This is their tradition. So these are the same fifty-six recipes that Lord Chaitanya tasted when he was in Jagannath Puri 500 years ago. They are the same as those that were tasted by devotees who visited 2000 years ago! That impressed me. The only ingredients used in the food preparations are the locally grown fruits, vegetables and spices. There are no potatoes, tomatoes, no cauliflower… not even chilies. They use ginger and mustard instead.

Everyday they cook in new pots because everything has to be new and fresh for God – clean and pristine. Potters are always making pots. Every morning I would see the potters coming to the Temple with huge carts filled with pots of all sizes.

Another part of the tradition is that human beings don't cook for the Deities. Lakshmi Devi alone does the cooking. All that the *pujaris* do is to get the ingredients together for the ancient recipes. They have many open fire pits and they stack the clay pots in descending size one on top of the other nine pots high over each fire. Then they leave and let Goddess Lakshmi take over. After some time, and I guess after thousands of years they know how long it takes, they knock on the door. They don't get an answer, so they look inside. Oh! Lakshmi Devi has gone. Everything is cooked and ready to be offered. Then they take all these pots into the temple and place them on the altar as an offering to the Lord. Not just a portion, but all of it – every single pot. That is why even the pots are considered to be *prasad*. This *prasad* is considered to be so holy that it cannot even be called *prasad*. It must be called "*Mahaprasad*!"

Since *Mahaprasad* is non-different from Lord Vishnu Himself, the first Person to eat it is Bimala Devi, a form of Sri Durga. The *pujaris* take the *Mahaprasad* to Her temple first. Then it is distributed to everyone else. It is primarily through the sale of *Mahaprasad* that the temple is supported.

Mahaprasad is served on a banana leaf plate. You must sit on the floor with no *asana* under you because you cannot be higher than the *Mahaprasad* which is non-different from the Lord. Secondly, since you are in the presence of the Lord, everyone is equal. All are served together whatever be their caste, whether a man or a woman, a *sannaysi* or a householder. All are considered equal before God.

Jagannath Temple, Puri

I loved these ancient traditions. I loved the austerity of it. I loved the high thinking. Everything was done as a service to the Divine. The entire focus of the culture and tradition is to get out of this material energy and to go through the transcendental door to our eternal home which is in the spiritual realm; to transcend *samsara*, the repeated rounds of births and deaths where everything is *asat,* temporary, *achit*, full of ignorance, and *nirananda,* full of anxiety, and to return to the eternal realm, characterized by *sat*, eternal existence, *chit*, full knowledge, and *ananda*, complete bliss.

The Vedic culture of India is based on devotional service: service to God, respect for the individual and reverence for all life – seeing all living beings as part and parcel of the one Supreme Lord. Material consciousness, because it is temporary, is always decreasing. In the end there is nothing left. We return to ash. On the other hand, that which is spiritual is always increasing. There is no end to the divine soul qualities of peace, love, wisdom, joy and beauty which continue to increase without limit.

A prominent feature of traditional Indian culture is the ideal of *nishkama seva*, selfless service. All men and creatures are seeking to fulfill their own needs and desires, yet in their striving there is always an element of fear, pain, emptiness and insecurity. A saint, on the other hand, lives a perfect life because he or she is always striving to make others happy. Their own happiness becomes of secondary importance.

Today, as we know, there is an obvious dichotomy in India. On the one hand, India is chasing after materialism in a big way. Yet spiritual India is also expanding both at home and throughout the world. My spiritual master would compare India with the lame man and America with the blind man. The lame man can't walk properly and the blind man can't see. But when the blind man takes the lame man on his shoulders, together they can walk and see much better. So we can see that with Indian culture and American efficiency, the world can be a better place. India extends her arm to shake our hand – and we *pranam* in response!

Sivananda Yoga Center, Bahamas

Vaiyasaki Das is a kirtan leader extraordinaire and one of the greatest Western exponents of raga kirtan. He has numerous CDs to his credit. He is also the author of "Sri Radha-Damodara Vilasa: The Inner Life of Vishnujana Swami and Jayananda Prabhu," a 620 page book chronicling the history of the Hare Krishna movement in America.

Touching Sri Agni Dev's Lotus Feet

Vaiyasaki Das

While I was living in Bangladesh there were times when I would be out traveling doing *kirtan.* At other times I would go to places where the professional *kirtan* bands were performing. The Indian people would love to hear us singing *kirtan* since we were from the West. Once we were doing our own *kirtan* program in a village. The next morning a gentleman told us that there was a very ancient temple nearby. "It is an *Agni Dev* temple," he said. "A temple dedicated to God manifesting as fire. It is the only temple of its kind that I know of on the whole planet, and it is very remote," he told us. "Would you like to go there?"

There were three of us: one god-brother from New Zealand and another from Canada. We unanimously said, "Yes, of course!" Driving for a while we turned onto a side road which soon became a dirt road, ending in a grassy area by a stream. The car couldn't cross over the stream so we had to walk from there. We had been told to bring *gamchas,* simple wrap-around waist cloths for bathing, so we put them on and waded through the stream. It was about waist deep. We kept walking, going deeper and deeper into the hills and through a pass that led to a horseshoe shaped valley. There were tribal people living there with oriental-looking eyes. We finally reached a place where there was a small wooden structure with a door – but the door was locked. Our friend told us not to worry, we were early. "The *pujari* always arrives at nine o'clock," he said.

The bottom part of the door was made of old wood and the top was just metal bars. I noticed that hot air was coming out through the bars. It was really dark inside and obviously going down into something.

The *pujari* arrived and was very surprised to see three Westerners there. He actually seemed overjoyed to see us! "Did you bring your *gamshas*? Put them on." We did and he opened the door. There were stone steps leading down into the darkness. We climbed down the steps to a flat level, turned and went down to another level and then down yet again to a third level. Finally we reached the bottom. It was a small underground room only about 12 feet square. The *pujari* lit many oil lamps, so the lighting was good. In the middle of the room was a *kund* measuring about 6 by 8 feet. It was bubbling and the room was filled with hot air.

He told us, "Just get into the tank." There were small stone steps along the edge, so we got into the water up to our necks. It was quite warm but not too hot. Once we were in we noticed that at one end of the tank there was fire – fire burning on the water! "This is the ancient temple of *Agni Dev*," we were told. "During the *Treta Yuga*, Sita, Rama and Lakshman came here during their years in exile." Then he began the *puja*, chanting all the appropriate *mantras*. When he had completed the formal worship, we chanted the *Gayatri Mantra* on our own.

Then came the climax. The *pujari* said, "Would you like to touch *Agni Dev's* lotus feet?" "Sure." "Just put your hands under the water and come up to the flames from underneath." So we did, touching our fire-blessed hands to our foreheads in awe. Where else could one have such an experience but in India? The ancient traditions are still very much alive!

Divine Sight

Kaisori Devi Dasi

I grew up in a family in Mexico that was well-versed in Vedic culture and already practicing *sadhana*. I also learned a lot from Bhaktivedanta Swami's teachings and his Bhakti Yoga centers. So when I first went to India it was not a big shock in the sense of being unfamiliar with the culture. Rather, it was an awesome experience. I was there for the first time in this body but not the first time in the spiritual sense. When my husband, Vaiyasaki Das, took me to Vrindavan, tears came to my eyes. The energy of the place – of spiritual Vrindavan – was indescribable! I was feeling something that I had never felt before anywhere else. It was so deep and so moving, seeing the humility of the people – how their whole lives were turned toward God. You see spiritual musicians on the streets singing to God for hours and hours every single day. Seeing their commitment to spiritual life was unbelievable. The way so many of the children were singing *bhajans*, worshipping or doing *sadhana* was amazing.

We attended the *Ganga Arati* at the Parmarth Niketan Ashram in Rishikesh where children, many of whom had been orphans, are receiving spiritual and academic training in the *gurukul*. I had never seen so many 'old souls' in the bodies of such small children. They were singing from the heart with so much devotion – and it was not just ordinary singing. They were connecting to something higher. I was really moved. They worship God every day, and *Ganga Ma* every night. You won't see that anywhere else in the world!

If you look beyond the faults of India – and of course they are there – yet if you look a little deeper and see Her essence, there is no place that can compare with India. The Divine Presence there is hard to explain. You really don't get that feeling so much in the West. The God-Presence in India is very tangible. Coming from the West to India we soon discover that there is something more to life than what we are used to!

When I was just four years old I had a unique mystical experience. My parents were devotees of Satya Sai Baba, and we children loved to sing and chant during the *kirtans* and *bhajans*. We also had weekly classes at the Sai Baba Temple every Saturday and Sunday, and we would study the lives of all the great saints, prophets and *avatars* from the religious traditions of the world.

One night after I had lain down to go to sleep, I felt someone push my arm. This happened again. The third time I started to complain, thinking it was my mother, so I said, "I'm trying to sleep." But when I turned to look, it was Sai Baba. He was standing next to my bed! He said, "Would you like to come to India with me?"

I was only four, so I asked, "How will we get there?" He replied, "Just hold my hand." He took me by the hand and we rose high up above the house. As I looked down I saw that our whole house was filled with angels – so many. It looked like a crowd of angels. They were so beautiful! I said, "I have never seen them before," and he replied, "They are always there to look after you and your family." Who knew!

Immediately we were at Sai Baba's Ashram in India and he was showing me around. I remember everything in great detail. There was a large lotus sculpture with petals dedicated to thc different religions of the world. Suddenly, right next to me, I saw a large and beautiful statue of Lord Ganesha with his hand raised in *abhaya mudra,* the traditional gesture of fearlessness. I remember the colored lights everywhere that looked so beautiful. Soon I was back at home in bed.

When I awoke I was very excited, of course. I told my mother, "Last night Sai Baba came and took me to India!" Of course, she thought that it was just a beautiful dream. It wasn't until several years later, when I was nine, that friends began sending photos back from Sai Baba's Ashram. My mother recognized in those pictures exactly what I had described to her as a small child. She showed them to me and I said, "Oh yes, that's Sai Baba's Ashram. That's what I saw!" She was amazed.

When I was in India for the first time in this life, I was careful not to become distracted by its material side. What drew me to India was Her spiritual potency. I remember thinking, "This is really something special. This is holy land."

When we arrived at the New Delhi airport I was so happy and so excited to be in India! The immigration official recognized my *Tulsi mala* and asked if I was a *Vaishnava*. When I said I was, he became excited also. Later, while we were waiting to retrieve our luggage, he sought us out and asked many questions about our spiritual interests, where we were going and so on. He even gave us his telephone number and begged us to stay in contact with him. Where else would you find an immigration officer like that!

I discovered that the Indian people usually feel honored when people from the West take a sincere interest in their religion and culture. Nowadays, of course, there is so much westernization in India, like the wearing of American clothes, and so on. Still, when they see people coming from the West who are living, imbibing and dedicating their lives to the ancient culture which has been part and parcel of India for thousands of years, they find it astonishing.

Even though there may be a trend toward westernization, there is still the *sadhu* tradition in India wherein millions of people leave every material pursuit and comfort in pursuit of the Divine. You still will find souls who are highly advanced spiritually. In the midst of what appears, at times, to be external chaos, you meet saintly people who will inspire you in your own spiritual aspirations.

To receive Her greatest blessings you must go to India with a spirit of humility and reverence. Then everything becomes magical. In the Bhagavad Gita, Lord Krishna says to Arjuna, "You cannot see Me with your present eyes. Therefore, I give you Divine eyes by which you can behold My mystic opulence." If, through God's grace, you are able to get even a tiny glimpse of that Divine sight, a whole new India is open to you.

In India you will find remnants of ancient civilizations from the higher ages when mankind was much more advanced than it is today; when the great *lila avatars* like Rama and Krishna lived on earth. In the Himalayan village of Devaprayag, for example, we saw a rock in which were imprinted the lotus feet of Sri Ram. We come to understand that the various gods and goddesses are not just mythological. They actually existed; and having once existed, continue to exist on earth in their subtle forms, and in all their glory and magnificence on the spiritual planes.

Beautiful Lord Krishna is a real being. Shiva is a real being. Hanuman is still living on earth in a real spiritual body. You see remnants of that; reminders of that truth. People may wonder why devotees are worshiping this rock, that tree, this mountain, that river. Many are associated with the lives of these great divine beings, and all are various manifestation of God. In fact, the whole universe is the body of God.

There are places with the footprints of Sri Chaitanya and the *danda* that he used. Scientists can see from satellites the bridge under the ocean that Hanuman and the monkey army built in service to Lord Rama to cross over to Lanka. You will find amazing spiritual archeology like that throughout India.

All these things are there. They reveal themselves to you more and more as divine sight unfolds within you. Take the Ganga as another example. When I first saw Her I felt Her *shakti*, her divine energy. She is not just an ordinary river. She is actually the manifestation of Sri Ganga Devi. Her waters are so holy, so special. The spiritual life of anyone who sees Her or bathes in Her waters goes up tremendously through Her mercy.

To understand the power of *Bhakti Yoga*, I came face to face with death while in India. I had to have surgery and during that surgery the anesthesia wore off. I couldn't speak or move, but I could feel tremendous pain. It was unbelievable! All I could do was to focus on the Hare Krishna Mantra as chanted by Bhaktivedanta Swami Prabhupada. The amazing thing was that I was able to do so! Later, when we looked at the chart of my vital signs, there was an area that was flat; 'flat lining', they call it, when you are clinically dead. I was that close to leaving the body yet I was never afraid for a moment. I saw the inestimable value of creating the habit of spiritual practice.

We never know what's going to happen in life or what circumstances may change from one moment to the next. Yet when you are connected to God and your spiritual master, no matter what situation occurs you are always going to be protected. You will have that deep understanding as to what the purpose of your life is and what the final destination is. That is why we go to India: to imbibe the spiritual culture so that no matter where we are in the world we will always have that inner divine connection. In the end that is all we have. Everything else we have to leave behind.

Vaiyasaki Das and Kaisori

Experiences with Anandamayi Ma

Madhava Johnson

I went to India for the first time in April of 1975 for Sri Anandamayi Ma's birthday celebration in Calcutta. It was a really big event. I arrived about a week before her birthday and went to see her at a remote village in North India called Naimasharanya. Naimasharanya is an ancient and very holy place where Sri Krishna had given *satsang* to a group of *rishis*. There is also a temple there where Veda Vyasa had composed portions of the Mahabharata and other sacred texts. Ma inaugurated a temple while we were there named the Purana Purusha Temple in honor of the Puranas, some of the holy scriptures of India. The Deity in the temple, the *murti* as it were, had the head of a parrot. There's a bathing *kund* there in the shape of Vishnu's *chakra* (discus) which is called Chakra Tirtha. Bathing there is said to grant great purification and spiritual upliftment. There is also a temple to Lord Hanuman with a huge stone Hanuman *murti* that must be fifteen to eighteen feet tall, carved into the stone.

It was unbelievably hot at that time of year. Even the Indians were passing out from the heat! We would get a soaking towel and wrap it around our heads and it would be dry in half an hour. We had to drink water continuously. Although it was well water, we still got sick. There were four or five of us foreigners there and we all had dysentery.

On the last day of the dedication of the Purana Purusha Temple there was a huge celebration and a *bandhara*. The trouble was that since we were all having stomach problems we were only supposed to eat a little plain rice with *dahi*. They actually recommended rice and yogurt with a little bit of lemon and sugar on it; nothing spicy, oily, greasy or sweet. I knew from experience that if I tried to eat those kinds of foods it only made matters worse, so we weren't planning to take the *prasad* from the *bandhara*. Then Ma said, "Tell them to go ahead and eat." We had to follow her instructions. After all, she should know what was best for us. We ate everything and after that we weren't sick anymore. Everyone was fine!

We then went on to Calcutta for Ma's birthday celebration. It takes place four days after *Buddha Purnima*. The event was held in a huge pandal. There must have been 10,000 people present. It was nice, of course, yet I had enjoyed being with her in the more intimate environment of Naimasharanya.

Then one night were heard that Ma was going to a devotee's home. We followed her car through a jungle-like area where there were just a few houses and arrived right after dark. We walked into the beautiful garden of a home that was obviously owned by a wealthy person. There were roses and an amazing variety of exquisite flowers everywhere. In the midst of the garden was a small covered pavilion. It was just about ten feet square with a roof and no sides. It seemed like we were in an astral dream. Ma was sitting in the pavilion with flowers and lights twinkling all around her. Music was playing. The expression "died and gone to heaven" is probably the most apt expression that comes to mind. It was so exquisite! Ma was sitting there like the Queen of the Universe.

We found accommodations at a boarding house in Calcutta that had a connection with Rabindranath Tagore. It was near the location where the birthday functions were being celebrated. Somehow – and I don't recall how it happened – I had injured my back and was experiencing intense pain, especially between my shoulders. There were two or three days when I could barely move. I couldn't go to the ashram or see Ma so I stayed in bed most of the time. Even getting in and out of bed was difficult. I had only been in India for about ten days and was feeling so uplifted and inspired being with Anandamayi Ma, and now I was in this terrible pain. Furthermore, it didn't seem to be getting any better. I started to think, "Am I going to have to go back to America?" I really didn't know what I was going to do, and I was feeling pretty upset because I had so much been enjoying being in the presence of Ma.

After not going to see Ma for a couple of nights, I heard that she was going to be holding *satsang* in a devotee's home that night. I said to myself, "I'm just going to go no matter what I feel like." I decided to pray intensely and ask her for help. The *satsang* was on the top floor of a large high rise. The view was spectacular. The room was large and very crowded. At least a hundred and fifty people were there. Next to Ma was a very great and well-known saint from Bengal whose name was Sitaramdas Omkarnath Thakur. He must have been close to a hundred years old at the time. He was very thin, with long matted hair piled on top of this head.

The scene was like this: Ma was sitting in the middle of the living room; she was about 80 years old. Next to her was this ancient looking man who was at least 95. They were holding each other's hand and looking into one another's eyes like a couple of young lovers – and radiating incredible bliss!

I was still in a lot of pain and didn't want to try to sit down so I stood at the back of the room praying to Ma. I was telling her that I didn't want to have to leave her and go back to America. I wanted to spend more time with her. I don't know how it happened but toward the end of the evening I started to test my back by moving a little. The pain was gone. I mean completely gone. And it never came back!

After that I remained in India for four more months or so on that first trip, and most of that time I spent with Ma. I later made four subsequent trips to India to be with her, the last being in January, 1982, when we were with her at the *Kumbha Mela* in Allahabad. At that time we were able to bathe with her on the most auspicious bathing day of the *Mela.* She attained *mahasamadhi* just seven months later. As you can well imagine, that was a very difficult time in my life.

Once, when Ma was questioned as to who, in reality, she was, she replied: "Purna Brahma Narayana," i.e., the full and complete manifestation of Divinity, both personal and impersonal. Being around her I can only say that that was certainly my impression. It wasn't that she was God but that there was no one there but God. The way she would walk, the movement of her hands, the sound of her voice and everything about her was so beyond what a human being could do or express. There was such grace, perfection and beauty. When Ma sang it was absolutely transcendental. The chants she sang were simple yet permeated with so much bliss. Her voice transported you to another realm. It wasn't subtle at all. She was pure Divinity.

A Pilgrimage to Kedarnath

At one point during that first trip to India, Anandamayi Ma announced that she was going to go into seclusion, so I decided to make a pilgrimage to the Badrinath and Kedarnath temples in the high Himalayas. I went on my own. It was truly a wonderful experience. Cars and buses can drive up to

Badrinath, but Kedarnath is a long climb. The last twelve miles to the temple is all on foot and uphill. Every step of the way is up, up, up. By the time you get to the village and the temple itself, you are at an elevation of about 12,000 feet. The Kedarnath Valley is completely surrounded by snow capped peaks. It is an exquisitely powerful place to be.

It was a tough hike, and as I recall, it took almost eight hours. I was so impressed because there were many older people in their sixties, seventies and even eighties making the climb. Here I was in my twenties, and although my strength wasn't a hundred percent, it was not an easy climb. Here were these people, many of them barefoot and walking on rocky paths. It was amazing to see, and very inspiring. I've been back to Badrinath since then but not to Kedarnath. I would love to go there again.

Pilgrims at Kedarnath
September, 2006

One thing I would like to mention is the way we were treated as Westerners in India back in the 1970's. We had no caste, and as such we were almost lower than the so-called "untouchables." There was definitely a certain amount of prejudice. Often we were kept separate from the Indian devotees or not allowed in certain places where Ma was. I came to understand that to their way of thinking we were from a country where most of the people ate meat, drank alcohol, took drugs, smoked and had sex out of marriage. That is the way the Indian scriptures describe demons, you know, and after thinking about it, I can't say that they were too far from wrong. Of course we felt that we were really sincere and that some of those things were unfair. Not all of the Indian devotees felt that way. Many were very cordial and kind. They would recognize our sincerity and treat us with great respect. Yet there were others would treat us like dogs.

So one time I asked Ma, "Why do you let these people treat us like that?" Ma always had the perfect answer for everything. This time she gave three answers, and each one, I thought, was right on. First she said, "You have come here for Ma. You didn't come for this ashram or these people, so what do you care?" Then she said, "You may want to experience a rose, but you will have to take the thorns with the rose." Her third answer was, "These people have their way. Let them." The strict Brahmanical caste system was their way of maintaining high standards of purity and discipline. If she were to say that they didn't need to live that lifestyle, they may have started to lose their focus on that high plane which has been the bedrock of Vedic culture for thousands of years. She didn't want to break down a time-honored structure which may have led to less pure modes of living. Ma herself, of course, always treated us like we were her own divine children.

Then along came Ammachi, who accepts and embraces everyone. All are welcome in her ashram right along side the Indian swamis and *brahmacharis*, who are living a very disciplined and pure life. And it works. It is an amazing balance to maintain. It is interesting to see the different roles that the great world teachers come to play. Over the last thirty years or so, the Indian people, as a whole, have become much more tolerant. It seems to be an ongoing stage in their cultural development. On the other hand, we have seen Westerners who were not living a very pure life come to Amma's ashram and be touched so deeply that their lives were completely transformed.

Madhava Johnson resides in Encinitas. He is active in the San Diego Ammachi Satsang.

Discovering Ammachi

Madhava Johnson

It was during my fourth trip to India, in 1980, that I discovered Ammachi. I was with Anandamayi Ma and she was going into seclusion. I was upset about that because I just wanted to be with her every minute that I could. Ma has an ashram on the banks of the Narmada River in Gujarat at Bhimpua. It is a very beautiful ancient and holy place in a quiet and remote area. Exquisite. I had been there before, yet this time they weren't letting people go with her. I realized that I was going to have a month without Ma so I decided to go on a pilgrimage.

The first place I went was Arunachala, the famous mountain identified as a physical embodiment of Lord Shiva by the great *avadhut*, Ramana Maharshi, and other masters. It is in the South Indian village of Tiruvannamalai. I had been to the Ramanashram before and felt that it was an incredibly powerful, beautiful and inspiring place, so I decided to go there.

Not long after I arrived in Tiruvannamalai I met an American *sadhu* whose name was Neelu. He later took *sannyas* and became known as Swami Paramatmananda, Ammachi's only non-Indian *swami*. Later he wrote about his life as a *sadhu* in India and how he came to Ammachi, in his book, *On the Road to Freedom: A Pilgrimage in India.*

Neelu had lived for twelve years as a *brahmachari* in Ramanashram. I had met him on a previous trip and we connected again on this visit. He had just heard about Ammachi from a devotee named Chandru who had spent some time with Amma and then came to Tiruvannamalai.

Later Chandru became very close to Amma and stayed with her for a number of years.

My plan was to go from 'Tiru' to Anandashram in north Kerala, founded by Swami (Papa) Ramdas. Neelu told me: "If you're going to Anandashram you really have to go down to south Kerala. There is a young girl in a fishing village there who is a great saint."

I did first go to Anandashram where I met two young ladies from Italy. When I mentioned where I was going, one of them wanted to come along, so from Anandashram we went down to south Kerala to see if we could find the young saint. It is wonderful to note that in recent years, the same lady who accompanied me on that journey has become a dedicated disciple of Amma.

It was a long day's ride, first on the train, then by bus, and finally in a taxi to the backwaters. From there we took a ferry across the river. By that time I was pretty tired from traveling all day. When I asked where Amma lived someone pointed to her parent's house. Once there we were told that she was in another village. I wasn't looking for another guru since I was already with Anandamayi Ma, so I almost gave up at that point. But they said that it was only half an hour's drive from there to the village where she was staying and they gave directions. I remember thinking, "Well, I've come this far…," so I went back to the taxi and we drove to the other village. Inquiring again we were shown a simple village house. There seemed to be no one around. Amma wasn't famous in those days, of course, but in the area surrounding her own village she was already recognized as a saint.

I walked through the front door of that little village house and, I tell you, having spent so much time around Anandamayi Ma I had had some experience of being in a vibration of purity, bliss and God-consciousness. When I walked through the door I didn't even see Amma but I felt that bliss, that Presence. My mind said, "Oh my God!" I knew she really must be something special. Before that experience I had been skeptical. Someone pointed to a doorway and I entered a small *puja* room with a dirt floor. There was Amma sitting by herself. I went over and bowed down in front of her.

Amma was twenty-six at that time but she looked like a girl of eighteen. She was very pretty. My experience of being around Anandamayi Ma was that it was a very rigid structure set in the orthodoxy of Hindu society. This was especially true where men and women were concerned. The sexes were always segregated in religious gatherings. Yet when I bowed in front of Amma she took my head and put it in her lap! We couldn't even touch Anandamayi Ma. I was feeling so drunk with peace and bliss that I wasn't about to move. I must have stayed in that position for five minutes. I don't recall whether she lifted me up or if I did it on my own. After that I was so completely convinced as to her spiritual identity that I didn't want to go

anywhere else. I stayed there for a full week and she let me stay with her almost constantly.

With Anandamayi Ma, *everyone* would come to see her: Indira Gandhi, the Shankaracharyas, many great saints. Everyone in India seemed to feel that she *was* the Divine Mother. Amma, on the other hand, was a young penniless village girl who was not even a *brahmin.* Even those who were close to her at that time didn't have a clue as to *Who* she really was. They loved her and they knew she was divine, yet they had no idea that she was destined to become a world teacher. They were drunk on her love and her bliss. There was none of this "respectful distance" either. She was just a girl who loved God. I didn't see her remotely like I saw Anandamayi Ma. In retrospect I feel she was definitely in that same state, although I wasn't able to perceive it. No one was treating her that way yet. They were respectful, yes, but there was a charming informality about the way we related to her.

One thing I recall, though, really tripped me out. At that time Amma was doing both *Devi Bhava* and *Krishna Bhava.* They were beautiful and powerful but they were also wild and 'out there'. I didn't know what to make of it. When she was in *Krishna Bhava* she would be dancing in ecstasy and jumping up and down all over the place. I didn't understand what was going on. They said that Krishna had come and taken her over. When she was in *Devi Bhava*, the Goddess would come in and take her over. My background was in the teachings of Paramahansa Yogananda. He would say that a real master never allows another soul or entity to possess them. When she was in *Devi Bhava* she was manifesting Ma Kali, running wildly around the courtyard with a sword and swinging it like a mad woman! That really threw me because my first impression was that she was very peaceful and divine, much like Anandamayi Ma. Yet when she entered into these *bhavas* it was like she was 'gone' and another force was operating through her. Later on I came to understand that it was just a play. She would allow the energy of who Krishna is, or who Devi is, to manifest through her. She could allow Ganesh or Shiva or any form of God to manifest through her because she *is* all of them. That's the difference.

Because I was unable to perceive her true spiritual stature and greatness, I saw Amma simply as a very saintly village girl. Sometimes she would feed me with her own hands. At other times she would hold my hand. It was so sweet. There was an intimate loving feeling around her. One time, in my ignorance, I said to her, "Amma, you need to find a husband. Otherwise, how will you support yourself?" There was no ashram in those days; no support system at all. She just burst into hilarious laughter, totally cracking up. Then she said so sweetly, "Don't worry! Krishna is taking care of me!" I didn't have a clue!

Sometimes people, having heard that story, come to me and say, "Oh, Madhava, I hear you proposed to Amma!" No, not really. I was truly concerned about her. She was twenty-six years old – way past marrying age, with no visible means of support – and she was a beautiful and radiant being. How could one not be attracted to her? Maybe one percent of my mind was thinking in that direction. I suppose that if she had said, "Well, how would you like the job?" I would have been quite interested!

Years later when I was traveling with Amma in the States, there was a group of us who went to see her off at the airport in Boston. She was on her way to Europe. When she got out of the car she came right over to me, gave me a hug, and told everyone that I had been the first to come to her ashram. I'm sure she meant that I was the first Westerner to come. Many others came later and had the good fortune to stay with her. At least I had enough good *karma* to meet her during those early days and to spend a week with her. I was with her nearly twenty-four hours a day – very close, and I was fortunate to have been able to take some beautiful photos of her also.

At the end of that week I went back to be with Anandamayi Ma. I was still thinking that Ma was the Divine Mother incarnate and that Ammachi was a beautiful village saint. This was my fourth trip to India and previously I had had several private interviews with Ma. I had always felt that she was my guru. She always treated me like I was her own. During this trip I had tried to arrange a private appointment with her on several occasions but was always told that she was too busy and so on. As soon as I got back from seeing Amma, however, that door opened. I may have asked Ma directly, I'm not sure, but within a day or two of my return I had a private interview with her.

I had several questions in mind that I wanted to ask her. As I started to ask the first question she looked at me with that peaceful, all-knowing look that she always had and said, "Who is your guru?" I was shocked and replied, "Ma, you are!" I was wondering why she was asking me a question like that. She didn't say anymore about it and went ahead and answered my questions.

Amma began making world tours in 1987 and from 1988 onwards, for many years, I would go to see her only when she was in Los Angeles. I was still concentrating on Anandamayi Ma. Yet as the years went by I was greatly missing the physical presence of Ma. More and more I was feeling an inner pull toward Amma. I felt that she really was at that same level of pure Divinity. Around 1995 or 1996 I finally said to her directly, "Amma, I want to stop resisting you." She turned and looked at me with a look of all-knowing love and said, "Amma knew you would come back to her. Don't worry. You shouldn't see any difference between Amma and Anandamayi Ma. We are the same." I had never said a word to her about Anandamayi Ma – at least in 16 years. I really do believe that what she said is true. Sure, Amma has a different body and a different role to play in the world – but the consciousness is the same.

I then remembered something very interesting that happened when I was sitting with Swami Vijayananda at the Anandamayi Ma ashram in Kankal near Haridwar. It actually happened on two occasions. Swami Vijayananda is a very beautiful saint who has spent more than sixty years meditating twelve hours a day. He is just "pure Anandamayi Ma."

We were sitting together one day and he said, "Have you met Ammachi?" I replied, "Yes, but I don't think she is as great as her disciples think she is." Can you imagine! I was still resisting her at that time. Swami Vijayananda lifted his finger and said emphatically, "No. I have not met Amma physically, but I assure you she is a great *rishi*. Go to her!"

Now here was one of Ma's greatest disciples literally pushing me to go to Amma. Even then his words didn't have a great impact until Amma herself said those words to me. Then I flashed back on Anandamayi Ma's words, "Who is your guru?" as soon as I had returned from meeting Amma. I thought of Swami Vijayanandaji, whom I see as a pure vehicle for Anandamayi Ma, telling me, "Go to Amma!" and I realized that Divine Mother had been pushing me in that direction all along. **Jai Ma!**

Sunrise – Nandi Hill, Karnataka

Swami Shantananda Giri

Ensconced on flying stone crag above Rishi Cave
High over ochre earth lost in darkness beneath,
Friendly forest trees chant *Aum* in a fresh east wind –
All clasped in blue-black sky sparkling with clear star lights.

Indistinct cloud buds floresce on horizon far
Lavender, purple, wine – exquisite bloom on bloom.

Fast racing clouds plashed by playing molten colors –
Ruby, scarlet, orange – carnelian crowned on high –
The vast billowy cover flies over mirrored plain
Drawn by an enchanted wind straight to Nandi Mount.

Gay, mischievous leprechaun mists come tumbling up
To enfold rocks, mandir, trees – all – in streaming white.
Eastern sunrise glow dims, enlightening the north,
Then northern light fades, again brightening the east.
Orient clouds blaze with a lucent eye, then form
Empyreal gold cobra with coral-eyed hoods –
Evanescent heralds of the Effulgent One.

Cobras candesce to a resplendent golden swan
Majestically riding a scintillant sea –
Ineffable cloud reliefs enhaloed in flame.

Aureate Sun now born of glittering waters
Dazzles sky and cloud-sea with gleaming yellow beams.
Leaping vapors strive hard to veil the fiery orb
By them transformed into a spiritual eye –

Turquoise blue – silver – soft gold – iridescent rings.

Flecks of light frolic throughout the lambent whiteness
Dancing about the ever-changing aureole.

Cloud spume tries to subdue His splendor, creating
Lustrous shield – septagon form – again sphere on fire
As the Radiant Beloved will not be masked.

The Brilliant-hued One – now complete – free – untouched –
Climbs above the obscuring flight of swirling mists –
A calescent white disc over glowing white sea –
An empyrean of love divine embosoms all –
Joyful breeze, bright blue sky, the universe and I.

©Self-Realization Fellowship
Used by permission

In the Presence of the Saints

India is India because her soil is favorable to the growth of saints.

Dilip Kumar Roy

We may well ask, "Who exactly is a saint?" I have found a satisfying definition in these words of the great Swami Sivananda:

Who is a saint? He who lives in God or the Eternal, who is free from egoism, likes and dislikes, selfishness, vanity, mine-ness, lust, greed and anger, who is endowed with equal vision, balanced mind, mercy, tolerance, righteousness and cosmic love, and who has divine knowledge, is s saint.

The lives of the great saints and masters of India create an ever-expanding *mandala* of sanctity that is a prominent feature of Hindu culture. Each one of their lives is unique. How they perceived and related to the world, how they struggled to attain self-mastery and divine communion, and how they expressed the Divinity that they perceived reflect an infinite spectrum of variety and creativity. How did God use their lives as His vehicles in this world? Like scintillating facets of a precious jewel, such are God's expressions in the lives of saintly men and women. How much we can learn from their examples! How much we can become transformed through the silent benediction of their unseen blessings!

I once ventured to ask Baba Hari Dass, a silent yogi, an interesting question: "How can we benefit the most from being in the presence of a saint?" I supposed I was expecting a more esoteric answer. His reply was characteristically practical: "By doing what they say."

During a *satsang* with Swami Shantananda Giri of Yogoda Satsanga Society at Yogoda Math, Dakshineshwar, someone asked a similar question. The devotee also asked about the subject of loyalty to one's own guru when visiting other saints. Swamiji replied that there is certainly nothing intrinsically disloyal in receiving the blessings of saints. He reminded us, in fact, that Paramahansa Yogananda has given a technique in the Self-Realization Fellowship Lessons instructing students how they may tune in and receive the blessings of such divine personages. Swamiji did caution, however, that it would not be proper or appropriate to receive a mantra, a spiritual technique (*upadesh*) from another saint once a devotee has accepted *diksha* from a true guru. Loyalty, after all, lies in the heart. It is an expression of the intimate relationship that exists between our soul, God and our Guru. Who else can judge it? Once, when asked during a *satsang* to explain the meaning of loyalty, Sri Daya Mata simply responded: "Loyalty means never to forget God."

Personally, I have never put too much importance on being in the physical presence of saints. I don't find it necessary. If the opportunity arises in a natural way, I may go for *darshan*, yet I know that spiritual work is done almost entirely on the subtle planes. The more we look for it outwardly in material creation the less likely we may be able to find it. Yet I love to read about the lives of the great ones. I find it absolutely thrilling. It has been my 'food' on the spiritual journey. I'm not too much for intellectual study, yet it is in reading the lives of the saints on the path of Hindu Devotional Mysticism that has kept my heart burning with the desire to know and commune with the Divine Beloved.

In essence all say the same thing. "The only purpose of life is to know God," they tell us; and, "God responds only to love." How we learn to develop pure love for God and to focus our attention on that One Divinity to the exclusion of every lesser thing we can discover through the example of their lives.

The essence and the expression of spirituality is manifest in the lives of the saints and sages of every clime and time. Since before the dawn of recorded history India has specialized in the science of God-realization. Even in this day and age – and perhaps especially in this day and age, when spirituality is so much needed to transform world consciousness – in India we find true devotees who have reached the summit of spiritual attainment.

In the West we are somewhat familiar with a few of the spiritual luminaries of India. Swami Ram Tirtha and Swami Vivekananda were among the first men of God-realization to brave the frontiers of 20th Century America. Indeed, it was the illustrious Swami Vivekananda who brought to our awareness the divine life and teachings of Ramakrishna Paramahamsa, one of the most spiritually influential masters of modern times. Through those early teachers, Americans were introduced to the great teachings of Vedic culture and the possibility that each and every person might achieve the exalted state of God-communion exemplified in the life of Lord Jesus Christ: "Know ye not that ye are gods and children of the most high?"

Sri Ramakrishna was the embodiment and personification of the God-intoxicated sage. Through his words and actions he amply demonstrated that divine communion could be achieved through all true religious paths when they are practiced deeply and sincerely, with one-pointed concentration and devotion. Yet he did not bring to the world at large practical techniques of God-realization.

Arriving in the United States at conservative Boston on September 19th, 1920, Paramahansa Yogananda brought scientific techniques of meditation and God-communion. Through the highly evolved liberating techniques of Kriya Yoga, he gave to all earnest aspirants the key to the divine kingdom awaiting discovery behind the darkness of closed eyes and in the temple of their own hearts.

The 1960's and early 1970's were a time of radical awakening in the lives of many young people, myself included. We were questioning everything, looking for the meaning behind appearances. There was a blessing and grace of a higher consciousness at work in the world at that time. I am sure of it. The so-called 'flower children' may have been naïve in their outlook, yet there was a guileless simplicity and a far-reaching idealism that was beautiful – although it was also fragile. In retrospect, I often feel that a little drop of the Christ-Consciousness must have descended upon the world at that time. It touched our hearts and inspired our souls even though we were not spiritually mature enough to grow the seed of love that had been planted in the temple of our hearts.

It was against this background of individual and cultural transformation that a wave of interest in all forms of yoga, Indian music and Hindu spirituality began to awaken in the West on a much wider scale. Several eminent disciples of the great Swami Sivananda of Rishikesh, founder of the Divine Life Society, had a great impact on our developing spirituality. Swami Satchidananda founded the Integral Yoga Institute, and Swami Vishnudevananda, the Sivananda Yoga and Vedanta Centers. The exalted Swami Venkatesananda also left a significant influence, though he spent considerably less time in the West than did some of his brother disciples. Swami Sivananda Radha, the well-known woman *sanyassini* who founded the Yasodhara Ashram in British Columbia in 1963, spread the teachings of *Sanatana Dharma* through her life, her classes and her highly acclaimed books on yoga and spirituality.

Awareness of the path of *Bhakti Yoga* was brought to national attention rather dramatically by the Hare Krishna movement founded by H.H. AC Bhaktivedanta Swami Prabhupada, known as Srila Prabhupad to his many followers and admirers. A simple swami who arrived in New York harbor in 1965, the only passenger on a weathered cargo ship on which he had begged passage, Srila Prabhupad had with him a supply of dry cereal, a few boxes of books and about seven dollars worth of Indian rupees. He was utterly alone, knowing no one and without any visible means of support.

Twelve years later, Srila Prabhupad left this earthly stage in holy Vrindavan at the age of eighty-one. He had spread the message of Krishna Consciousness to every major city in the world, and had established 108 temples. He had trained literally thousands of students, given innumerable talks and discourses and written fifty-one books in twenty-eight languages!

The time was ripe for the 'yogi invasion'. Beginning in the early 1970's, Swami Muktananda Paramahansa began coming to the West for varying periods of time. He was a disciple of the great Bhagavan Nityananda, a true *avadhut.* Many others also came during that time period including Swami (Papa) Ramdas; Swami Rama of the Himalayas, founder of The Himalayan Institute; Shiva Bala Yogi; Swami Amar Jyoti; Sant Keshavadas; Sri Chinmoy; Swami Chinmayananda; Swami

Kripalvananda (Bapuji); Dhyanyogi Madhusudandas and his successor, Anandi Ma; Yogi Bhajan, the Sikh guru who established the Healthy, Happy, Holy Organization (3HO), teaching 'Kundalini Yoga;' and Baba Hari Dass, the silent yogi.

Baba Hari Dass was brought to our attention in the pages of the spiritual classic, *Be Here Now,* authored by university professor turned yogi and spiritual teacher, Baba Ram Dass. Ram Dass made us aware of another exalted divine being: his own guru, Neem Karoli Baba (aka Neeb Karori Baba), or simply, 'Maharaj-ji'. Neem Karoli's influence continues to spread throughout America and the world through the dedication of many of his close disciples, and by the *kirtan* singers he attracted and nurtured on the path of *bhakti*: Bhagavan Das, Krishna Das, Jai Uttal and Jai Lakshman and many others. They are now being followed by the 'next generation', so to speak, including Durga Das (David Newman) and Govindas.

I was first attracted to yoga and Hindu spirituality by reading *The Complete Illustrated Book of Yoga,* by Swami Vishnudevananda. It had been given to me by my father, who was also attracted to yoga. Although I was fascinated by the *asanas* that were so deftly demonstrated in the photographs, it was the chapters on yoga philosophy and meditation that I found most intriguing. Along with my daily practice of *asana*, I began incorporating various classical *hatha yoga pranayamas* and short periods of meditation. Swami Vishnu mentioned the benefits of long concentration on *ajna chakra*, at the point between the eyebrows. I soon discovered that Paramahansa Yogananda, who was to become my own Guru, also counseled his disciples to meditate on the spiritual eye center. When asked by a student if there was any practice other than

Kriya Yoga that would greatly accelerate one's own spiritual development, the master replied, "Always keep your attention at the spiritual eye." That became the center of my meditation practice. From time to time I would see a circle of beautiful opalescent blue light which seemed to be coming down over me. As much as I tried to go into it or through it, though, I was unable to do so.

Yet it was in reading *Be Here Now* that I really began to awaken to the spiritual life. I know that many of us in my generation can say the same thing. Reading that book I became inflamed with the desire to know God – to actually experience higher states of consciousness. Imbibing the contents of that book was, for me, the perfect set-up for *Autobiography of a Yogi* which hooked me for life!

When I first read Paramahansaji's life story, all I wanted to do was to meditate and read that book. I find that almost everyone I meet on the spiritual path today was greatly influenced by reading the Master's inspiring story. On my own behalf, I knew in my heart that I had found my ever-living Guru and would follow his path until the goal was achieved, no matter how long it took and no matter what I had to go through.

Even though many of the great saints and masters of this century such as Neem Karoli Baba, Swami Sivananda, Satya Sai Baba and Anandamayi Ma, never left the shores of India, their indelible influence on truth seekers in this country is inestimable.

In more recent years there has come another wave of savants from India, led by the 'Divine Mothers': Ammachi (Amritanandamayi Ma), Karunamayi Ma (Vijayeswari Devi), and Sri Maa of Kamakhaya, amongst others. Many have expressed the feeling that now is the time of the Mother – a time when qualities of the Feminine Divine are so much needed in the world. Who can deny that such qualities as forgiveness, compassion, sympathetic understanding and unconditional divine love are vital if we are to progress as a civilization? Indeed, we may say that our very survival depends on them.

The saints of India are true emissaries of these essential qualities. I find it fascinating that so many of the great masters of our times have designated women as their spiritual successors: Ramakrishna: Sarada Devi; Aurobindo: Mother Meera; Dhyanyogi Madhusudandas: Anandi Ma; Neem Karoli Baba: Siddhi Ma; Swami Muktananda: Gurumayi Chidvilasananda; Paramahansa Yogananda: Sri Daya Mata.

Though born in the West, Sri Daya Mata was personally trained by Paramahansa Yogananda to carry on his worldwide mission after his *mahasamadhi*. As *Sangamata*, she continues to guide Self-Realization Fellowship, the organization he founded, to disseminate his teachings worldwide.

As impressive as this collection of stellar spiritual giants may be, it represents only the tip of the iceberg of Hindu spirituality and its inherent tradition of sanctity. In *Autobiography of a Yogi* alone, so many saints are mentioned. Most were Paramahansaji's contemporaries, residing close to his family home in Kolkata (Calcutta). In Bengal today you will see many pictures of Yogavatar Lokanath Baba. Have you heard of him? After renouncing the world at a young age, he was ultimately successful in his spiritual practices, attaining the summit of God-realization at the age of 90. He then began his world mission. For the next 50 years Lokanath Baba walked all over India teaching, finally attaining *mahasamadhi* in 1890 at the age of 160 years. What are *your* plans after retirement?

Have you heard of Sri Swami Purushottamananda Maharaj of Vashishta Guha? When asked if there were any genuine saints around at the time, Swami Sivananda mentioned him by name. He lived in a wonderful cave 22 kilometers north of Rishikesh near the small village of Shivpuri. Vashishta Guha is one of our favorite places to meditate in all of India. The cave extends about 50 feet into the hillside near the banks of the Ganga. The *asan* is still there where Swamiji Maharaj used to sit enrapt in *samadhi* meditation. The cave is said to extend much beyond its current depth, having been closed off by Swami Purushottamanandaji as a place where highly advanced *siddhas* could remain in unbroken ecstatic divine communion.

This brings to mind an incident in the remarkable life of Shiva Bala Yogi, who was staying for a time in an ashram in the Nandi Hills area of Karnatika. The Yogi enjoyed going for walks in solitude after midnight. One night, when he was accompanied by a devotee, he sat down and meditated for a long time. After he arose from his mediation, the devotee asked what his experience had been. To this inquiry, Shiva Bala Yogi replied, "There is a great saint here who is doing *tapas*. I wanted to contact him."

There was a long-held belief that yogis were meditating in hidden caves around that area, so Baba's words created a lot of interest. One devotee wanted to explore the caves in search of the yogis but Yogi-ji reprimanded him saying, "Why do you want to do that? There are people there who are doing *tapas*."

The devotee argued, "If I have your blessing, I should be able to go and see them."

Swamiji said, "All right. Will you do as I tell you?"

The devotee replied, "Whatever you tell me to do I will do."

Swamiji said, "Go to your home. Tomorrow come to the ashram and sit for meditation. Then you can have *darshan* of the yogis."

The next day that devotee went to the Dodballapur ashram to meditate. In his meditation he entered a cave that led up a hill, then steeply down. The cave opened into a field with dried grass that was flooded by a soft light. There he saw a yogi sitting in meditation. His matted hair was piled on top of his head. The devotee walked around him in respect and then came out of the cave.

On their next meeting Shiva Bala Yogi asked the devotee, "Did you have *darshan* of the *swamiji*?" He then went on to say that the yogi's name was Krishnappa, and that he was 450 years old. He said that there were several other yogis who were also doing *tapas* in those caves and added, "All of those great yogis come to the *bhajans* at the Nandi Hills ashram each evening."

Perhaps you have heard of Devraha Baba, who was more than 300 years of age when he took *mahasamadhi* in 1989. He was said to be a direct disciple of Mahavatar Babaji. Usually residing near Brindavan, he was a regular feature at the Kumbha Melas for many years, living in a small thatched hut built on a raised platform about eight feet above the ground. He would bless visitors by throwing fruit to them.

During our *yatra* in 2004, Hilary and I were privileged to have the *darshan*, on *Diwali* night, of Brahmarishi Barfani Dada, also reputed to be more than 300 years of age, although he didn't look at day over 150 to us! His name literally means 'ice brother'. It is said that he spent 100 years amongst the eternal snows of the high Himalayas, including

30 years with Mahavatar Babaji near Mt. Kailash in Tibet. Once he was trapped under a mountain of snow during an avalanche. Using the mystical heat of the yogi's inner fire, he melted the snow and emerged unharmed. That is how he became known by the name 'Barfani Dada'!

After spending some time in India as a pilgrim and a devotee, the awesome realization begins to dawn on one's heart and mind what a land of sages and saints India really is! Every *tirtha* and temple seems to be associated with one or more great spiritual personages of the past or the present.

Once while walking in the Himalayan foothills by the Ganga near Kodyala, my wife and I passed through the outskirts of a village looking for a small Shiva *mandir* on a hill. When we arrived, the morning *puja* had been completed and no one was around. We meditated in what felt like an otherworldly environment – partially in this realm of existence and partially on a transcendental plane. Across the courtyard, shaded by an ancient tree under which were installed two small stone *lingams* was the concrete shrine of a saint. Whether it was a *samadhi* or a *kutir* was not clear to us. The door was locked, yet an old picture of the saint hung on an interior wall. We were left to wonder: Was it his holy presence in subtle form or the location itself that made this place so special, so divine?

When as a young boy, Mukunda Lal Ghosh, later known to the world as Paramahansa Yogananda, sat on his bed one morning in deep reverie, a probing thought came powerfully into his mind: "What is behind the darkness of closed eyes?" In *Autobiography of a Yogi* he writes: "An immense flash of light at once manifested to my inner gaze. Divine shapes of saints, sitting in meditation posture in mountain caves, formed like miniature cinema pictures on the large screen of radiance within my forehead. 'Who are you?' I spoke aloud. 'We are the Himalayan yogis.' The celestial response is difficult to describe; my heart was thrilled. 'Ah, I long to go to the Himalayas and become like you!"

Who are these divine yogis? Although the great Himalayas are well known since ancient times to be the 'abode of saints,' the *mahayogi*, Ram Gopal Muzumdar told Mukunda, "Masters are under no cosmic compulsion to live on mountains only."

Indeed it is true that the saints of India come in all strata of society and from every corner of this vast land. Many are hardly to be recognized by society. They hide their innate glory from the masses while revealing their teachings and blessings discreetly to those who are receptive; whose good karma and spiritual earnestness has drawn them into the sphere of their influence.

Pandit Rajmani Tigunait, spiritual successor to Swami Rama of the Himalayas, and director of the Himalayan Institute, told author Linda Johnsen, "If you go into the Himalayas you will find many *bhairavis*, female yogis who live in caves and forests doing penance. But most of the women saints remain with their families, purifying themselves by serving others. Every morning before their family awakens they sit before the altars in their homes, worshipping and praying. They don't care for name and fame. Even people in the next village do not know who they are. In your country you believe that no one can be a saint unless they give seminars!" (*Daughters of the Goddess: The Women Saints of India*). The same may be said of many saintly men as well.

Who then, exactly, is a saint? What are the qualifications? Definitions vary subjectively from an embodied soul who has attained complete freedom in Spirit – a *jivanmukta* – to highly advanced aspirants whose hearts and minds are immersed continually in the thought of God and service to humanity. Swami Sivananda's description offered at the beginning of this chapter provides a beautiful and all-encompassing definition. A tall order it may indeed seem, yet that is the inevitable goal set before us by God and the propensity of our own soul's evolution. We are seeking complete freedom in Spirit, and many are the souls on the 'Satchidananda Highway' who are drawn to this holy land of holy lands: Mother India, land of saints and sages!

Swami Mangalananda, an American direct disciple of Sri Anandamayi Ma who currently resides at her ashram in Omkareshwar, Madhya Pradesh, has perceptively written: "India is, and always will be, a land of living saints. The rich spiritual tradition, and the esoteric knowledge of yoga and meditation that is inherent in the culture, allows evolved souls the capacity for continued spiritual growth and attainment."

Swamiji recounts this wonderful episode from the time he spent in the company of the great Anandamayi Ma:

"Once I witnessed an event that might seem small, but has a wonderful charm to it. In the dead of night, we were waiting on a railroad platform in a small town in Uttar Pradesh. There was just a small group of us with Ma, and someone brought a chair out and placed it on the platform for Ma to sit on. I saw that sitting right next to the chair was a little village woman, squatting on her luggage. Ma leaned over to her and started a friendly conversation. I could follow enough to tell that they were just discussing their destinations, the weather, and such not, but the lady was looking up at Ma with such love and joy, not knowing who She was, but experiencing a strange happiness she herself could not describe. After some time one of the *brahmacharis* wanted to show Ma something, so a flashlight was brought and shone on the object in Her hand. The light illumined Ma's face in the darkness of the night. I saw the simple woman sitting so close to Ma, staring up at Her face with reverent awe. I thought, 'Only in India can one have a casual conversation with God while waiting for a train!' "

Recounting his experience as a youth in the holy town of Hardwar during his "interrupted flight toward the Himalayas," Paramahansa Yogananda tells the story of the police officer who had assaulted a *sadhu* with his axe, thinking him to be a dangerous criminal. The *sadhu*, who was in truth a great master, had forgiven his attacker saying, "Son, that was just an understandable mistake on your part. Run along and don't reproach yourself. The Beloved Mother is taking care of me." He invited him to return and meet him after three days, at which time he found the saint completely healed with "no scar or trace of hurt!"

"I am going via Rishikesh to the Himalayan solitudes," said the exalted *sadhu*. He blessed them quickly and departed. The officer concluded, "I feel that my life has been uplifted through his sanctity."

God is love, and the devotee wants to feel the love of God and His mystic embrace. God is beautiful, and the devotee wants to adore Him, worship Him, praise Him, and offer all that is best in him to God. God is merciful and appears to the devotee in the form of avatars, prophets and saints to show His compassion. God comes in these forms to sustain the world, to destroy evil and to uphold righteousness.

Saints are beyond caste, creed, color and country. They belong to God and their approach is universal. Their lives are examples for all of us... Mother India has given birth since time immemorial to many avatars, sages and saints. When the caste system was threatening the structure of society in India, saints showed the way of universal brotherhood. When scholars were engrossed in arid philosophical speculations, saints spoke from the joyful experiences of the heart. When people were thinking that monkhood is essential to attain God, saints lived as householders and worked as potters or gardeners to show that a saint is not a superhuman being, but has his feet on earth and his head in heaven. When God was considered as an impersonal entity, saints made Him appear and walk among them.

The future religion of the world will be mysticism. Its scriptures will be based on the teachings and lives of saints of all world religions... May God and saints inspire and bless you to realize and to share the love of God with all.

Sant Keshavadas

Paramahansaji remarks: "Amar and I lamented that we had missed the great yogi who could forgive his persecutor in such a Christlike way. India, materially poor for the last two centuries, yet has an inexhaustible fund of divine wealth; spiritual 'skyscrapers' may occasionally be encountered by the wayside, even by worldly men like this policeman."

In his book *The Path to Love*, Dr. Deepak Chopra tells of an incident experienced by his friend, Lakshman, who was then living in the city of Bangalore, in Karnataka, where his parents owned a factory in the center of town. Lakshman wasn't a believer in saints. His family did their daily *puja* prayers, but as he puts it, "It was merely a formality." He admits that he wasn't what one would call a deeply religious person.

It seems that instead of fighting traffic one morning, Lakshman decided to walk to work: "Ten minutes from home I was totally frustrated," he relates, "pushing my way through a sea of peddlers, beggars, layabouts, and twenty thousand other people trying to get to the same place I was…." He was feeling irritated and exhausted. "Rounding a corner I saw a knot of people gathered around something. Of course they blocked the whole sidewalk, and this being India, traffic had stopped while taxi and lorry drivers got out to have a look. Something in me snapped, and I furiously pushed through, shouting for everyone to get out of my way. No one did. In five seconds I was embedded in a pack of shoving bodies, unable to escape.

"You can't imagine how I felt… but there I was, on the verge of screaming, when I suddenly felt everything in my mind stop. My anger and frenzy, my preoccupations, the constant flow of associations – the whole baggage simply disappeared, leaving behind an empty mind. I'm no fool; I had read scriptures and knew all that stuff about an empty mind being the silence of God. But on the streets of Bangalore! Somehow I managed to push my way forward. There in the middle of the pack was a small woman in a white sari sitting with her eyes closed. She must have been about thirty, I suppose, and something about her told me she was from a country village.

"To this day I have no idea why she stopped in the middle of the sidewalk like that. She sat completely still, not minding the crush around her. Actually, the crowd was acting quite respectful on the whole; she was surrounded by a ring of people on their knees. I got a little nearer, and the most remarkable thing happened. My empty mind began to have something in it, not a thought but a sensation. *Mother.* That's the only way I can describe it. It was as if all the mothering feelings that women give to their families were inside me, but with much greater purity and clarity.

"I wasn't thinking of my own mother. There was just this feeling. It grew stronger, and I saw, like a revealed truth, that this woman on the sidewalk was emanating the energy of 'Mother' from its very source. I also saw with complete clarity that my own mother had been trying to express this same energy. However imperfectly, she was connected to a reality that doesn't depend on this mother or that mother. It is just 'Mother,' the endless love of the feminine toward everything in creation.

"The next second I was on my knees, only a few feet from the saint on the sidewalk. She had her eyes open now and was smiling at all of us. Her smile somehow made my experience far more intense. I had a flashing glimpse of thousands upon thousands of souls wanting to be here on earth to experience the preciousness of being a mother… What came to me then was forgiveness…"

Dr. Chopra remarks, "Although his encounter had lasted only a few minutes, its effect was permanent. He (Lakshman) remains awed that the mere presence of a saint can uplift ordinary awareness. (This effect is known as "*Darshan*" in Sanskrit). More important, he became convinced that a path to the divine is real, since he had now met someone who was at the end of that path." (From THE PATH TO LOVE, by Deepak Chopra, M.D., copyright © 1996 by Deepak Chopra, M.D. Used by permission of Harmony Books, a division of Random House, Inc.)

Swami Jnanananda Giri, in his extraordinary autobiography, *The Transcendent Journey,* (yet to be published in English), tells the following remarkable story. It poignantly illustrates the truth that saints can live anywhere, unbeknownst to even their closest associates.

In this narrative, when Swami Jnanananda refers to "Master," he is speaking of his own Guru, Swami Atmananda, an eminent disciple of Swami Kebalananda, Paramahansa Yogananda's Sanskrit teacher and exalted disciple of Lahiri Mahasaya. Swami Atmananda received *sannyas* from Rajarsi Janakananda, spiritual successor of Paramahansa Yogananda. Paramahansaji left Swami Atmananda, known at the time as Brahmachari Prakashdas Maharaj, in charge of his Yogoda ashrams during his years in America. He was a close childhood friend of Paramahansaji.

"One day the Master returned to the hermitage late in the evening. The young Swami (Jnanananda) had been expecting him and waiting in the prayer hall. The Guru appeared pensive, rather in an abstract mood. He sat quite close to his disciple, and they remained silent for a while. No one else was present. The *Swami* sensed something unusual. After some time, the Master began: This morning he had been called to attend the funeral of an elderly *brahmin.* After all the ceremonies were over, the wife of that gentleman confided to the Guru (himself) that she and her husband had been practicing Kriya Yoga for many years. Now that her husband had gone, she had no more duty in this life. She wanted to follow him – in other words, to die! She then asked his permission to do so.

Continuing, the Guru said that of course he discouraged such a drastic step, as he thought that the lady was infatuated by grief. But the woman had insisted and explained that she knew the secret method of Kriya by which she could consciously leave her body and not return. She would do so in her *puja* room and would like to have him there, observing her. He was too intrigued to refuse, and consented. He did wonder what would happen.

They both had sat on special *asans* and remained in silent meditation for nearly two hours. He watched her practice continuously Kriya, then a higher Kriya, until she was able to gather up all her *prana.* She then centered her life-force at the point between her eyes. Thus, remaining composed and withdrawn, the *Yogini* gave up her body as her *prana* passed through the fontanel in the skull on top of the head. The body remained in that pose for a few moments and then sank slowly to the ground.

That night, the atmosphere of the hermitage was highly charged. It was inspiring to know that even now-a-days true yogis exist; a testimony to Indian spiritual culture."

Study the lives of saints; you are inspired at once. Remember their sayings; you are elevated immediately. Walk in their footsteps; you are freed from pain and sorrow… May this world be filled with good saints and sages! May you all attain the supreme goal through their satsang and advice!! May the blessings of saints and sages be upon you all!!!

Swami Sivananda

Mahasamadhi Commemoration Service for Paramahansa Yogananda, Haridwar, 2001

Man has come on earth solely to learn to know God; he is here for no other reason.... This is the true message of the Lord.

Paramahansa Yogananda

Man's Eternal Quest

No one can find God without continuous love for Him in the heart... There is nothing greater than the love of God. If a devotee has found that, his work in the school of life is finished.

Paramahansa Yogananda

The Second Coming of Christ

Mahasamadhi Commemoration Service for Sri Sri Paramahansa Yogananda, Haridwar, 2001

We were nearing the conclusion of a seven week pilgrimage to India which had begun with the *Mahakumbha Mela* at Prayag Raj. We had stayed at the main ashrams of Paramahansa Yogananda at Dakshineswar and Ranchi, visited Kolkata, Varanasi and Puri, and had just completed a more than three week trek in the Himalayas. Our group of twenty-nine pilgrims was staying at the Alakananda Guest House on the banks of the Ganga in Haridwar. Adjacent to the guest house is the Keshabananda Ashram wherein is enshrined a portion of Yogavatar Lahiri Mahasaya's ashes. It was March 7th, the day, in 1952, that our Gurudeva left this world for the eternal shores.

We decided to walk upriver to Hari-ki-Pairi Ghat to attend the famous Ganga *Arati* in the evening and then return to our hotel to conduct a commemoration service for Gurudeva on the lawn beside the river. Our tour leader, Gangadas, asked the hotel personnel if they would obtain some flowers and set up a table with the Master's picture on it so everything would be in readiness when we returned. What awaited us far exceeded our expectations.

When we got back to the guesthouse we found the entire garden and lawn area decorated with 'Christmas' lights and candles. A table had been set up beneath a large tree as the centerpiece for the altar. 'OM' symbols had been traced on the lawn on both sides of the altar in flower petals. There were piles of flowers and garlands just waiting to be offered by the devotees in loving devotion.

The commemoration service was truly heartfelt. We read from the Master's poem, *My India*: "Where Ganges, woods, Himalayan caves, and men dream God – I am hallowed; my body touched that sod," realizing that we had just come from those very places. While we were at the *Ganga Arati* we had offered our individual leaf boats with camphor flames to the river, sending our prayers along the joyful current in the darkness. Unbeknownst to the group, however, Gangadas had ordered a very large leaf boat – big enough for twenty-nine flames, one for each member of our group. After the conclusion of the service we all went down to the banks of Mother Ganga, lit the flames and pushed the boat out into the swiftly flowing current while chanting *Brahma Stuti* from *Sri Guru Gita*, translated by Paramahansaji in his book, *Cosmic Chants*, as "Hymn to Brahma." The flaming leaf boat took off rapidly yet it became caught in a swirling eddy and came right back to us. We chanted once more and again sent the boat out into the current, yet the results were the same. The feeling we had was that this special sacred boat containing the essence of our Guru's love just didn't want to leave us! On the third attempt, however, while we were chanting and blowing the conch, off she went, carrying our hopes and our prayers to that mystical place where *Ganga Ma*, God and Guru unite and are one.

Almost unnoticed during the commemoration service, a group of visitors from Europe, who were also staying at the guesthouse, had been sitting toward the back. When we returned from the *ghat* we found that they were kneeling in front of Guruji's picture. Tears were streaming down their faces. They knew nothing of Guruji or our path, yet had been deeply touched by his living presence. Such is the unseen power of those who know God. **OM TAT SAT**

My Native Land

By Paramahansa Yogananda

The friendly sky,
Inviting shade of banyan tree,
The holy Ganges flowing by –
How can I forget thee!

I love the waving corn
Of India's fields so bright,
Oh, better than those heav'nly grown
By deathless gods of might!

My soul's broad love, by God's command,
Was first born here below,
In my own native land –
On India's sunny soil aglow.

I love thy breeze,
I love thy moon,
I love thy hills and seas;
In thee I wish my life to cease.

Thou taught'st me first to love
The sky, the stars, the God above;
So my first homage – as 'tis meet –
I lay, O India, at thy feet!

From thee I now have learned to see,
To love all lands alike as thee.
I bow to thee, my native land,
Thou mother of my love so grand.

©Self-Realization Fellowship
Used by permission

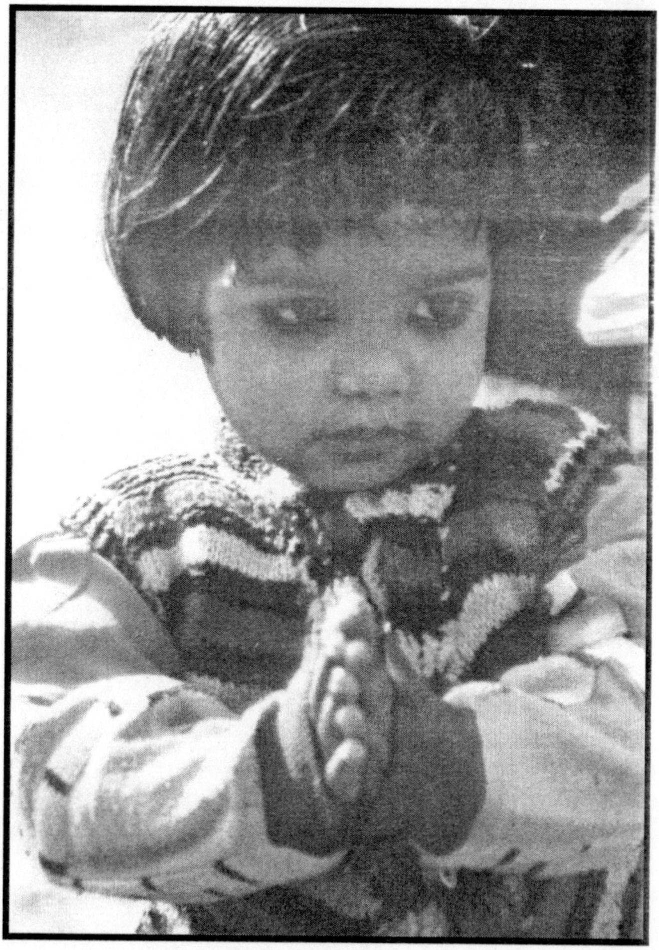

Appendix I

India

Swami Sivananda

India is the sacred land which has given birth to countless sages, *Rishis*, *Yogins*, saints, and prophets. India is the land that has produced many *Acharyas* or spiritual preceptors like Sri Shankara, Sri Ramanuja; many saints like Kabir, Ramdas, Tukaram, Gouranga Mahaprabhu; many Yogins like Jnandev, Dattatreya, Sadashiva Brahman; many prophets like Buddha and Guru Nanak. Buddha is our flesh and blood.

India is proud of Guru Govind Singh and Shivaji. India is proud of King Bhoja and Vikramaditya. India is proud of Shankara and Kabir. India is proud of Kalidas and Valmiki. Krishna, Rama and all Avataras were born in India. How sacred is India! How sublime is India! The dust of Brindavan and Ayodhya, the land trodden by the sacred feet of Krishna and Rama, still purifies the heart of countless people. Even Jesus, during the missing period of his life, lived in Kashmir and learnt Yoga from the Indian Yogins.

India is the sacred land with several holy rivers and powerful spiritual vibrations. It is a land peculiarly suitable for divine contemplation and Yogi's practices. The hoary Himalayas attract the people of the whole world.

How charming is the Himalayan scenery! How sweet is Mother Ganga! How soothing and elevating are their vibrations! How soul-stirring is the company of the Yogins! How beautiful and lovely is Rishikesh, with Yogins, Ganga, and Himalayas!

India is a spiritual country. Religion governs all the departments of Hindu life. The Hindu must realize the freedom of the soul in every department of life. Religion affords the greatest scope to him for the culture of true freedom.

It is in India alone that every man knows something of philosophy. The cowherd who tends the cattle, the peasant who ploughs the fields, the boatman who pulls at his oar, sings songs replete with philosophical truths. Even the barber repeats *Om Namah Shivaya, Sivoham,* before he takes up the razor. The *Paramahansa Sannyasins*, the itinerant monks of Hinduism, have disseminated the highest of *Vedanta* from door to door. In exchange for a handful of rice, they have distributed from door to door, through religious songs, the priceless gems of Hindu religion and philosophy.

History of Indian Civilization

Indian civilization has had a long history. It has influenced the history of the world at every stage.

Hindus have had a culture, civilization, and religion millennia older than those of any other country or people. When the ancestors of the Westerners were completely uncivilized savages, India was full of sages, saints, Yogins, seers, and *Maharshis* with Self-realization, and the highest culture and civilization. Hindu culture and Hindu civilization were at their zenith in days of yore. The Greeks and the Romans imitated the Hindus, and absorbed Hindu thoughts.

The *Ramayana* and the *Mahabharata* tell us clearly about the ancient India, about her people, her customs, her ways of living, her arts, her civilization and culture, her manufacturers. Even today, our domestic, social, and national ideals are copied from the noble characters in the *Ramayana* and the *Mahabbharata*. The great national heroes stand even today as beacon-lights to guide and inspire the people of the whole world. If you read these two books, you will come to know how great India once was, and you will be inspired to make her great once more. No other country has produced so many great teachers, great Yogins, great seers, great *Rishis*, great prophets, great *Acharyas*, great kings, great heroes, great statesmen, great patriots, and great benefactors as India. Each and every province of the country has produced intellectual giants, poets, and saints. Even now India abounds in sages and great souls. The more you know of India and Hinduism, the more you will honor and love it and the more thankful to the Lord you will be that you were born in India as a Hindu.

Spirituality – The Bedrock of Indian Culture

England is famous for coal and iron, America for dollars, Italy for sculptural works, but India is famous for its religious devotion, Yogins, and saints. The history of India is a history of religion. Its social code and regulations are founded upon religion. Minus its Yoga, religion and its regulations, India will not be what it has been for millennia. India cannot be India without the *Gita* and the *Upanishads*. The culture of India is built round the central idea of *Dharma*, or righteousness. India is the land of *Dharma*. Her breath is *Dharma*. Her life and light is *Dharma*. She moves and has her being in *Dharma*. *Dharma* protects India and She shall protect *Dharma*.

The solid foundation of Indian culture has enabled it to withstand the rigors of political strife and alien invasions.

Temporary periods of political bondage have not sullied the soul of India. The passage of time has not diminished the glory of Indian culture. The civilizations of ancient Egypt, Assyria, Babylon, Greece, and Rome have faded out; but the ancient civilization of India lives through ages.

Self-restraint and mastery over the senses have been the keynote of India's culture from the earliest period of her history. The goal of India is Self-realization through renunciation and knowledge. The national ideals of India are renunciation and service. The ideal of renunciation and detachment is the one factor that has kept intact the virility of *Bharatavarsha* as a nation.

India is a garden rich with the fragrance of the flowers of tolerance, virtue, love, and goodness cultured out of the seeds of the recognition of universal brotherhood and oneness of mankind. Unity of mankind and universality of religion are the prerogatives of the Indian tradition.

India is the most tolerant country in the world. She has a very expansive heart. She includes all nations in the embrace of her love. For more than eight centuries, she was oppressed by some greedy men. And yet, she served them and made them happy and rich. She is ever rich, liberal, and catholic. She nourishes the whole world. Her resources are inexhaustible.

Indian culture is not a dead culture. It has an undying vitality. It can be revitalized age after age to suit the needs of changing times. There is a fundamental vitality which has enabled India to carry on through all these millennia in spite of her weaknesses.

India and the West

To India, Brahman is the only reality. Its nature is *Sat-chit-ananda.* To the West, matter is the only reality. To have plenty of dollars is freedom. To have abundant atom bombs and airplanes is freedom. To India, Self-realization is the goal. To the West, power and dominion is the goal. To India, self-restraint gives happiness. To the West, self-indulgence gives pleasure. To India, renunciation bestows joy. To the West, possession gives joy. To India, the practice of *Ahimsa* is the ideal. To the West, 'kill and conquer' is the idea.

In the West, he who has many wants is the most civilized man. A Westerner calls a man who has few wants a barbarian. A Yogi or a devotee of the East is a savage in the eyes of a Westerner. The Westerners have not realized the axiomatic great truth that 'the fewer desires the greater the happiness.' This is, indeed, a great pity.

Western culture is for the self-aggrandizement of the Westerners; Eastern culture is for the whole world. Western culture turns the mind outward; Eastern culture turns the mind inward. Western culture thickens egoism and strengthens the personality. Eastern culture annihilates egoism and individuality, and leads to universality. Western culture brings bondage; Eastern culture leads to salvation. Western culture makes a man materialistic and *Asuric.* Eastern culture makes a man divine.

The West is material. The East is spiritual. Science is the offspring of the material force, and Yoga is the child of the spiritual force.

India will not be able to rival the West in physical science, but in the spiritual field, she will certainly be unparalleled.

She will always guide the entire universe in spiritual matters, in Yoga, *Vedanta*, etc. She will ever be the world's preceptor. India will always lead the world in spirituality. She does not stand in any need of spiritual enlightenment from others.

India's Contribution to the World

India has given much to the world in the form of mental and spiritual culture. The Indian *Rishis* of yore rejoiced in spiritual wisdom, communed with God, and enlightened the world with divine knowledge. The spiritual literature of India, given by her *Rishis*, will ever continue to retain their infinite brilliance through ages to come.

The teachings of India's ancient seers are, indeed, the most universal. The works of Yoga belongs to the entire world. They are also practical to the core.

Numerous persons are turning from a war-torn and sullied atmosphere to India and her ancient, divine wisdom which is found in the *Gita*, the *Upanishads*, and *Advaita Vedanta* philosophy.

India, due to her glorious heritage, can show the right road to all, and lead all to prosperity, peace, and perpetual bliss. Let India lead the countries which are spiritually bankrupt. She alone can undertake this gigantic task. India alone can lead the world towards better understanding, harmony, fraternity, and peace.

The Future of India

India's mission is different from that of others. The mission of India is the achievement of spiritual greatness, but not political eminence and military power.

Military glories are not the criterion of a nation's progress. India has never sought them at the cost of other people's freedom. India has never attached importance to wealth and power, from the beginning of history.

India is always a land of seers, sages, Yogins and Munis. If she imitates the West, she will lose her spiritual glory, for everything Indian should have a spiritual basis. Her conquest is through *Ahimsa*, love, and wisdom. She should ever maintain her ancient culture, ancient wisdom, and Yogic attainments. She cannot become glorious through building of more airplanes and warships. She should produce more Yogins, and victors over self. The governors of India should consult saints on important matters of administration. They should accord them a high place of honor. Then and then alone will the India Government be righteous, divine, and peaceful.

India has attained freedom now, but her problems of poverty, ignorance, and economic crises remain still unsolved. There is the great need for cleansing the public life and ridding it of those excrescences which are poisoning the springs of national life in India at its very source. Let all live the *Gita*-life.

Those in India who imitate the West have lost their soul. This is a great pity, indeed.

The future of India depends on her spiritual strength rather than upon her material wealth. *Atman*, or the Spirit, is the rock foundation of wisdom, prosperity, strength, and peace. Be ever a beacon-light of the spiritual essence of *Bharatavarsha* culture. Live an exemplary personal and social life of the ideal Hindu.

India will rise. India must rise. It is a glorious land of *Rishis* and sages. It is a *Punyabhumi* with Ganga and Yamuna. It is the best of all lands.

Appendix II

Swami Avdheshananda Giri: Spiritual Practicality in Action

Author's Note: *I first became aware of Swami Avdheshananda during my one-month stay at the Mahakumbha Mela at Prayag Raj in January, 2001. He and Tapasvi Baba, of Amarkantak, were two saints who immediately drew my attention in the assembly of mahants and religious leaders that attended the parliament sponsored by the Himalayan Institute. He was one of the two mahatmas (the other being H.H. Swami Chidanand Muniji) who hosted the Dalai Lama's first visit to the Kumba Mela that year. I was fortunate to have been at the camp of Swami Avdheshanandaji during that historic occasion. Many thousands of people attended that day.*

Interview by Rajiv Malik, New Delhi, for Hinduism Today

For years, I had wanted to do an extensive interview… I was not expecting the mix of modernity and unapologetic tradition that followed. Swami's speech was articulate, contemporary and relevant, yet not a grain of Hinduism's cultural richness was lost in his translation from the ancient to today's world. In his quarters, where a couple of his *sannyasin* initiates are always present to help turn decisions immediately into actions, his personal secretary held fast to his laptop during the interview, using wireless connection to send e-mails and gather information. Professionalism and efficiency seem to be the order of the day in the 21st Century Juna Akhara. I found Swamiji to be sharper and more agile than a corporate CEO. Yet, after attending all the four

Kumbha Melas and meeting hundreds of swamis, I can say that Swami Avdheshananda is one of the most orthodox Hindu saints in India... Here now, are excerpts from that extemporaneous exchange with HINDUISM TODAY, in which Swami Avdheshananda Giri speaks of his life, his Order's work, and his vision for the future.

My Journey to Infinity

Sannyas is an unending journey. This is a journey that takes us to the infinity of God. The goal is discovery of one's own Self. When you realize that everything around you is not the Truth, and you feel that all that you see is perishable, that all is changing every moment, then you start aspiring for Truth. When the aspiration becomes a craving to know That, that intense desire slowly becomes a state of *sannyas.* It dawns on you. The solitude of mountains and caves becomes attractive. All this happened to me. I moved to the Himalayan mountains and lived there for a long time. During that stay, I realized how important it is to dwell with *satpurushas* (noble souls), those that are awakened and have the blessings of the Almighty on them. Those are the *jivanmuktas* (liberated ones). Such people are not much influenced by worldly things. I realized that until you come in close touch with such sages, you couldn't really understand life. This was my experience. That was what took me to the feet of the great saint, Swami Avadhoot Prakash.

Teaching by Example

I am the Acharya Mahamandaleshwar of Juna Akhara. My group has a few *mahamandaleshwars*, and our task is to lead and organize thousands and thousands of *sannyasins* associated with the *Juna Akhara*, all over India, who are serving the people. Our work, the sum of all of our efforts, is to create *samskaras,* deep impressions in people's minds. This is not done in the classrooms using the blackboards. We want to shape the devotee's character. If you want to civilize, educate and discipline someone to obey the law, or if you want a person to keep his equilibrium with nature, then a certain awakening has to catalyze in that person. These things can be taught only by example. We *sannyasins* use our conduct, character and thoughts to reshape society. Most of us may not do this in a very conscious or structured way. But that is the result of keeping full control over the senses and living according to the scriptures. By doing that, we are building the character of individuals. We develop the personality of those who come near. Our objective is to create harmony all throughout the world. Since it is today's wrong lifestyle which leads to the world's problems, the *sannyasins* are teaching people the art of living.

On India's Challenges

In India and all over the world, everyone fears terrorism. There are also many other challenges, like global warming and the caste system. But in my view, even bigger and more dangerous than all these problems in India is the problem of *bhogwad* (desire for things and pleasures). We are following the consumerism of the West without understanding it. The lifestyle of blindly fulfilling desires is having an adverse impact on our relationships. This lifestyle is making us focus just on ourselves. I think we have to create proper *samskaras* to educate people on this. We are using my *kathas* to do it, which is also a form of group counseling.

Hindutva and Ahimsa

We have to understand that a movement driven by devotion, faith and improvement of the world is good and acceptable. But when the movement's aim is power, it does not become successful. Today Hindus are recognized as important members of society in the Silicon Valley in Los Angeles, in Tokyo, in London, in Paris and even in China. Hindus are nonviolent. Hindus believe in the family system. Hindus are non-aggressive, not attackers. Hindus will never harm anyone. There are four reasons why I say this. The first is our principle of *vasudhaiva kutumbakam*, which means the whole world is one family. For us, the whole world is a big family. Second, *par dara matravat*, meaning women of others are like our mothers. Hindus are known all over the world to maintain the purity of relationships. Third, Hindus believe in *sarve bhavantu sukhina*, let all be happy and blissful. We want the whole world to be harmonious and joyous; we want the welfare of all beings. The fourth principal is *atmavrata sarvabhuteshu*; treat others as they would treat themselves. Hindus are believers in one God. This God is present everywhere and in every being, formless but also on Earth. Hindus are flexible and generous. They mingle freely with everyone. If there is a least harmful community on this Earth, that is the Hindu community.

Our Treatment of the Planet

Don't you feel that the laws of nature are being violated? Global warming, forests cut down, rivers drying up. Chemicals and fertilizers are destroying the soil. All the glaciers are melting. I have traveled to the North Pole and I have seen the angry mood of nature. The Vedas say that if you deprive anyone of his honor, that is a sin. We want to protect the rights of even a lion, an elephant, and for that matter, every element of nature, including a cloud. Such nature loving is our *dharma.* Just imagine the kindness and open-mindedness of our heritage and culture. We are the people who offer milk to poisonous snakes. We consider trees as our *devatas* (village gods). Hinduism and Hindus are the most nature and environment-loving people in this world. On this Earth, animals have never engaged in widespread killings as we do. Earth has never been divided by them. We are less civilized than animals. They have not encroached on our lands; it is we who have cut down the trees and attacked their places of living. In fact, there is a big debate about vegetarianism in the whole world. Research has highlighted that the production of white and red meat is behind global warming. Our teeth and mouth are not designed to consume non-vegetarian food.

A Message about Today's Youth

Today's youth have a lot of temptations before them, especially in India. There are a lot of chances of them moving in the wrong direction. One example is the tendency of trying to become rich overnight, and doing every single thing possible to achieve it. My message to youth is that without labor and *sadhana*, success cannot be attained. A youth must be focused, have the qualities of patience and control over the senses, and work hard on both his worldly pursuits and spiritual practices. But to have young people develop these qualities, we need to have a dialogue with them; we must motivate them. Before we guide the young, we must earn their trust and confidence.

My Adversities and Aspirations

In the life of every human being, times come when the circumstances are not favorable. He feels he is lacking something. He feels he is not capable. With the blessings of my gurus, I developed confidence and experience. I can face the worst of adversities. Adversities could never defeat me. It would be incorrect to say that I am beyond faltering. I also have *vasanas* and things to overcome. But I have always experienced that the inner presence of my gurus gave me such strength that when challenges came, I simply stood up and faced them. I have worked to realize my dreams of a better world with better people. Another dream I have is to convey the spirituality of India to the Western world. I want to let them know that Indian spirituality has the human *dharma* defined for the welfare of all beings of the world.

Only the spirituality of India has the power to overcome anything that mankind will face.

Sri Swami Avdheshananda Giri

OM TAT SAT

Posters on a wall in the Garwal Himalayas announcing a satsang with H.H. Sri Swami Avdheshananda Giri

Photographs

Most photos by the author may be ordered as beautiful full color enlargements. Please write for details:
HimalayanHeritage@JyotiMandir.com

By the author: **Page**

Contributors:

Nandi
Banares Hindu University, Varanasi

HIMALAYAN HERITAGE **MAGAZINE is a lively, informative and inspirational 12-page bi-monthly.**

Each issue includes an "India Dreaming" feature presenting stories from or about India, focusing on Her endlessly unfolding expressions of spirituality. We encourage your contributions.

...And a "Saints & Sages" column profiling the lives of the great masters which create an ever-expanding mandala of sanctity, which is a prominent feature of Indian culture.

... Plus many more articles of interest to everyone on the path of Hindu Devotional Mysticism.

www.HimalayanHeritage.org

Lord Ganesha
Outdoor Shrine, Devi Mandir, Ramnagar

India Stories Project

The collection of stories about Spiritual India such as are reflected in the pages of this book is ongoing. We warmly invite your participation. Stories should describe your own personal experiences in India from a spiritual perspective. Humor is appropriate in context. Please avoid social and political commentary.

Submissions may be published in a proposed second volume of *Where Souls Dream God*, or in our magazine, *Himalayan Heritage*. Submission does not guarantee publication.

If you would like to submit your story, please send to:
HimalayanHeritage@JyotiMandir.com

ॐ

Lord Hanuman

Mahakumbha Mela, Prayag Raj

Shantipuri Friends Foundation

The Shantipuri Friends Foundation was established in December, 2008, as a tax exempt nonprofit public charity dedicated to support poor and underprivileged children and their families in India. Our sponsored organizations provide education, school supplies, food, clothing, and a home for orphaned children, as well as moral training and spiritual education.

We have had the wonderful good fortune of becoming associated with two exceptional souls, both *sannyasis* of the Swami Order, and both of Western birth. Swami Nirvanananda, from Italy, has been staying with us most summers since 1995, bringing with him his soul-comforting, magical singing voice, and his peaceful, loving presence. Swamiji recorded the enclosed CD, *I Love You, India*, especially for inclusion with this book. For nearly 30 years, he has been traveling the world, singing devotional songs and kirtans for God and His Guru, Paramahansa Yogananda, while accepting donations for the charitable projects that he supports in and around the holy city of Puri, in Orissa.

Swami Mangalananda, who so graciously wrote the forward to this publication, became an instant friend when we stayed at the Sri Anandamayi Ma Ashrams in Indore and Omkareshwar during our visit to India in the fall of 2004. Swamiji is instrumental in bringing awareness about and raising funds for the Ashram School for poor village children of Omkareshwar, founded by H.H. Sri Swami Kedarnath-ji Maharaj, a Self-realized direct disciple of Sri Anandamayi Ma.

Swami Kedarnath has stated that the spiritual and educational ideals that are being taught in the Ashram School will one day spread throughout India.

We encourage the reader to visit these wonderful websites for more information, and to become involved.

www.ShantipuriFriends.org

www.Nirvanananda.org

www.ChildrenofMa.org

50% of the profits from the sale of this book will be donated to the Shantipuri Friends Foundation

Bibliography

A.N. Sharma. Modern Saints and Mystics.
Shivanandnagar, India: The Divine Life Society, 1997

Chopra, Deepak. The Path to Love.
New York, New York: Harmony Books, 1997

Daya Mata. Self-Realization Magazine, July - August, 1959
Los Angeles, California: Self-Realization Fellowship

Johnsen, Linda. Daughters of the Goddess:
The Women Saints of India.
St. Paul, Minnesota: Yes International Publishers, 1994

Keshavadas, Sant. Saints of India.
Washington, D.C.: Temple of Cosmic Religion, 1975

Mangalananda, Swami. Om Ma: Anandamayi Ma, a Short
Life Sketch. Omkareshwar, MP, India, 2006

Palotas, Tom. Divine Play: The Silent Teachings of
Shiva Bala Yogi.
Langley, Washington: Shivabalayogi Seva Foundation, 2004

Patil, Vimla. Celebrations: Festive Days of India.
Bombay: India Book House Pvt. Ltd, 1994

Satchidananda, Swami. The Gospel of Swami Ramdas.
Kanhangad, India: Anandashram Publications
Shantananda, Swami. Self-Realization Magazine, Spring, 1976
Los Angeles, California: Self-Realization Fellowship

Sivananda, Swami. Lives of Saints.
Shivanandnagar, U.P. India:
The Divine Life Trust Society, 1993

Sivananda, Swami. India, Peace & Science.
Mumbai, India: Divine Life Society, 2000

Yogananda, Paramahansa. Autobiography of a Yogi.
Los Angeles, California: Self-Realization Fellowship, 1946

Yogananda, Paramahansa. Man's Eternal Quest.
Los Angeles, California: Self-Realization Fellowship, 1975

Yogananda, Paramahansa. The Divine Romance.
Los Angeles, California: Self-Realization Fellowship, 1986

Yogananda, Paramahansa. Journey To Self-Realization.
Los Angeles, California: Self-Realization Fellowship, 1997

Yogananda, Paramahansa. Songs of the Soul.
Los Angeles, California: Self-Realization Fellowship, 1983

Yogananda, Paramahansa. The Second Coming of Christ: The Resurrection of the Christ Within You.
Los Angeles, California: Self-Realization Fellowship, 2004

Glossary

AGNI: Fire; fire god; God manifesting in the form of fire.

AKANDANAM: Continuous chanting or repetition of a Name of God, usually for an extended yet specific period of time.

AKHARA: Seven subdivisions of *Naga Sadhus*, originally organized along militant lines in response to aggressive Muslim invasions. They include the Ananda, Niranjani, Juna, Avaham, Atal, Nirvani and Agni Akharas.

AMAVASYA: The new moon night, especially sacred to Goddess Kali.

ANANDA: Bliss-consciousness; the state of ever-new joy.

ANJALI MUDRA: Traditional gesture of *pranam* with the hands folded in prayer position. "Anjali" means "to offer."

ARATI: The circling or waving of a lamp or flame before a holy person or deity. The flame is then presented to the assembled congregation, each person passing his or her hands through the flame and bringing them to their eyes, thus receiving the blessings of the Divine. **Arati** may be performed on its own as a short *puja.*

ASAN: Meditation seat.

ASANA: *Hatha Yoga* posture.

ASHRAM: A place where God or "Ram" abides; a hermitage or a place of spiritual practice. Also refers to the four **ashramas** (stages) of life. See: *brahmacharya, grihasta, vanaprastha and sannyasa.*

ASURA / ASURIC: Demon / demonic. In Hindu parlance, often used to describe those beings who are addicted to materiality and sense gratification, and who have no interest in spirituality, or those who work in opposition to spiritual values and teachings.

ATMA: The soul, the transcendental Self; a person's true nature, one with omnipresent Spirit.

AVADHUT: A saint who is beyond identification with the body.

AVATAR: The descent of Divinity into flesh; an incarnation of God, or that of a soul who has achieved perfection in a previous life, who then returns to earth for the upliftment or salvation of others.

BABA: "Revered father;" a respectful name for a holy man; also, ***babaji***.

BAKSHISH: Begging for alms.

BALA YOGI: A child yogi.

BANDHARA: Feast on a religious occasion.

BAUL: Literally, "mad;" a subculture of folk musicians in Bengal who sing of ecstatic love for God and humankind.

BHAIRAVI: A woman ascetic; especially a female *Shaivite sadhu*.

BHAIYYA: Brother.

BHAJAN: A devotional song; also, to worship with devotion; from the root *bhaj*, to love and revere.

BHAKTA: A devotee of God.

BHAKTI: Devotion to God.

BHAKTI YOGA: The path of union with God through devotion and self-surrender.

BHARAT / BHARATAVARSHA: India.

BHAV / BHAVA: Divine mood; experiencing or manifesting higher feelings and transcendental emotions; also, allowing a certain manifestation of the Divine to manifest through a saint, i.e., *Krishna Bhava, Devi Bhava,* etc.

BIKSHA: Begging for alms by a religious mendicant.

BRAHMAN: Transcendental Spirit beyond creation; becomes "*Sat,*" or God-the-Father in relation to creation; also called *Parabrahma, Paramatman, Paramashiva.*

BRAHMACHARYA: "Teacher of God;" usually taken to mean continence, self-control, sexual restraint; also, the first *ashrama* (stage) of life: that of the celibate student.

BRAHMACHARI (male), BRAHMACHARINI (female): One who is practicing *brahmacharya*; a celibate student, monk or nun.

BRAHMARISHI: The highest scriptural demarcation of a sage.

BRAHMASTHANAM: A ceremony in which the living presence of God is infused into a *murti.*

BRAHMIN: A person belonging to the priestly caste.

BUDDHA PURNIMA: Birthday of Lord Buddha; the full moon night in the Hindu month of Vaishakh, mid-April to mid-May.

CHALISA: "Forty;" A devotional song or poem consisting of forty verses such as the Hanuman Chalisa, Shiva Chalisa and Durga Chalisa.

CHAR DHAMS: "Four holy temples;" refers to the four main pilgrimage destinations in the Himalayas, the temples of Badrinath, Kedarnath, Yamunotri and Gangotri.

DAHI: Yogurt.

DAMARU: A ceremonial drum carried by Lord Shiva, and often by His renunciant devotees, *Shaivite sadhus.*

DANDA: Walking staff; ceremonial staff often covered by an ochre cloth, carried by certain orders of *swamis.*

DARSHAN: Literally, "Sight." Seeing and being seen by the Divine; being in the presence of a holy person or a manifestation of Divinity.

DEVA: Being of light; God, or a messenger of God, i.e., an angel.

DEVI: Denotes a form of the Divine Mother; "Goddess."

DHARMA: Duty or righteousness; thought and action which is in accordance with universal Divine principals.

DHARMASHALA: A rest house for pilgrims.

DIKSHA: Spiritual initiation, wherein divine energy is transmitted from guru to disciple.

DIYA: An open-flamed ghee, oil or camphor lamp.

DHOLAK: A two-sided folk drum.

DHOTI: A traditional lower garment of unstitched cloth worn by men.

DHYANA: Meditation. The sixth step in Patanjali's eightfold path of Ashtanga or Raja Yoga.

DHUNI: Sacred fire.

DWAPARA YUGA: One of four vast cycles of cosmic time: Satya Yuga (or Krita Yuga), Treta Yuga, Dwapara Yuga and Kali Yuga.

GAMPSHA: A thin towel worn by men as a wraparound for bathing purposes.

GANGA: The holy Ganges River, personified as a form of the Divine Mother.

GANGA MA / GANGA MAIYYA: "Mother Ganges."

GARUA: Ochre color; the color of a *swami's* robe.

GAYATRI MANTRA: Called the 'Mother of the Vedas,' this ancient Sanskrit *mantra* is often considered to be the holiest of all *mantras.* It is said to contain the blueprint of creation: *Om Bhur Bhuvaha Swaha / Tat Savitur Varenyam / Bhargo Devasya Dhimahi / Diyo Yo Naa Prachodayat.*

GHAT: Bathing place with steps leading down to the water.

GOPARAM: Temple towers characteristic of South Indian architecture.

GOPI: Milkmaid girls of Brindavan who were intoxicated by passionate and ecstatic love of God in the form of Lord Krishna.

GRIHASTA: The second *ashrama* or stage of life: that of the married householder.

GURU: One who removes the darkness of delusion by bringing in the light of wisdom; "The awakened God in the Guru awakening the sleeping God in the disciple," (*Satguru*). In its less exalted form can also mean "teacher."

GURUKUL: A residential school under the auspices of a *guru.*

HALWA: Sweet semolina pudding, usually served hot.

HANUMAN CHALISA: A famous and oft-sung hymn consisting of forty verses describing the exploits of Lord Hanuman, epitome of the ideal devotee and servant of God as Rama. Composed by the 16th Century poet-saint, Tulsidas.

HARINAM: "Name of God."

HOMA: Sacrificial fire; the fire altar for the performance of *yajna.*

JAGATGURU: "World teacher;" a title given to the great *avatars*, and the *Shankaracharyas.*

JAPA: Repetition, usually of a *mantra* or name of God.

JAPA MALA: A rosary.

JAYANTI: "Victory day;" often refers to the birthday of a saint or an *avatar.*

JIVANMUKTA: "Freed while living;" a saint who has achieved *moksha* while still living in the physical body.

JYOTIR LINGAMS: Twelve famous and powerful Shiva temples and their corresponding *lingams* which are considered to be highly important pilgrimage destinations: (1) Somnath; (2) Mallikarjuna; (3) Mahakal; (4) Omkareshwar; (5) Kedarnath; (6) Bhimashankar; (7) Kashi Vishwanath; (8) Trayambakeshwar; (9) Baidyanath; (10) Nageshwar; (11) Rameshwaram; and (12) Grishneshwar.

KARMA: Literally, "action;" the cause and effect relationship between thoughts, actions, and their results; the cause of rebirth.

KARTAL: Hand cymbals used in *kirtan.*

KATHA: A devotional performance or presentation combining music, singing, drama and storytelling.

KAUPIN: A strap-like undergarment of cotton used by *sadhus.*

KHEYAL: A Bengali word meaning "imagination;" often used by Sri Anandamayi Ma to describe her spontaneous and often unconventional divinely guided words and actions.

KIRTAN: Congregational devotional chanting with instrumental accompaniment. Also: *sankirtan.*

KIRTANIYA: A person who sings *kirtan* as a livelihood.

KIRTAN WALLAH: Same as *kirtaniya.*

KRIYABAN: An initiated practitioner of *Kriya Yoga.*

KRIYA YOGA: A highly advanced psycho-physiological *pranayama* technique that rapidly accelerates the soul's evolution; brought to the West by Paramahansa Yogananda.

KUMBHA MELA: The largest congregational gathering on earth; religious fair held every three years in four different cities: Allahabad (Prayag Raj); Haridwar; Nasik and Ujjain.

KUND: A bathing tank; usually a square or rectangular manmade pond used for bathing purposes.

KUTIR / KUTI: A small hut or room occupied by a *sadhu* or *sadhaka* for the purpose of performing spiritual practices.

LADDU: A traditional sweet favored by Lord Ganesha.

LAMA: A Tibetan Buddhist monk.

LAKH: 100,000

LILA: The Divine play; a worldview in which creation is seen as a great and magnificent drama conceived of and acted by God as divine entertainment.

LILA AVATAR: Often referring to the Divine Incarnations of Rama and Krishna; those *avatars* who play a world drama for the inspiration and edification of a large segment of humanity.

LINGAM: An oblong stone or vertical column symbolizing the Formless and Infinite nature of God as Shiva.

LUNGI: A cotton cloth worn by men as a bottom garment.

MADHUKARI BIKSHA: The practice of begging food from certain specific homes on a regular basis; practiced by monks belonging to certain religious orders.

MAHABHARATA: "Great Epic of India;" The world's longest epic poem revolves around the conflict between two royal families, the Pandavas and the Kauravas, culminating in the great battle at Kurukshetra. The holy Bhagavad Gita is set in the midst of the Mahabharata. Its central figure is Lord Krishna. The Mahabharata is considered a holy scripture in the *Vaishnava* tradition.

MAHAMANTRA: "Great *mantra*;" commonly used to refer to the Hare Krishna *mantra*, *Hare Krishna Hare Krishna Krishna Krishna Hare Hare / Hare Rama Hare Rama Rama Rama Hare Hare*; may also refer to other great universal *mantras* such as *Om Namah Shivaya, Om Namo Bhagavate Vasudevaya, Om Sri Ram Jai Ram Jai Jai Ram*, etc.

MAHANT: The head of an *ashram* or Hindu religious institution.

MAHAPRASAD: Literally, "that *prasad* which is most holy."

MAHARAJ / MAHARAJ-JI: "Great king;" a reverential title often given to exalted holy men.

MAHASAMADHI: "The great *samadhi*;" a *yogi's* final conscious exit from the body.

MAHATMA: Great soul.

MAHAYOGI: Great yogi.

MAIYYA: Mother.

MALA: A rosary, usually containing 108 beads plus one central or Meru bead. Shorter malas may contain 27 or 54 beads; also, a flower garland.

MANASA PUJA: Mental worship.

MANDALA: A circular or concentric geometrical design symbolizing the wholeness and interconnectedness of the universe.

MANDIR: Temple.

MANGALA ARATI: "Blessing *arati*;" refers to the first *arati* of the morning in a Hindu temple, usually at 4:30 AM.

MANTRA: Literally, "to control the mind;" vibrationally potent Sanskrit words which may be repeated audibly, silently or in writing. Though mantras may serve many purposes, their highest purpose is to purify the thought processes leading to spiritual unfoldment and divine communion.

MATA / MATAJI: Mother.

MATH: The center or headquarters of a Hindu religious organization.

MELA: Hindu religious fair.

MOKSHA: Liberation from the cycle of forced reincarnation; salvation.

MOUN / MOUNA: Silence; or the practice of silence for spiritual purposes.

MRDANGAM: A two-ended drum used in *kirtan.*

MUDRA: Literally, "to give joy;" hand or body positions that lock *prana* in the body, leading to purification and higher states of consciousness.

MUKTI: Freedom from bondage to the world and compulsory reincarnation

MURTI: A sanctified statue or image of God in one of His or Her manifestations which is considered to be a living embodiment of that Divine form.

NADASWARAM: Temple horn or trumpet used in South Indian temples and holy festivals.

NAGA BABA: "Naked renouncers;" *Shaivite sadhus* who are 'sky clad,' wearing only ashes.

NAMASKAR / NAMASTE: Spoken greeting with hands held in *anjali mudra* while honoring the Divinity in another person.

NARMADESHWAR LINGAM: "Lord of the Narmada Lingam;" A special type of natural stone Shiva *lingam* which comes from the holy Narmada River.

NIRVANA: The state of enlightenment wherein one is freed from the influence of *karma* and the mind has achieved at state of utter tranquility. The *Moksha Dharma* from the *Mahabharata* says, "Yoked by that joy, the *yogi* delights in the practice of meditation. Thus do they go to Nirvana, free from all forms of suffering."

NISKAMA (NISHKAMA): Without desire; selfless activity.

OM / AUM: Called *Pranava*, the primordial sound; the vibrational substratum of creation, and the creation itself. Paramahansa Yogananda says, "Audible utterance of 'AUM' produces a sense of sacredness… At the beginning of all acts and rituals, repetition of the holy syllable… removes the taints and defects that adhere in all human activities… However, the real understanding of *Aum* is obtained only by hearing it internally and becoming one with it in all creation, (*God Talks With Arjuna: The Bhagavad Gita*, Self-Realization Fellowship, 1995). OM is the bridge between human consciousness and divine consciousness.

OM TAT SAT: The Holy Trinity: *Sat*, God-the-Father, transcendental Spirit beyond creation; *Tat*, the Son or Christ-consciousness inherent in creation; *OM* the creation itself, also called the Divine Mother, Mother Nature or the Holy Ghost in Christian terminology. *Om Tat Sat* is a sacred *mantra* often used to conclude religious ceremonies.

PANDIT: A scholar; someone well-versed in the scriptures, or in a specific field of knowledge.

PARAMATMA: "Supreme Soul;" identical with *Brahman* or *Parabrahma*.

PARIKRAMA: The sacred act of circumambulating a sacred temple or holy location; also, *Pradakshina*.

PRANA: Life force or life energy in the body; also, specifically one of the five *pranas* or electricities in the body which is the cause of inhalation.

PRANAM: To bow to, salute or honor the image of God residing in another person or persons, or in a *murti*; usually performed with hands held in *Anjali Mudra*, or *danda pranam*, with the body outstretched on the ground.

PRANAVA: OM

PRANAYAMA: Control of *prana*, usually through yogic breathing techniques combined with energy locks (*bandhas*), physical postures and mental control.

PRASAD / PRASADAM: Food or other offerings which are offered to God in a temple or religious function and then returned to the assembled devotees as a blessing from the Divine.

PREM / PREMA: Divine Love.

PREMA SAMADHI: Oneness or absorption in Divine Love; feeling only that Love; seeing everyone and everything as an expression of God's Love.

PUJA: "To worship;" a ritualistic worship of a form of God either outwardly or mentally (*manasa puja*); can be as simple as offering a flower, some water or incense, or long and elaborate *pujas* which are described in the scriptures; *puja* is one of the nine forms of devotional service in *Bhakti Yoga*.

PUJARI: One who performs *puja*; a priest.

PUNYA: Religious merit.

PUNYABHUMI: India – land of virtuous actions.

PURANAS: "Ancient;" Hindu folk narratives and tales expressing ethical, religious and cosmic teachings.

PURIS: Delicate bread that puffs up when deepfried.

RAGA: The framework or structure of Indian classical music. Each raga has its own flavor, *rasa,* and mood *bhava*. Ragas may reflect a mood, either human or divine, and are often intimately connected with the rhythms and cycles of nature.

RAMAYANA: "The Story of Rama;" a great epic poem narrating the life and exploits of Rama (Sri Ramachandra), who is considered to be an incarnation of God as Vishnu. Many 'Ramayanas' have been written by various saints through the ages, most based on the original Ramayana of Valmiki, a contemporary of Sri Rama. Valmiki's Ramayana consists of 24,000 perfectly rhymed Sanskrit couplets. In the 16th Century, the great *bhakti* saint, Sant Tulsidas, wrote a new and very devotional re-telling of the story entitled, *Ramcharitamanas*, "The Lake of the Mind Overflowing with the Exploits of Lord Rama."

RANGOLI: Symmetrical designs often painted in colorful rice powder on the ground in front of a temple or home; a sign of auspiciousness.

RASA: Sweet divine emotion of ecstatic love for God.

RASALILA: A specific divine play of Lord Krishna in which He expands Himself in order to dance individually with each *gopi* on moonlit nights in the forest of Brindavan; a symbol of the highest ecstatic love between God as Beloved and the soul as Lover.

RINPOCHE: Literally, "Precious one;" a title of respect given to a master in the Tibetan Buddhist tradition.

RISHI: Seer or sage; often referring to the great masters of the past who composed the authoritative scriptures of Hinduism; or to any God-realized master who is a transmitter of great wisdom.

ROTI: Handmade unleavened bread; also *chapati.*

SABJI: A general term for any food preparation made of vegetables.

SADHAKA: Spiritual seeker; one who performs *sadhana.*

SADHANA: Spiritual practices.

SADHU: A person who has renounced the world to seek spiritual advancement, whether or not he has taken formal vows.

SADVI / SADHAVI: A female *sadhu.*

SAMADHI: Union; merging of the individual consciousness in God-consciousness, or some aspect of divine consciousness. The eighth and final step in Patanjali's eightfold path of Yoga.

SAMPRADAYA: Religious order with varying backgrounds and traditions.

SAMSARA: The relative world of time and change; the repeated cycle of birth and death and the sufferings inherent in it.

SAMSKARAS: Seed tendencies carried over from past lives; also, a sacramental rite performed to mark a significant transition of life such as name-giving, first feeding, commencement of education, graduation, coming of age, marriage and death.

SANATANA DHARMA: "Eternal Religion;" that which is eternal, and those principals that are in exact correspondence with Truth or Ultimate Reality.

SANDHYA: Twilight.

SANGAM: Merging; where two or more rivers join.

SANKALPA: A strong spiritual intention or determination.

SANT: Saint.

SANNYASI / SANNYASIN: A monk; a male who has taken formal vows of renunciation, especially in the ancient Swami Order; also, the fourth *ashrama* or stage of life, that of the renunciant; anyone who, regardless of their external mode of living, has attained complete non-attachment to worldly life.

SANNYASINI: A female renunciant; a nun.

SATCHIDANANDA: Descriptive Sanskrit word for God as "Ever-existing, Ever-conscious, Ever-new Joy or Bliss."

SATGURU / SADGURU: "True Guru;" one who has attained highest enlightenment in God-consciousness and has been divinely directed to guide others toward their own salvation.

SATPURUSHA: "True soul;" a saint who expresses the highest state of consciousness.

SATSANG: Literally, to be 'in the presence of Truth'; a gathering during which spiritual principals are taught or discussed; a group that meets for the purpose of sharing the teachings of a saint.

SEVA: Selfless service.

SHAIVITE: A devotee of Lord Shiva.

SHAKTA: A devotee of the Divine Mother.

SHAKTI: Primal energy of creation; the Divine Mother who carries on all the activities of the universe.

SHANKARACHARYAS: Adi Shankaracharya (the first or 'original' Shankaracharya) established four *maths* in the four corners of India at Mysore, Puri, Dwaraka and Badrinath. A fifth *math* was later established at Kanchipuram. The heads of these *maths* are referred to as Shankaracharyas.

SHANTI: All-satisfying, transcendental Peace.

SHASTRAS: Holy scriptures.

SHIVARATRI: Night of Shiva; the day before the new moon in the Hindu month of Phalgun, between mid-February and mid-March; especially sacred to God in the form of Shiva. Devotees maintain vigil throughout the night, praying, chanting or performing *puja*, often during the four quarters of the night. A celebration and feast are held at sunrise.

SIDDHA: Perfected being; a master.

SLOKA: A Sanskrit verse from the scriptures.

SRIMAD BHAGAVATAM: A sacred scripture; one of the principal *Puranas*, written by Sage Vyasa and describing the glorious, exploits and pastimes of Bhagavan Krishna.

SRUTI BOX: A small musical instrument pumped by hand to sustain the *sruti* or drone, the main tonic of a *raga*. Now days, an electronic drone is often used.

STUPA: A Buddhist monument; usually a mound commemorating a certain incident from the life of the Buddha, or containing a sacred relic.

SUNDARKAND: "The Beautiful Story;" Book Five of the Ramayana of Tulsidas, *Ramcharitamanas*, describing the wonderful exploits of Lord Hanuman.

SWAMI (male) **/ SWAMINI** (female)**:** Renunciants of one of the eight branches of the Swami Order, reorganized by Adi Shankaracharya in the 8th Century. Although vows may vary slightly between branches, all swamis take a vow of celibacy, non-possession and accepting all of mankind as one's greater family.

SWAMIJI: A respectful way of addressing a *swami*.

SWARG LOKA: Heaven.

TAL / TAAL: Rhythm structure in Indian music.

TAPAS / TAPASYA: Literally, "burning, as in a fire;" denotes intense spiritual practices leading to purification.

TILAK: Forehead marking indicating Hindu denominational affiliation, or received as a blessing during a *puja* or religious ceremony.

TIRTHA: "To cross over;" a holy place of pilgrimage; holy water from a sacred source.

TRISHULA: Trident usually associated with Lord Shiva, or Durga, the Goddess of Protection. The three points represent the three worlds or vibrational planes: the physical, astral and causal; and the three *gunas*: the activating, darkening and purifying qualities of nature. Symbolically, He or She who is "Trishuladhari" – who carries the trishula – has complete control over all three worlds and all the forces of nature.

TULSI MALA: Holy rosary made from wood of the sacred Tulsi (holy basil) tree; especially sacred in the *Vaishnava* tradition.
UPADESH: Spiritual instructions, usually imparted by one's *guru*.

VAISHNAVA: Devotee of Lord Vishnu and His *avatars* such as Rama and Krishna.

VANAPRASTHA: "Forest dweller;" the third *ashrama* or stage of life wherein a person retires from involvement with mundane affairs in order to concentrate on spiritual development.

VIBHUTI: Sacred ash prepared by burning dried cow dung along with milk and ghee; symbolizes purity and is a sacrament in many *pujas*, especially in the *Shaivite* tradition.

VIPASSANA: A form of Buddhist meditation wherein one observes ones thoughts and dissociates oneself from them.

VISION, THE: Ashram publication begun by Swami (Papa) Ramdas, who founded Anandashram in Kanhangod, Kerala, South India.

YAJNA: (Pronounced yag-ya). Worship; sacrifice; a fire ceremony in which ghee and various pure offerings are presented to God manifesting in the form of fire (*Agni*); also, the inner spirit of sacrifice wherein all actions are performed as an offering to the Divine.

YATRA: Pilgrimage.

YATRI: Pilgrim.

YSS / YOGODA SATSANGA SOCIETY: Founded in India by Paramahansa Yogananda; sister organization to Self-Realization Fellowship in America.

Oh, I will be Thy gypsy;
I'll roam and roam – through aeons roam.
But when 'tis time my soul to rest,
I'll dream of Thee whom I love best
And wake from many lifetimes' dreams fore'er.
Then Thou and I, as one, shall gypsy everywhere.

From "The Divine Gypsy," by Paramahansa Yogananda
(Songs of the Soul)

Sundaram La Pierre's great interest is Sanatana Dharma, the "Eternal Religion," kept for all the world by the Himalayan sages and great masters of India. He enjoys photographing and writing about its endlessly unfolding expressions of spirituality.

Sundaram and his wife, Hilary, live in Encinitas, California, where they coordinate a weekly Kirtan Circle which is open to all who enjoy Indian devotional chanting.

Kirtan has become a genre of music in its own right in the West. They host many of the traveling kirtan artists who are bringing this soul-uplifting and transforming music to the world. It is their conviction that the true purpose of music is to uplift the consciousness, leading to actual communion with God.

In May of 2005, Sundaram began publishing Himalayan Heritage Magazine to bring a greater awareness of the vast and sublime teachings of Sanatana Dharma and its tradition of saints. Published six times a year, each issue contains an "India Dreaming" section featuring stories from or about spiritual India, a "Saints and Sages" feature, highlighting the life of one of India's great masters, and many other stories of interest to all on the path of Hindu Devotional Mysticism.

Sarvam Sri Gurudeva Arpanam Astu!